SHANAHAN LI
MARYMOUNT MANHA
221 EAST 71
NEW YORK, N

D0076943

Meredith Kimball

Feminist Visions of Gender Similarities and Differences

Pre-publication
REVIEWS,
COMMENTARIES,
EVALUATIONS . . .

"**A**s a feminist clinician who has struggled with the similarities/differences debate, and repeatedly seen both points of view used to oppress/exploit women or as fuel in the current backlash, I welcome this much-needed book. Drawing on many years of experience and reflection, Kimball writes clearly and persuasively about the need for a 'double vision' and a multiplicity of feminisms. Her use of historical material adds focus and cogency to her arguments, demonstrates difficulties engendered by the choice of one tradition over another, and shows how dominant groups can appropriate radical ideas and use them to further their own ends."

Dr. Sue Penfold
Professor, Department of Psychiatry,
University of British Columbia

"This well-crafted book examines traditions in feminist theories and research that minimize the differences between women and men (similarities) and traditions that emphasize gender differences and the positive aspects of characteristics undervalued because they are 'feminine' (differences). After carefully describing the similarities and differences traditions, Kimball illustrates each with an example from the history of psychology (Leta Stetter Hollingworth and Karen Horney), an example of contemporary feminist scholarship (gender and math and gender and moral theory), and an application (women in science and caregiving). Each pair of chapters is a fascinating contrast and will be more or less useful depending on one's particular interests (e.g., historical or contemporary, theoretical or applied). Always there is an honesty in highlighting both the strengths and weaknesses of each approach, not only their theoretical strengths and weaknesses but also their political strengths and weaknesses as tools for ending domination. It is significant too that while the focus of the book is on gender similarities and differences, throughout Kimball acknowledges other important differences such as race, class, and sexual orientation.

While the six illustrative chapters are very valuable, for me the most exciting contributions are found in the first and last chapters in which Kimball argues compellingly for 'double visions'–the value, depending on the context, of using each tradition. They also provide a valuable challenge to those who hold doctrinaire views that women and men are either 'almost the same' or 'very different' from one another. As one who has 'double vision' but occasionally feels uncomfortable with positions that are 'contradictory,' the opening and closing chapters provide me with powerful arguments for embracing both. Meredith Kimball has illustrated, analyzed, and justified the double visions so many of us experience. We are reminded, however, to use them very carefully; she shows how each can, so easily, be distorted and misused to the detriment of women. This focus on the political implications of our theories and research is one of the real strengths of the book. In a time when academic feminisms seem in danger of losing touch with activist feminisms, Kimball's book is an important contribution."

Beth Percival, PhD
Associate Professor of Psychology &
Coordinator of Women's Studies,
University of Prince Edward Island

More pre-publication
REVIEWS, COMMENTARIES, EVALUATIONS . . .

"**T**his book offers a highly intelligent as well as engaging exposition and evaluation of the similarities and difference traditions in feminist thought. Whereas many authors have entered the debate by opting either for similarity or for difference, it is Kimball's genius that she shows how the tensions between the two positions provide constructive opportunities for enlarging and enriching feminist visions. Along the way she illustrates her arguments with fascinating material about such diverse topics as the work and lives of Leta Stetter Hollingworth and of Karen Horney, gender differences in mathematical ability and in moral reasoning, women as scientists, and the paradox of a culture that simultaneously values and oppresses women as caregivers.

I feel privileged to have been one of the early readers of this fine book, which makes an invaluable contribution to the sometimes acrimonious debate about similarities and differences. It is an important step in reconciling the two traditions, not by oversimplifying them, but rather by fully recognizing their complexities. Yet it is one of the pleasures of this book that,

although she writes about complexity, Kimball's prose is clear and accessible."

Olga Eizner Favreau, PhD
Professor of Psychology,
University of Montreal

"**K**imball puts forth an argument many will find utterly astonishing: social scientists and laymen alike should embrace two different sets of opposing ideas—i.e., men and women are the same/men and women are different. In building a case for the paradox, Kimball looks at a vast range of gender research and theorizing. Kimball's argument is bold, far ranging, and careful. It is extremely interesting reading. If we were to stretch ourselves to encompass the contradiction, our thinking about gender and the human condition would suddenly become less muddled and more adequate to the task."

Mary Field Belenky, EdD
Research Professor,
University of Vermont

"**U**sing as illustrative vehicles the topics of variability, motherhood, morality, and mathematics, Professor Kimball deconstructs the gender similarities/differences debate. Drawing from historical as well as contemporary discussions of this issue, while linking it to the main theoretical traditions in feminist thought, Kimball provides a unique contextualization of the complexity of this key controversy. Readers will be exposed to an exceptionally lucid account of some of the philosophical orientations underlying sciencing and feminist theorizing–logical positivism, social constructivism, and essentialism. Kimball's balanced treatment, replete with fascinating detail of the lives and work of feminist scholars, Horney and Hollingworth, is a welcome relief from the unnecessarily abstruse or conversely, oversimplified presentations of this subject in the feminist literature and is the best exposition of this contentious topic currently available. The finished product is an elegant, seamless tapestry, reflecting a meticulous interweaving of theory and empiricism, present and past, research and social action, a credit to Kimball's respect for diversity and her intolerance of intolerance. In sum, this work is an exemplar of the very best in feminist scholarship."

Sandra W. Pyke, PhD
Professor and Chair, Department of Psychology, York University

"**M**eredith Kimball has written a lucid, comprehensive review of a number of the most important feminist visions in the field of gender differences and similarities. A must-read for all who are interested in psychology of women and gender issues."

Paula J. Caplan, PhD, C. Psych
Co-author with Jeremy Caplan of
Thinking Critically About Research on Sex and Gender

More pre-publication
REVIEWS, COMMENTARIES, EVALUATIONS . . .

"**M**eredith Kimball's book, *Feminist Visions of Gender Similarities and Differences*, seems destined to become a classic in both women's studies and psychology. Kimball is already well-known for her work on gender and mathematics and on older women. I am also familiar with her paper on similarities and differences, presented at the Canadian Psychological Association meeting several years ago. Based on that superb paper, this is the book I had hoped she would write.

Kimball has a remarkable ability to present complex material clearly, without oversimplification. Thus, she can write effectively for two audiences, the psychologists who are familiar with empirical testing and meta-analyses, and the feminists who come from a humanities tradition. Her inclusion of poetry is also a nice, humanities-oriented touch.

Furthermore, Kimball is one of the few psychologists who is 'bilingual,' able to talk knowingly and fairly from both a similarities perspective and a differences perspective. No other book accomplishes this task so effectively. Furthermore, it's a real advantage to have a single author's voice providing continuity across chapters; an edited volume is nowhere nearly as satisfying.

Kimball also provides a valuable international perspective, with a comprehensive review of research in countries outside of North America. I also admired her coverage of the motherist movements in Latin America.

In short, you have a winner in Kimball's new book. It is clearly written, comprehensive, interesting, and remarkably even-handed in its treatment of gender issues."

Margaret W. Matlin, PhD
Distinguished Teaching Professor,
SUNY Geneseo

"**I**n *Feminist Visions of Gender Similarities and Differences*, Meredith Kimball gives us a balanced view of two feminist traditions that have persisted from the early days of Western feminisms to the present: the tradition that seeks women's equality with men and denies or attempts to transcend gender differences, and the tradition that celebrates women's differ-

More pre-publication
REVIEWS, COMMENTARIES, EVALUATIONS . . .

ences from men and seeks to give the activities, characteristics and values associated with women more recognition and more influence in the world. She describes in lively and absorbing detail historical and contemporary examples of both traditions from feminist psychology and philosophy, arguing that the insights and discoveries of the two traditions offer a richer and more complex understanding when combined than they do alone.

For everyone who has felt the pull of both approaches to feminism and the pressures to choosebetween them, this book will be a vindication and a relief. Kimball's approach is remarkably accessible, careful and fair to her subjects, and her deep appreciation and respect for both traditions and for their applications to contemporary feminist issues come through clearly throughout the text."

Susan Wendell, PhD
Associate Professor
of Women's Studies,
Simon Fraser University

Harrington Park Press
An Imprint of The Haworth Press, Inc.

NOTES FOR PROFESSIONAL LIBRARIANS AND LIBRARY USERS

This is an original book title published by Harrington Park Press, an imprint of The Haworth Press, Inc. Unless otherwise noted in specific chapters with attribution, materials in this book have not been previously published elsewhere in any format or language.

CONSERVATION AND PRESERVATION NOTES

All books published by The Haworth Press, Inc. and its imprints are printed on certified ph neutral, acid free book grade paper. This paper meets the minimum requirements of American National Standard for Information Sciences–Permanence of Paper for Printed Material, ANSI Z39.48-1984.

Feminist Visions
of Gender Similarities
and Differences

HAWORTH Innovations in Feminist Studies
Esther Rothblum, PhD and Ellen Cole, PhD
Senior Co-Editors

New, Recent, and Forthcoming Titles:

When Husbands Come Out of the Closet by Jean Schaar Gochros

Prisoners of Ritual: An Odyssey into Female Genital Circumcision in Africa by Hanny Lightfoot-Klein

Foundations for a Feminist Restructuring of the Academic Disciplines edited by Michele Paludi and Gertrude A. Steuernagel

Hippocrates' Handmaidens: Women Married to Physicians by Esther Nitzberg

Waiting: A Diary of Loss and Hope in Pregnancy by Ellen Judith Reich

God's Country: A Case Against Theocracy by Sandy Rapp

Women and Aging: Celebrating Ourselves by Ruth Raymond Thone

Women's Conflicts About Eating and Sexuality: The Relationship Between Food and Sex by Rosalyn M. Meadow and Lillie Weiss

A Woman's Odyssey into Africa: Tracks Across a Life by Hanny Lightfoot-Klein

Anorexia Nervosa and Recovery: A Hunger for Meaning by Karen Way

Women Murdered by the Men They Loved by Constance A. Bean

Reproductive Hazards in the Workplace: Mending Jobs, Managing Pregnancies by Regina Kenen

Our Choices: Women's Personal Decisions About Abortion by Sumi Hoshiko

Tending Inner Gardens: The Healing Art of Feminist Psychotherapy by Lesley Irene Shore

The Way of the Woman Writer by Janet Lynn Roseman

Racism in the Lives of Women: Testimony, Theory, and Guides to Anti-Racist Practice by Jeanne Adleman and Gloria Enguidanos

Advocating for Self: Women's Decisions Concerning Contraception by Peggy Matteson

Feminist Visions of Gender Similarities and Differences by Meredith M. Kimball

Feminist Visions
of Gender Similarities
and Differences

Meredith M. Kimball

Harrington Park Press
An Imprint of The Haworth Press, Inc.
New York • London

Published by

Harrington Park Press, an imprint of The Haworth Press, Inc., 10 Alice Street, Binghamton, NY 13904-1580

© 1995 by The Haworth Press, Inc. All rights reserved. No part of this work may be reproduced or utilized in any form or by any means, electronic or mechanical, including photocopying, microfilm and recording, or by any information storage and retrieval system, without permission in writing from the publisher. Printed in the United States of America.

The author gratefully acknowledges permission to reprint the following material:

"The Courtesans" by Leta Stetter Hollingworth, from *Leta Stetter Hollingworth: A Biography* by Harry L. Hollingworth, © 1990 Anker Publishing. (Original work published in 1943.)

"Salutation" by Leta Stetter Hollingworth, from *Radical Feminists of Heterodoxy: Greenwich Village, 1912-1940* by J. Schwarz, © 1986 New Victoria Publishers, Inc.

"The One Girl at the Boys' Party" from *The Dead and the Living* by Sharon Olds, © 1983 by Sharon Olds, reprinted by permission of Alfred A. Knopf, Inc.

"Variation on the Word *Sleep*" from *Selected Poems II: Poems Selected and New, 1976-1986*, © Margaret Atwood, 1986. "There is Only One of Everything" from *Selected Poems*, © Margaret Atwood, 1976. Reprinted with permission of Oxford University Press Canada, Houghton-Mifflin Co., and Virago Press. All rights reserved.

"Here Are Our Albums," © 1992. Reprinted from *Circles of Madness: Mothers of the Plaza de Mayo*, by Marjorie Agosín, with permission from White Pine Press, Fredonia, NY.

Library of Congress Cataloging-in-Publication Data

Kimball, Meredith M.
  Feminist visions of gender similarities and differences / Meredith M. Kimball.
      p.   cm.
  Includes bibliographical references and index.
  ISBN 1-56023-870-4 (alk. paper).
    1. Sex role. 2. Sex differences (Psychology) 3. Feminist theory. I. Title.
HQ1075.K54 1995
405.3–dc20   95-8959
                                                                                                      CIP

To my parents:
Donna Jane Delzell and Marvin Mahlen Fink,
who gave me the dual gifts of knowing
how to get the job done
and
how to have fun along the way

ABOUT THE AUTHOR

Meredith M. Kimball, PhD, is Associate Professor in Women's Studies and Psychology at Simon Fraser University in Burnaby, British Columbia. She has been actively involved in the development of Women's Studies since the early 1970s. Her research has focussed on gender differences in cognitive skills, especially mathematics and visual-spatial skills. She teaches courses in Feminist Psychoanalytical Theory; Theories of Gender, Women, and Aging; and Female Roles in Contemporary Society. Dr. Kimball is a member of the Canadian Psychological Association, the Canadian Women's Studies Association, and the Association for Women in Psychology.

CONTENTS

Preface

This book was 20 years in the making and six years in the writing. For all of my professional life, feminisms have captured my intellectual interests and informed my political life. However, it took some time for me to realize that I was unwilling to settle for a unidimensional vision of feminism. For a number of years, I have been privileged to have a joint appointment at Simon Fraser University in both Psychology and Women's Studies. As a psychologist I have studied empirical gender differences in achievement, particularly visual-spatial skills and mathematics. In this work I was concerned with minimizing gender differences and arguing that not only were these differences smaller than many people thought, but also that they could be explained better by environmental than biological factors. Most important, it was obvious to me that the differences that I found could not begin to account for observed gender differences in the labor force, particularly those in fields of science and technology. This work centered me in the similarities tradition as I describe it in this book.

In addition to the empirical research I conducted, I was teaching a course in Feminist Psychoanalytic Theories in the Women's Studies Department. This brought me into contact with a very different set of feminisms, ones that emphasized gender differences, the importance of women's agency in traditional settings, and the importance of women's subjectivities. Although my students and I were very critical of the essentializing aspects of these feminisms, we were also excited by the validation of many of our experiences, particularly the validation of the feminine in our worlds. In short, this has been some of the most exciting teaching and learning I have done. This work centered me in the differences tradition as I describe it in this book.

Throughout these years I was well aware of the contradiction of the two sets of feminisms I espoused, and more important, believed in. That they occurred in two largely different arenas allowed me to continue to believe in both. I never seriously considered giving up either. Both were central to what I wanted feminisms to include. Finally, I came to the conclusion that these two sets of feminisms could coexist and inform each other within the cover of one book. What you read here is the result of my refusal to give up either of the two experiences I describe above, and therefore, my refusal to resolve the contradictions between them. Thus, I do not attempt to reduce the differences among feminisms to a single or best vision. I do aim to describe both traditions of feminisms accurately and to explore the limits and advantages of each of them. I am convinced that what I call practicing double visions allows the tension of contradictions among feminisms to exist and to inform feminist theories and actions. The world is not simple. Even the best theories about how it works and the most successful attempts to change it are always partial, always have strengths and weaknesses. I consider feminisms to be among the best explanations of human social worlds and the most useful guides to actions. However, there is neither a complete, nor a best feminism for all contexts. In a particular situation, for a particular woman or group of women, one vision of feminism may be more accurate or effective. Both empirical and political considerations are useful in judging the effectiveness and limitations of a particular partial vision in a specific context.

Because I believe in the necessity of a multiplicity of feminisms, I have chosen to consistently use the plural throughout this book. In many cases I have done this where the reader will expect the singular. For example I speak of maternal or equal-rights feminisms, ethics of care, moralities of justice. I do this on purpose, even when it jars, because I think it is critical not to presume to be able to define a best or most accurate theory or a single morality that incorporates what feminism, justice, or care is in a wide range of contexts. I am advocating diversity, I am not advocating relativism. Women are diverse and experience a diversity of oppressions. A diversity of feminisms is necessary to reflect the diversity among women. But not all that concerns women is feminist. My definition of the core, or essence, of feminisms is striving to end all forms of domination, those of men over women and those among women. To accomplish this it is important to understand, honor, and empower both what women do traditionally and what women do subversively (Fine & Gordon, 1991). Oppressions that arise out of existing social structures must be spoken and acted against. At the same time visions of what might be must be encouraged.

I have relied on the work of feminist psychologists, philosophers, and theorists throughout this book, and hope that many of them will find it a useful integration of ideas. However, I aim also to reach beyond academics interested in feminist and women's studies. Thus, I have tried to minimize the jargon and technical language in this book so that a wide range of people interested in gender similarities and differences will find parts or all of the book useful for their own thinking and political action. Some familiarity and sympathy with feminisms will be useful in reading this book. Some background in the social sciences and/or philosophy will facilitate reading some of the more technical parts of the book. However, the main points and many of the interesting illustrations will not require any technical expertise.

Writing a book is hard business. Over the years of preparing for this book, I have become an avid reader of the prefaces and acknowledgments through which authors introduce their books to me. As with most authors, I have many people to thank for encouragement, comments on chapters, help with the physical acquisition of materials, and being an audience to my ideas, my excitements and frustrations, and my obsessions.

I needed documents from the early twentieth century to books published this year in order to research the range of topics in this book. Living and working in Canada adds one step of difficulty to this process. Thus I am most grateful to the people who helped put the printed words that I needed in front of me. *The Women's Review of Books* was a valuable guide to the most recent feminist work in all the areas I researched for the book. Carolyn Jones and Honorée Newcombe found books, as did George Kimball and the mail order people at Elliott Bay Bookstore. The staff at Simon Fraser University Interlibrary Loan, Frances Fournier of the SFU Archives, and the staff at the University of British Columbia Library who retrieve books from storage all persevered in tracking down the older documents I needed for the history chapters. Joan Wolfe of the Psychology Department provided state-of-the-art word processing information. Jacky Coates did bibliography work for Chapter 2 and Jodi Jensen shared references from her own work that were useful for Chapter 6. Donna Jane Fink helped with the reference check on the completed manuscript. The very generous administrative leave policy at Simon Fraser University gave me the time necessary to complete the final manuscript.

I was fortunate to have several opportunities to share this work while it was in progress. I first developed the underlying thesis of this book in 1988 at the University of New Brunswick where I spent a sabbatical leave as a visiting scholar in the Women's Studies Program. My interaction and discussion with the Women's Studies faculty there were invaluable for inspiring me to undertake this project. Special thanks go to Gail Campbell, Vicky Gray, Jenny Hornesty, Joan McFarlane, Nancy Nason-Clark, Wendy Robbins, Janet Stoppard, and Gillian Thompson. At a critical point in my work, the Section on Women and Psychology of the Canadian Psychological Association nominated me to give an invited address at the CPA meetings in Québec in 1992. This was a valuable opportunity to develop many of the ideas included in Chapters 1 and 5, and to receive much-needed encouragement to continue with my work. This paper was later published in *Canadian Psychology* (Kimball, 1994), and I gratefully acknowledge their permission to use the previously published material in this book. I gave an early version of Chapter 4 as part of a panel at the ICMI Study 93, Gender and Mathematics Education conference in Hoor, Sweden. My particular thanks to Elizabeth Fennema for suggesting my name, and to Gila Hanna for convincing me that I really did want to take the time out from writing the book to travel to Sweden. The contact with leading feminist math educators from around the world informed and enriched Chapter 4. Similarly, thanks to Faye Crosby who convinced me it was worth a trip to Martha's Vineyard to attend the Nag's Heart Similarities and Differences Workshop. The chance to share ideas with an exciting group of feminist psychologists both informed and confirmed my views. Many thanks also to Gillian Thompson of the University of New Brunswick and Jonathan Vaughan of Hamilton College who arranged visits to their respective campuses where I presented draft versions of Chapters 4 and 6 and received very valuable feedback. At Simon Fraser University the Women's Studies brown bag group heard and commented on Chapter 3, and the Psychology developmental group discussed Chapters 4 and 6.

A number of individuals commented on one or more chapters, suggested references, or wrote to encourage my work on the book. They include Elinor Ames, Bill Andrews, Mary Barnes, Janet Beggs, Ann Bigelow, Leone Burton, Susan Chipman, Heather Davey, Sarah Dench, Alice Eagly, Olga Favreau, Elizabeth Fennema, Helen Forgasz, Andrew Gotowiec, Barbro Grevholm, Rachel Hare-Mustin, Carol Jacklin, Dana Janssen, Helga Jungwirth, Andrea Lebowitz, Sibyl Likely, Marilyn Mac Donald, Colleen MacQuarrie, Arlene McLaren, Jim Marcia, Jeanne Marecek, Honorée Newcombe, Joy Parr, Sandra Pyke, Diana Relke, Sandy Shreve, Claudie Solar, Janet Spence, Else-Marie Staberg, Mary Lynn Stewart, Janet Strayer, Gillian Thornley, Chris Tragakis, Rhoda Unger, Heather Walters, Sue Wendell, and Merle Zabrack. Many of their ideas and suggestions are incorporated into this manuscript, clarifying the prose and strengthening the logic. The problems that remain are my responsibility.

No book happens without a publisher. My thanks go to Ellen Cole and Esther Rothblum, Editors of the Haworth Women's Studies book program, for having enough faith in my proposed ideas to give me a contract at a point when I needed assurance that the ideas were worth pursuing. And special thanks to Patricia Brown and Peg Marr of The Haworth Press for their guidance through all the details involved in turning a computer printout into a real book.

Chapter 1

Introduction: Feminist Double Visions

Irony is about contradictions that do not resolve into larger wholes, even dialectically, about the tension of holding incompatible things together because both or all are necessary and true.

Donna Haraway
Simians, Cyborgs, and Women, 1991, p. 149

What is risky is giving up the security–and the fantasy–of occupying a single subject-position and instead occupying two places at once.

Diana Fuss
Essentially Speaking, 1989, p. 19

Throughout the history of Western feminisms, from Mary Wollstonecraft to the present, a consistent divide has informed feminist thought and action. On one side of the divide are feminists whose thoughts and actions work to tear down the category of woman, to promote the equality of women with men, and to deny or transcend gender differences. On the other side of this divide, feminists have worked to reclaim and revalue the category of woman, to promote change based on solidarity among women, and to celebrate gender differences (Snitow, 1990). As with most dichotomies, this one

---

Portions of this chapter have been adapted from "The Worlds We Live In: Gender Similarities and Differences," *Canadian Psychology, 35,* 1994, pp. 388-404. Reprinted here with permission.

does not clearly separate feminist movements or even individual feminists from one another. Both streams of thought have been present in the arguments of individual feminists, and used as political strategies. However, in spite of movement across the divide, debate about which approach is most progressive and most truly feminist has been persistent and at times fierce. This divide has been described in many ways: minimalists and maximalists, radical feminists and cultural feminists, social constructionists and essentialists, poststructuralists and cultural feminists (Snitow), beta bias and alpha bias (Hare-Mustin & Marecek, 1990, pp. 29-46), and individualist and relational feminists (Offen, 1992). Both approaches have had political successes, improving the lives of some women in some situations, but neither has eliminated women's subordination. The purpose of this book is to examine this divide, the two sides of which I have chosen to label the similarities tradition and the differences tradition, within feminist psychology. In addition to presenting history, research, and applications to illustrate each tradition, I hope to convince the reader that to choose one tradition over the other is to turn what is valuable as a partial vision into a flawed whole.

In this chapter, I will first outline the assumptions and major contributions of each tradition within feminist psychology and philosophy. Second, I will present my thesis that double visions are theoretically and politically richer and more flexible than visions based on a single tradition. In the chapters that follow I will explore the history, a modern area of scholarship, and an area of application for each tradition. In each case, I have not attempted to present a survey of the empirical and theoretical work that defines the tradition. Rather, I have chosen specific examples that illustrate the concepts and political concerns central to each tradition. I have made this choice for two reasons. First, by limiting my discussion to central examples, I can more clearly illustrate the history and modern uses of each tradition. Second, and more important for my thesis, this allows me to show, in each chapter, how double visions that include both traditions lead to more complex and richer pictures. In the historical section, I focus on the work of Leta Stetter Hollingworth as an example of the similarities tradition (Chapter 2) and Karen Horney as an example of the differences tradition (Chapter 3). As examples of modern feminist scholarship, I have chosen gender differences in mathematics achievement to illustrate similarities (Chapter 4) and gender and moral theories to illustrate differences (Chapter 5). In the third section, I turn to examples of applications of each tradition. For similarities I focus on women in science (Chapter 6) and for differences I explore the gendered nature of caregiving (Chapter 7).

SIMILARITIES TRADITION

Feminist psychologists working within the similarities tradition have sought to show that gender[1] differences in intellectual skills and social competencies are either nonexistent or far too small to explain existing gender differences in power, prestige, and income in public and private life. Through this work they seek to provide the scientific justification for political and social equality. Their work has occurred within academic experimental psychology and relies on empirical, especially statistical, techniques as the main sources of proof. Historically, this tradition can be traced to the earliest work in experimental psychology. From the turn of the century until 1920, several women who were among the first to enter the profession produced a sophisticated critique of the existing scientific view of gender differences. Their work illustrated the main arguments of the similarities tradition, including the importance of overlap between the genders, social origins of differences, and the contextual determinants of differences. In Chapter 2, I discuss the work of one of these women, Leta Stetter Hollingworth. After 1920, feminist work on gender difference receded and did not become a focus within academic psychology again until the early 1970s, with the rise of the modern women's movement.

Contemporary feminist work on similarities reflects the positivist approach of academic psychology with the view of good science as self-correcting (Grady, 1981; Eagly, 1987, pp. 1-6; Epstein, 1988). The use of well-controlled experiments, often conducted in the laboratory, is an important technique because they facilitate the study of gender with other potentially confounding social factors eliminated (Jacklin, 1981; Eagly, pp. 119-120). More recently, some feminist psychologists who are critical of this strong empiricist bias, have proposed social constructionist theories of gender, psychology's version of poststructuralism (Hare-Mustin & Marecek, 1990, pp. 22-64; Riger, 1992; Squire, 1989). What is common in this work, whether empiricist or constructionist, is a concern with the deconstruction of difference. The empiricist work has emphasized deconstructing difference through empirical sophistication, with the assumption that good methodology and accurate statistics will provide accurate information with which to combat misguided stereotypes (Eagly, 1987, pp. 1-6; Grady, 1981). The questions to be answered are: What differences are real and how real, i.e., large, consistent, or important are they? The social constructionist work has emphasized deconstructing difference through theory. The assumption is that all gender differences are socially constructed. The questions to be answered are: How and why are gender differences constructed?

The work of deconstructing gender differences through empirical sophistication has led feminist psychologists to important critiques of existing statistical techniques. Eleanor Maccoby and Carol Jacklin's *The Psychology of Sex Differences* (1974) reviewed psychological studies of gender differences for many intellectual and social characteristics. In attempting to draw conclusions from many individual studies of a particular characteristic, they calculated the percentage of studies that found statistically significant[2] differences between the sexes and the percentage that did not. Using this vote-counting (Hyde, 1986) or box-score approach (Eagly, 1987, pp. 34-41), each individual study was categorized as evidence for either similarities or differences. If the percentage of studies finding no difference was large, then a judgment was made that the sexes are more similar than different for that particular characteristic.

The box-score technique does not necessarily provide an accurate view of the size of gender differences across a number of studies. The main problem with its use is that the number of participants in the study is an important factor in determining statistical significance. Because statistical significance depends on sample size, two further specific problems arise. If very large samples are used, very small and meaningless differences will be significant. On the other hand, if small samples are used, even medium-sized and perhaps meaningful differences will not be statistically significant.

The researcher who attempts to compare across studies using the box-score approach also faces the problem that if some studies have large samples and others small samples, it may appear that the studies are contradictory when all studies reveal a difference of similar magnitude (Eagly, 1987, pp. 34-41; Hyde, 1986).

In order to overcome these problems, feminist psychologists have been instrumental in developing and applying a technique called meta-analysis. Ignoring the statistical significance of the findings, the first step in a meta-analysis is to calculate an effect size for each measurement of gender difference. An effect size is the difference between the female and male averages expressed as a proportion of the combined variability of male and female scores.[3] Individual effect sizes can be averaged across a number of findings, and statistical tests have been developed to determine the probability that an average effect size is different from zero and whether a group of effect sizes is consistent. If a group of effect sizes is inconsistent, the researcher then attempts to divide the studies into subgroups with similar effect sizes and to examine how the context of the studies, the samples used, and the definitions employed contribute to the differences in effect sizes found among the subgroups (Eagly, 1995; Hedges & Becker, 1986). By examining the research contexts that are associated with larger or smaller gender differences, these differences are shown to be specific to particular social contexts rather than universal. In Chapter 4, I review the large body of work examining gender differences in mathematics achievement based on the meta-analytic techniques.

One way of deconstructing difference is to focus on accurate portrayals of average differences between women and men. However, there is always variability within the groups of women and men studied. Thus, another way to take apart difference is to examine the distribution of female and male scores. As Olga Favreau (1993) points out, this is not often done, and important information about gender similarities and differences is thereby lost. For example, a large and consistent average difference between preschool girls and boys in the amount of rough-and-tumble play has been found (Di Pietro, 1981). However, the distributions of rough-and-tumble play for each sex revealed different patterns. All of the girls and most of the boys engaged in a low or medium level of rough-

and-tumble play. A few boys engaged in more rough-and-tumble play than all the other children. This difference in the distributions of girls' and boys' scores is missed when only average scores are reported, creating the mistaken impression that boys in general engaged in more rough-and-tumble play than girls did. A more accurate description of the data is that a few boys engaged in a very high level of rough-and-tumble play (Favreau, 1993).

The work of deconstructing difference through theory has led to an emphasis on the social construction of difference (Hare-Mustin & Marecek, 1990; Unger, 1989). In contrast to the view that empirical strategies can reveal similarity or difference, the social construction of difference emphasizes that "Knowing the truth about difference is impossible" (Riger, 1992, p. 735). Gender traits do not reside within the individual, but rather are constructed in a cultural context and through interpersonal interactions. Individuals do not *have* gender, rather they *do* gender (Bohan, 1993; Lott, 1990). It is assumed that if women and men are put in the same social context, exposed to the same social forces, they will behave similarly (Kahn & Yoder, 1989). Because women and men in our society engage in different interactions, most important interactions of unequal power and status, their behavior may be different in some situations. If women, more than men, are in situations that elicit a specific behavior, then that behavior will be constructed as feminine. What is crucial to these theorists is that these differences are not due to gender per se. Rather, they reflect different demand characteristics in the social contexts and interactions of women and men. Janis Bohan (1993) describes this as ". . . the difference between describing an individual as friendly and describing a conversation as friendly" (p. 7). Although biological differences are acknowledged, their meaning and importance are socially constructed. Biology is related to gender in variable ways across cultures, and within cultures across individuals. Gender constructions change or influence biology, as in the case of transsexuals (Unger, 1993).

If, as Bernice Lott says, ". . . behavior has no gender" (1990, p. 79), then to think in terms of gender differences is to reinforce stereotypes. Because stereotypes are the social constructions feminists want to change, it is dangerous to describe individuals or social contexts as either masculine or feminine. Thus most similarities theorists reduce gender symbolism to stereotypes. For example, it is thought unwise to describe experimental research methods as masculine or feminine because this implies that women ought to or in fact do different research than men (Eagly, 1987, pp. 142-144; Peplau & Conrad, 1989). This also reinforces the very constructions that need to change if women are to gain equality with men. In Chapter 6, I discuss this issue as an important aspect of the lives of women scientists.

DIFFERENCES TRADITION

Feminist psychologists, psychoanalysts, and philosophers working within the differences tradition have focused on positive human characteristics, such as a sense of human connection and caregiving, that have been undervalued because they are associated with women and with the symbolic feminine. The primary political goal is not equality within the status quo, as much as it is the creation of a different, more humane world that incorporates traditional feminine values as a central human focus. Gender differences are stressed because out of these differences visions of better worlds are possible. Historically, one antecedent of this tradition can be found in the early development of psychoanalysis. In Chapter 3, I discuss the work of Karen Horney, in particular her debate with Sigmund Freud in the 1920s and early 1930s about the value of female biology and psychology.

Contemporary feminists working in the differences tradition emphasize the construction of both individual and symbolic gender differences. They emphasize the study of individual gender differences that are embedded in social contexts. Thus they look to women's lives, especially the experience of motherhood, as an important source of difference. Equally important, they emphasize the power of gender symbols in the construction of social institutions and discourses within which all of us live our lives.

The construction of difference through women's experience of motherhood is central to the differences tradition. Nancy Chodorow's *The Reproduction of Mothering* (1978) is a feminist psychoanalytic theory of the development of gender differences. Central to this development is the social fact that most infants are cared for primarily by women. Nancy Chodorow is most interested in explaining how women develop both the necessary relational skills and the desire to become mothers. The mother is more likely to treat the infant daughter as an extension of herself. Later, the daughter takes with her a strong sense of her own connection with her mother as she also turns to her father in an attempt to differentiate herself from her mother. Her relationship with her father builds on but does not displace her emotional closeness with her mother. Because the girl does not repress or deny the early connection with her mother, she is able to develop a rich set of relationships, a desire for complex relational patterns, and an openness to the experience of others (Chodorow, 1978). She can live more easily in ". . . the domain between one and two, where self and other are never . . . cast in opposition" (Keller, 1992a, p. 50). The woman comes to adulthood with a need for close emotional connections. Her heterosexual mate is unable to meet her need because of his early denial and repression of the feminine relational abilities in himself and his greater investment in difference and separation (Chodorow, 1989, pp. 99-113). To meet her own needs and desires for relationships, the woman chooses to have children and to mother them (Chodorow, 1978, pp. 199-205).

What is important in Nancy Chodorow's description is the validation of women's relational skills and desires to engage in close emotional relationships, especially those with children, and the success of most mothers in raising daughters who recreate these skills and desires in themselves and in their daughters. She does acknowledge the ambivalence of the early mother-infant relationship. Indeed, both gratification and frustration are necessary for development. However, this ambivalence is not often paralyzing; rather, the daughter is able to tolerate and use the ambivalence to create connection with others.

Whereas Chodorow examines the mother-daughter relationship from the perspective of the daughter, Sara Ruddick (1989) locates gender differences in the maternal practice of women. She defines maternal practice not in terms of characteristics of women, but in the universal demands that human children present for protection, growth, and training. The goals of protecting, nourishing growth, and training, and the conflicts that necessarily arise within and among these three aims, define maternal thinking. The specific ways these aims are carried out and the contexts in which women carry out maternal practice vary greatly across cultures, historical periods, ethnic and racial groups, sexual orientations of mothers, and many other individual differences in values and life experiences. However, the essential aims of maternal practice are to protect children's lives, to nourish or at least not to interfere with their growth, and to train them so that they become socially acceptable members of society, hopefully people their mother can decidedly appreciate (Ruddick, 1989, pp. 13-27, 65-123).

Sara Ruddick is clear that she is not describing an achievement in maternal practice but rather a struggle. She defines failure of maternal practice as a failure to struggle or to acknowledge conflict and ambivalence, not as a failure of behaviors, feelings, or motivations (1989, pp. 160-184). Mothering is not nonviolent; however, at its best it is a struggle toward nonviolence. "I can think of no other situation in which someone subject to resentments at her social powerlessness, under enormous pressures of time and anger, faces a recalcitrant but helpless combatant with so much restraint" (p. 166).

Neither Sara Ruddick nor Nancy Chodorow is arguing that there is anything inherent in women's nature that makes them more able to mother than men. Both argue that if men nurtured and cared for infants and children, both sexes would develop the relational skills and desires to parent (Chodorow, 1978, pp. 211-219) and learn maternal thinking (Ruddick, 1989, pp. 42-45). However, both base their theories in the social reality that it is primarily women who mother, however variably this activity is constructed in different contexts. Because women are most often involved in maternal practice, it is important to acknowledge and validate the consequences of this social difference for our ways of thinking, our visions of the future, and our understanding of women's lives. For difference theorists, maternal identity is not primarily an empirical generalization, but a political act. That is, maternal identity is not meant as a statistical statement of what mothers do, so much as a potential for moral and political action that is based in what some mothers do some of the time (Offen, 1990; Ruddick, 1989, pp. 55-56, 160-164). In Chapters 6 and 7, my analyses of moral theories and caregiving are informed by feminist maternal theories.

Difference theorists have explored the role of gender symbols in the construction of social worlds and discourses. In symbolic gender systems, human characteristics are arranged in binary opposites, associated with gender, and asymmetrically valued (Cohn, 1993; Harding, 1986, pp. 52-57). Symbolic gender systems describe beliefs people hold about gender rather than the behavior of individual women and men. For example, conversations that are constructed as friendly (Bohan, 1993) can also be constructed as feminine or masculine. Even though these gendered beliefs do not accurately describe individual behavior, nevertheless they have very real effects on what people do, say, and think. Symbolic gender norms are beliefs that influence the construction of our social and natural worlds, including worlds women never enter. To the extent that the masculine is assumed to be the human, these organizing beliefs remain silent (Keller, 1992b, pp. 15-36). For example, as I discuss in Chapters 4 and 6, women and men are equally skilled at math and science and there is no evidence that women scientists practice science differently. However, cultural symbol systems that structure the discourses of math and science as masculine create beliefs that influence men and women differently.

A particularly chilling example of the effects of gendered discourses is given by Carol Cohn (1989, 1993) in her analysis of defense intellectuals' thinking about weapons and war. She describes how symbolically feminine values such as peace and disarmament are devalued and therefore difficult to speak and hear by either men or women. In contrast, symbolically masculine values such as aggression and strengthening deterrence become rational, neutral, and objective in these discourses. Furthermore, because no one can express concerns marked as feminine in this context and maintain legitimacy, ". . . gender discourse becomes a 'preemptive deterrent' to certain kinds of thought" (1993, p. 232). Often these are the very kinds of thought that might save lives and limit destruction in an international conflict. Gendered discourses do not originate in the individuals who use them, but in the broader social context. Although they do not shape decisions, they do function ideologically to legitimate certain outcomes and foreclose others (Cohn, 1987).

The political goals of feminist difference theorists are not only to recognize the prevalence of gendered discourses, but also to undermine the devaluation of the feminine common to these discourses. In traditional Western philosophical discourses women have had no essence. To give women an essence can be an act of resistance that seeks to undo Western phallocentrism, allowing women to be the subjects of our own lives (Fuss, 1989, pp. 55-72). Luce Irigaray's claim "That we are women from the start" (1978/1985, p. 212) has ". . . a political advantage . . . that a woman will never be a woman solely in masculine terms, never be wholly and permanently annihilated in a masculine order" (Fuss, 1989, p. 61). For difference theorists it is important that women do not settle for being equal in a man's world. "When women want to escape from exploitation, they do not merely destroy a few 'prejudices,' they disrupt the entire order of dominant values, economic, social, moral, and sexual. . . . They challenge *the very foundation of our social and cultural order,* whose organization has been prescribed by the patriarchal system" (Irigaray, 1978/1985, p. 165). In Chapter 5, I draw on feminist attempts to disrupt the asymmetrical nature of gender symbolism through the reconstruction of moral theory.

PRACTICING DOUBLE VISIONS IN THEORIES AND POLITICS

The central thesis of this book is that feminist theories and politics will be richer and stronger, and that each of us will provide a better criticism of our own work if we engage in practicing double visions. By situating double visions as a practice, I borrow from Sara Ruddick's ideas about maternal practice. A human practice is a socially constructed activity that is defined by the assumptions, aims, and goals without which the practice would cease to be recognized as itself. Engaging in a practice generates knowledge that must be sharable with some human community. Consequently, such knowledge does not transcend its human origins (Ruddick, 1989, pp. 3-27). The major goal of practicing double visions is to resist the choice of either similarities or differences as more true or politically valid than the other. Practicing double visions does not preclude making choices for one side or the other in particular contexts

(Davis, 1992), nor does it deny the existence for some individuals of a subjective preference (Snitow, 1990). However, it does mean that neither alternative is foreclosed, the tension between alternatives is engaged, and the partiality of any particular view is recognized. Central to the practice is a respect for theoretical diversity (Martin, 1994). Ideally, by resisting choice and engaging the tensions of double visions in creative ways, the possibility of a stereographic view that brings reality into a three-dimensional focus is created (Cott, 1987, p. 20). Both the realistic visions of the world as it is and feminist future visions of how it might be are recognized through "two sights seeing" (Raymond, 1986, p. 207).

In this book I apply the practice of double visions primarily to gender similarities and differences. However, practicing double visions also applies to the understanding of similarities and differences among women across races, classes, sexual orientations, abilities, and ages. No two women are alike in every situation and no two are different in every respect (Martin, 1994). By practicing double visions with respect to differences and similarities linked to all socially constructed categories, the complexities of human social and political worlds become more apparent. Thus, throughout this book I attempt to construct double visions of gender that also take into account similarities and differences among women.

Why not give up both gender similarities and differences? This is a possibility and one that some feminists, particularly feminist poststructuralists, have proposed (Freedman, 1990). It is, however, not my choice. To some extent my choice reflects my own history, which I describe in the Preface. However, I am also convinced by the arguments that the divide has been around for the 200 years of modern feminisms and that to change history requires more than a linguistic maneuver (Offen, 1990; Snitow, 1990). Or, as Luce Irigaray puts it, one cannot leap outside phallocentrism (1978/1985, p. 162), even though we may occasionally transcend it. I like Irigaray's view that we may first transcend it in laughter (p. 163). At least laughter is a better bet than theory at this point in history. Furthermore, in a culture that is constructed by gender and other hierarchies, a too-ready deconstruction of categories risks reinforcing relations of domination. If feminist theorists abandon gender, gender will not disappear. Rather, male-dominated theories of gender will define the field. In this sense, gender skepticism may operate to sustain white, male knowledge and power (Bordo, 1990).

Resisting choice will result in better theories and politics in the sense that they will be richer, have more depth, and be less myopic. To illustrate my point that practicing double visions will enrich theories, I want to examine three ways in which the work coming out of a single tradition fails to apply thoroughly and consistently the principle that gender is a social construction. First, work in the similarities tradition has failed to adequately address the construction of gender similarities. Second, work in both traditions has failed to examine how essentialisms are socially constructed. Third, gender and other differences are not consistently treated. The differences tradition tends to construct gender as central and overlook other socially constructed differences. On the other hand, the similarities tradition tends to deconstruct gender differences and reify differences among women. In contrast to these limitations, practicing double visions leads to the following assumptions: (1) similarities are constructed, (2) essentialisms are constructed, and (3) differences should be consistently constructed and used.

First, similarities are constructed. Although this may seem obvious, it is not the impression conveyed by much of the similarities literature. Theorists acknowledge the importance of values, and that to choose similarities or differences is to choose a bias (Hare-Mustin & Marecek, 1990, pp. 29-46; Kahn & Yoder, 1989). However, the emphasis on deconstructing differences, and statements about the impossibility of knowing the truth about differences (Riger, 1992) without similar statements about the impossibility of knowing the truth about similarities, reveal an implicit underlying assumption that if we deconstruct differences well enough what we are left with is real similarities. However, similarities also are constructed. I offer here two examples. The first is a quote from the work of Carol Jacklin:

> With fewer variables confounded with sex, sex will account for smaller percentages of variance. Thus, paradoxically the better the sex-related research, the less useful sex is as an explanatory variable. In the best controlled sex-related research, sex may account for no variance at all. (Jacklin, 1981, p. 271)

Many feminist psychologists would agree with her premise that the best way to study gender is to eliminate confounding variables (Eagly, 1987, pp. 119-120; Riger, 1992). What is happening here is the construction of similarity. If the only real gender differences are those that exist in isolation, and if the best sex-related research eliminates confounding variables, the construction of similarity becomes hidden behind scientific rhetoric. Gender differences in social roles, power, and oppression become confounding variables. The only differences that count as real are those that remain after the social context is stripped away. All other differences are only apparent and can be reduced to the social contexts that created them.

My second example is a more obvious question and one that has been addressed by feminist researchers. How small is small? Although meta-analysis does not inherently support either differences or similarities, it has been constructed mainly as a tool to show that women and men are more similar than different, that the differences that exist are too small to be meaningful, that there is much overlap in the distributions of scores, and that gender interacts with other variables (Favreau, 1993; Hyde, Fennema, & Lamon, 1990; Linn, 1986). Yet, as Alice Eagly (1987, pp. 114-147; 1995) points out, the size of a difference is a social construction. Evaluations of size will depend on the value of the difference in society, how it compares to other differences, and choices about how the numbers are displayed. Although gender differences are often labeled small, they are similar in size to other differences found in psychological research which are not described as small. No difference is simply large or small. As an example, consider the following interpretations of the gender difference in height. It is easy to construct this difference as quite large in terms of effect size, $d = 2.0$ (McGraw & Wong, 1992), minimal overlap (estimated 11 percent) of the male and female distributions (Eagly, 1987, p. 124), or the probability that, if women and men were randomly paired, in 92 percent of the cases the male would be taller (McGraw & Wong). All of these figures construct the height difference as very large. For example, the effect size of $d = 2.0$ is gigantic compared to gender differences in mathematics performance that I discuss in Chapter 4 which range from $d = .15$ to $d = .4$ (Hyde, Fennema, & Lamon, 1990). In contrast, Alison Jaggar (1990) describes the mean difference as only a few inches, contrasts this with a variability in height of over two feet within each sex, and points out that our perception of difference is exaggerated by the norms of heterosexual coupling (p. 247). These arguments construct the gender difference in height as much smaller, and as influenced by the social construction of heterosexuality.

Second, essentialisms are constructed. Essentialism is not a unitary construct; indeed, to assume so is to engage in essentialist thinking (Fuss, 1989, pp. 1-21). Rather than using essentialism as a thought-stopper and infallible criticism, I would argue that we gain more by examining how essentialisms are constructed and how they are used. An essentialist argument is one that attempts to describe the properties, qualities, and necessary attributes without which a group of people, a culture, an historical period, or a social institution would cease to be recognized as itself. Such a project tends to ignore differences within the construct being defined and exaggerate differences from other constructs. This has its dangers. However, it is also impossible to make any generalization without engaging in essentialist thinking. Furthermore, an overemphasis on differences also has its dangers. In avoiding the traps of essentialisms and false generalizations, we may fall into the trap of false differences with its political dangers of overdistancing ourselves from others who then cease to share any common humanity with us (Martin, 1994; Scheper-Hughes, 1992, p. 355).

Labels of essentialism have been most often applied to difference theories and theorists, and often these theories do emphasize generalizations about women at the expense of examining differences among women. However, to imply that women and men are the same is not necessarily less essentialist than to say they are different. Essentialisms are constructed about groups of people, and they are also constructed about historical periods and social forces. For example, to say that oppression is universal is an essentialist construction. Constructionist theories often displace essentialism from the individual to a social reality or social forces (Fuss, 1989, pp. 2-6).

Because essentialisms are constructed, who is considered an essentialist is also constructed. An interesting example is the work of Nancy Chodorow (1978, 1989), which has often been labeled essentialist. Much of her work supports such a construction. However, she argues:

Feminist theories and feminist inquiry based on the notion of essential difference, or focused on demonstrating difference, are doing feminism a disservice. They ultimately rely on the defensively constructed masculine models of gender that are presented to us as our cultural heritage, rather than creating feminist understandings of gender and difference that grow from our own politics, theorizing, and experience. (1989, p. 113)

One could claim that she is making an essentialist statement here; however, she does not construct it that way. And to argue that all statements about difference are essentialist does not get us very far. Others have argued that Chodorow is not essentialist because she posits modern capitalism, not socialization practices, as the ultimate cause of women's feminine characteristics (Kahn & Yoder, 1989). Such a reading is clearly possible, but it is also possible to argue that Chodorow's construction and use of capitalist forces essentializes modern economies. Politics can also be constructed in essentialist ways. To assume that *any* positing of internal causes of gender differences ". . . is necessarily supportive of the status quo and, hence, antithetical to a women's movement" (Kahn & Yoder, p. 428) constructs a political essentialism by assuming that certain causal explanations are always oppressive.

Third, differences should be consistently constructed. In the differences tradition, gender differences are socially constructed through women's mothering. What is often ignored is the way other differences are constructed within a group of women who are mothers and how privileging mothering supports the domination of some women over other women. What is argued as true for all women, is often most or only true for white middle-class women who may even rely on the labor of poor women to carry out the mothering that is valorized. Jane Flax points to the racist implications of valorizing white women for exclusive motherhood when black women doing the same are constructed as dangerous matriarchs (1993, pp. 68-69). Privileging of gender differences through mothering also privileges heterosexuality and helps construct lesbianism as deviant. And intimacy between men becomes totally invisible in theories that focus on mother-child emotional bonds (Fuss, 1989, pp. 45-49).

Differences are also constructed inconsistently within the similarities tradition. Gender differences that are socially constructed are not regarded as real but only as apparent (Kahn & Yoder, 1989), and to focus on them is dangerous and politically conservative (Mednick, 1989). On the other hand, differences among women, also socially constructed, are real, important, and celebrated (Bohan, 1993; Griscom, 1992). Susan Bordo (1990) asks: "Why . . . are we so ready to deconstruct what have historically been the most ubiquitous elements of the gender axis, while so willing to defer to the authority and integrity of race and class axes as fundamentally *grounding?*" (p. 146). There is no a priori reason why any difference is more important than any other difference. A more useful and consistent theory of difference would argue that many differences are important and that all differences are socially constructed. The more differences that are explored, the less central any single difference will be (Unger, 1992).

CONCLUSIONS

Not only feminist theories, but also feminist politics will be richer and more useful if we practice double visions. Both similarities and differences have political dangers and strengths. To illustrate some of these strengths and dangers, I turn to a brief examination of victimization, oppression, and women's experience from the view of each tradition. A clear risk of the differences view is that it is easy to engage in victim blaming. This is particularly true if women's agency and choice are seen to be limited to traditional roles. On the other hand, the emphasis on social forces and coercion in the similarities tradition risks reducing women to victims for whom agency, choice, and subjectivity are delusions. Difference theorists, in their attempt to valorize women's traditional activities, also risk valorizing oppression. On the other hand, by emphasizing the power of oppression, similarities theorists risk eliminating agency, choice, and subjectivity. Difference theorists validate women's subjectivity and often mistakenly treat experience as self-evident or true. In deconstructing subjectivity, similarity theorists sometimes deny the subjective, implying that the only reason women stay in traditional roles is false consciousness.

My main point is that it is important to understand how difficult it is to avoid reinforcing male domination in a male-dominated culture. And it is domination that feminists want to end, not difference, gender, or the feminine (Flax, 1992). Women are caught in a double bind. We are not heard because we are women and we are not heard because we are invisible men (Snitow, 1990). To deny difference and to claim difference can serve the gender hierarchy. To argue that women are the same as or different from men leaves men as the standard (Rhode, 1990). On the other hand, both views can be liberatory. Both ". . . breaking with the gender bargain" (Snitow, p. 32) and reclaiming womanhood on our own terms have motivated feminist actions and thoughts. Any critique of the dominant culture can be deflected, changed, and reconstructed to support the status quo. Work based in differences will be used to devalue the feminine and to keep women out of positions of power. Work based in similarities will be used to reduce women and the world to a male-dominated view. If women are just like men and can operate just as well in a male-dominated system, then the system will not be questioned. On the other hand, both differences and similarities can be used to undermine the status quo. Differences are visionary. And similarities are a powerful argument for demanding equality. For example, Eleanor Maccoby and Carol Jacklin's book, *The Psychology of Sex Differences* (1974) has been cited as often in equal rights court cases as in psychological studies (C. Jacklin, personal communication, October 1989).

Both traditions have important strengths to challenge the status quo, and both can be subverted to support it. Thus it is important to be aware of the contradictions that are embedded in our theories and in our attempts to change our world. Women are both responsible and lacking in power, and although our responsibility can be reduced to victim blaming and our lack of power to victimization, this reduction is not necessary. We have choices and our choices are limited by oppression. Feminist theories must include both critiques of existing cultures and utopian visions of the future.

NOTES

1. The use of sex and gender has been much debated. Throughout this book I use gender in preference to sex even when I discuss differences between groups of

women and men. I do this to emphasize that all differences, even if based in biology, are socially constructed. The use of gender is to remind myself and the reader that any particular difference or similarity is the result of complex and sometimes contradictory social processes that involve individuals, social institutions, and cultural beliefs. For a more detailed discussion of the use of sex and gender by feminist psychologists, see work by Kay Deaux (1993) and Rhoda Unger and Mary Crawford (1993).

2. Statistical significance is determined by a formula that includes the number of women and men in the study, the average score for each group, and the range of scores within each group. The conventional level for declaring a result significant is $p = .05$. What this means is that there are five chances out of 100 that the researcher would find a difference this large or larger if women and men really are the same, and 95 chances out of 100 that s/he would not. Basically, the researcher takes a gamble based on probability and declares a difference as real if the probability is small (5 percent or less) that s/he is wrong.

3. Technically, an effect size is determined by dividing the difference between the two means by the combined standard deviation for the two groups. This means that an effect size is dependent both on how large the difference between the means is and how much variability there is within each group. For example, an effect size of .5 reflects that the means differ by half of the combined standard deviation.

SECTION 1:
HISTORICAL ANTECEDENTS

In the next two chapters I begin my exploration of the traditions of gender similarities and differences by examining historical antecedents through the work of two women and the feminist contexts within which they worked. In Chapter 2 I have chosen to focus on the work of Leta Stetter Hollingworth, whose critical work on sex differences clearly reflects the assumptions of the similarities tradition. She was an active feminist, working for suffrage with the clear view that when the truth was told, women would not be found wanting in any intellectual endeavor. The context for her work was the equal-rights feminisms of the 1910s and 1920s in the United States.

In Chapter 3 I turn to the work of Karen Horney, who was a prominent psychoanalyst in Germany in the 1920s and later in the United States. Although she did not identify as a feminist, much of her work, particularly her early work in which she criticized Sigmund Freud's theories of female development, reflected the maternal feminisms of Weimar Germany. She emphasized woman's difference, in particular the primary nature of femininity and motherhood, in the theoretical work that brought her into direct conflict with Sigmund Freud.

Leta Hollingworth and Karen Horney, born within a year of each other, had different personal yet similar professional lives. Leta Hollingworth was born into poverty in rural Nebraska. Very early she saw, and was encouraged to see by her teachers, education as the way out of her very unhappy childhood. By the time she attended the University of Nebraska in the early 1900s, half of the undergraduate students were women. She met Harry Hollingworth there and a few years later they were married. Their marriage lasted until her death in 1939, and he wrote her biography a few years later

(H. Hollingworth, 1943/1990). Leta Hollingworth never had children. In contrast, Karen Danielsen Horney, who was born into a middle-class family, knew from the age of 13 that she wanted to be a doctor. She attended the first Gymnasium for women in Hamburg and was in one of the first classes of women medical students in Freiburg. She also married a man she met at the university, Oskar Horney, but differed from Leta Hollingworth in that she had three daughters, divorced Oskar after 17 years of marriage, finished raising her daughters as a single mother, and remained single until her death in 1952. She explored her own heterosexuality in premarital and extramarital relationships. Her heterosexual and maternal experiences were reflected in her theoretical position that femininity was primary and not derived from a basic masculinity as Sigmund Freud claimed.

Both women were pioneers in their professions, both worked in professions that were considered maternal, and both were highly successful. Most important for my purposes, both challenged dominant patriarchal ideologies in their professions. Leta Hollingworth directly attacked theories of inherent sex differences, attempting to disprove theories and discredit data and implied women were intellectually inferior. She provided the intellectual tools for feminists to argue for equal rights for women. Karen Horney, on the other hand, accepted the idea of inherent differences, but attempted to subvert the dominant discourses. Her goal was to revalue and reclaim femininity from the misogynist evolutionary and psychoanalytic theories of her time. In this she reflected the values and strategic discourses of the German maternal feminists who were her contemporaries. Although they used different arguments, both women took on, at considerable professional risk to themselves, major proponents of patriarchal scholarship. Leta Hollingworth debated Edward Thorndike on the issue of greater male variability and Karen Horney challenged Sigmund Freud's theories of femininity.

Karen Horney's debate with Sigmund Freud differed from the debate between Leta Hollingworth and Edward Thorndike in several ways. First, sexuality was a central issue for Sigmund Freud, whereas individual differences in variability was only one among many interests for Edward Thorndike. Also Leta Hollingworth's political and scientific foci included several issues, whereas for Karen Horney female sexuality was central. Thus the debate between

Karen Horney and Sigmund Freud had much more staying power and much greater personal involvement. Second, Leta Hollingworth and Edward Thorndike were first graduate student and supervisor and later colleagues at Columbia as well as neighbors. In contrast, Karen Horney and Sigmund Freud lived in different countries and met only formally and infrequently. Third, Sigmund Freud took Karen Horney's criticisms seriously enough to dismiss them in print, even misspelling her name in one reference to her work (Freud, 1931/1961, p. 243). Edward Thorndike, on the other hand, did not engage Leta Hollingworth's ideas and data in print, although he did know her work, and even asked her to speak to his class about sex differences in variability (Hollingworth, 1940, p. 11). The exchange between Leta Hollingworth and Edward Thorndike was more a set of parallel arguments than it was a debate. Finally, although Karen Horney, Leta Hollingworth, and Edward Thorndike were well known and respected in their fields, Sigmund Freud dominated psychoanalysis by the 1920s. Probably no one could have debated him and won. It is amazing that Karen Horney not only tried, but also that she persisted as long as she did.

Chapter 2

Saying the Truth:
Leta Stetter Hollingworth
and Equal-Rights Feminisms

THE COURTESANS

We were the courtesans of ancient Greece.
Nor time nor death can lull our hearts to peace.
Our hearts, once flaming with that subtle sin
Of women who will neither weave nor spin.

Half-stifled from those ranks of matrons fair,
That served the looms, we burst away! Undone!
Shame stricken, forth we fared; while there
With bated hearts and muted breath they spun.

Outcast, but free, we went, with skirts that flowed,
And took the body's rhythm in the breeze.
Sappho was of us, and Aspasia bode
With us as one, and with her Pericles!

We watched the flocking boats wing out to sea.
The skies of Greece burned wide upon our gaze.
Dream-taught, we conjured up a prophecy
That brightened word by word, till in amaze

We glimpsed a vision on the sands dim brown,–
All women, walking free, within the town!

We were the courtesans of ancient Greece;
Nor time nor death can lull our hearts to peace.

Leta Stetter Hollingworth
Leta Stetter Hollingworth: A Biography, 1943/1990, pp. 82-83
by Harry Hollingworth

The similarities tradition in modern feminist psychology has historical antecedents in North American experimental psychology as well as in Western equal-rights feminisms. All of the important ideas of the similarities tradition are found both in Leta Stetter Hollingworth's work published between 1913 and the late 1920s and in the individual rights feminisms of the same period. These ideas include the social construction of women's inferior status, the importance of within sex variability, the absence of inherent differences between the genders, and faith in science as a source of progress. Leta Hollingworth (1927) traced her feminism to Mary Wollstonecraft who first put forward the central tenet of the similarities tradition, that a woman's disadvantage in society is a result not of her inherent nature, but of the social disadvantages she endures (Shields, 1975; Snitow, 1990). I will begin this chapter with a brief description of Leta Stetter Hollingworth's life. In the rest of the chapter I will examine how the ideas current in the feminisms of her time interacted with her own critical work on sex differences.

The life of Leta Stetter Hollingworth could have served as a plot for one of the New Woman fictional stories published in popular women's magazines in the 1910s and 1920s. In an anthology of these stories, Maureen Honey has described these fictional women. They grounded their hostility to patriarchy in a desire for self-actualization, and either found supportive mates or made a life for themselves outside of marriage. The heroine was often an artist or a woman of action who moved from the confining small town in which she was raised to the big city. Most of these women battled alone against prejudice, sometimes with the help of other women, sometimes in spite of the betrayal of other women. They were all white, heterosexual, young, middle-class women who believed in the importance of progress and individualism (Honey, 1992, pp. 3-36). "The New Woman heroine overcomes prejudice against her gender within a system that is basically open to any person with talent, fortitude, and ambition even if backward beliefs and individuals put women at a disadvantage" (p. 25).

Leta Stetter Hollingworth was born May 25, 1886 in a dugout near Chadron, Nebraska, the oldest child of Margaret Elinor Danley Stetter and John G. Stetter. Her father did not return home until eight days after her birth, and then promptly declared that she was the prettiest baby he had ever seen and "I'd give a thousand dollars if it was a boy" (H. Hollingworth, 1943/1990, p. 16). When Leta was three years old, her mother died while giving birth to her third daughter. Leta and her two sisters, Ruth Elinor and Margaret Carley, lived until 1898 with their maternal grandparents, Mary and Samuel Danley. Although her grandparents were poor, they provided a loving home for the three girls and Leta later dedicated her book on gifted children (Hollingworth, 1926) to them. In 1898 Samuel Danley died and their grandmother Danley returned to Chadron to live with her son. The three girls moved into the home of their father and stepmother, Frances Barling Stetter, in Valentine, Nebraska. Leta lived there until 1902 when she graduated from high school and moved to Lincoln to attend the University of Nebraska (H. Hollingworth, 1943/1990, pp. 1-38; Roweton, 1990). In contrast to their grandparents' home, the home of their father and stepmother was emotionally, and perhaps also physically, abusive. Her father was a great storyteller, but an unreliable family man who made and lost several fortunes in his life, owning meat markets, ranches, and saloons with his two brothers, Henry and Jake (Roweton, 1990). Her Uncle Henry joked that "Women and dogs . . . belong at home and in the front yard" (p. 137). Her stepmother was, from the beginning, hostile to the girls, punishing them excessively, even to the extent of not letting them speak to their Grandmother Danley when she came from Chadron to see them, which she did from time to time until her death in 1904. Her father, although kinder, was unable or unwilling to act as a mediator. Just how strongly Leta Stetter felt about these years is reflected in a letter she wrote in August 1907:

> When people break The Law, as it is writ large on the world for all, I *want* them to suffer. I have a perfect passion for wishing to see them "pay." If they seem not to suffer retribution I feel somehow cheated. I cannot "from my heart" *forgive* them and wish to see them escape consequences. Oh, it is easy enough to speak with them as usual, to regard them without malice, to treat them conventionally. But I do not absolve them; I can't forgive them till they've paid . . . I don't mean at all my "enemies," that is those who may dislike me, or harm

me, or differ from me in values or opinions . . . there is nothing to forgive them for. But those who "offend against God's holy Law," for instance against the law of kindness, or of meekness, or of generosity. I just delight in seeing them suffer the penalty. (H. Hollingworth, p. 62)

Or, as she more succinctly quipped, "There's no place like home—thank God!" (p. 93).

Throughout these difficult years, Leta Stetter saw her salvation in education, and was encouraged to do so by her teachers who recognized her intelligence and promise. In 1902 she entered the University of Nebraska to study literature. Her father supported her for the first year, and she supported herself for the last three years of university. She excelled at both academic and extracurricular activities, graduating Phi Beta Kappa and serving as the Class Poet of the Class of 1906. After graduating she taught for two years in DeWitt and McCook, Nebraska. In 1908 she moved to New York City to marry Harry L. Hollingworth, a classmate of hers at the University of Nebraska who was studying psychology at Columbia University (H. Hollingworth, 1943/1990, pp. 39-74). They both agreed that she should continue to work, but her way was blocked by the New York City school system that did not hire married women to teach in the public school system.

For about two years, she was continually frustrated in her attempts to achieve more than "Staying at home eating a lone pork chop" (H. Hollingworth, p. 73). She continued to write short stories, but was not successful in publishing them. She considered graduate school, but she needed financial assistance and none of the 12 full fellowships ($650 per year) and only four of the 32 tuition scholarships ($150 per year) were open to women (Rosenberg, 1982, p. 87). She tried a few literature courses at Columbia, but found them too dry for her tastes. Throughout these frustrating and depressing two years, she received both emotional support and encouragement from her husband Harry. Then, in 1911, the Coca-Cola company, which was being sued by the government because the caffeine in Coke was considered a health hazard, offered a generous grant to James Cattell to study the effects of caffeine on human performance. Cattell refused the grant and it was offered to

Harry Hollingworth who accepted and hired Leta as director of the study. The stipend from the Coca-Cola company was generous enough to help finance her graduate education, and she received both an MA (1913) and a PhD (1916) in psychology from Columbia Teachers College (Silverman, 1992).

While still in graduate school, Leta Hollingworth trained herself to give the newly developed intelligence tests, and in 1913 she was hired part time by the Clearing House in New York City, a clinic for testing the mentally handicapped. In 1916, when she finished her PhD, she was offered two jobs. One was a faculty position at Teachers College, Columbia University as head of the school for exceptional children, and the other was as head of the psychological laboratory at Bellevue Hospital. She chose the Teachers College job and remained at Columbia for the rest of her life, receiving appropriate and timely promotions through the academic ranks. She was only 53 when she died in 1939 from a cancer she kept secret from even those closest to her until the last few months of her life. Her early death cut short an outstanding research and teaching career (H. Hollingworth, 1943/1990, pp. 75-80, 99-102, 149-151).

Throughout her life, Leta Stetter Hollingworth spoke out against the injustice and prejudice against women common in her society. While in high school she protested a fellow student's quotation from Caesar that included the expression "Women, children, and other household utensils," commenting that "If such is the case Caesar has lowered himself in the H.S. girls' estimation" (Roweton, 1990, p. 140). Later, she protested the proposal of the Phi Beta Kappa council to limit the proportion of women eligible for membership. In the council's view, women's better marks in college were resulting in too high a proportion of female membership and lowering the prestige of the organization. In her response Leta Hollingworth protested: "That a position so untenable and action so invidious should be taken by the representatives of a body supposedly recruited on the basis of superior intelligence, offers food for ironical reflection" (Hollingworth, 1916a, p. 932). She often appeared before school boards and state legislatures to speak out on issues of concern to her (Poffenberger, 1940). Much of her published work on the psychology of women, which I will be discussing later in the chapter, was a protest against the prejudicial attitudes common at that time among her male colleagues, including her supervisor in graduate school, Edward Thorndike.

Like the New Woman of popular fiction, Leta Stetter Hollingworth's life was a very privileged one and did not reflect the lives of most of the women of her time. In 1900 only 4 percent of the U. S. population between 18 and 21 were enrolled in degree programs (Cott, 1987, p. 40). However, in attending university, Leta Stetter did not find herself in the position of a token woman. At the turn of the century, women nearly equaled or outnumbered men at a number of midwestern and western universities, including the University of Nebraska (Rosenberg, 1982, p. 44). What was much more unusual was her attendance in graduate school. By 1920, women earned about 15 percent of the doctoral degrees (Rossiter, 1982, p. 131). Sixty-two women had received PhDs in Psychology, including nine from Columbia (Russo, 1983). Even more unusual was her full-time permanent employment as a married woman. In 1930 less than 12 percent of married women worked for pay outside the home and at least two-thirds of these wives worked in domestic or personal service, agriculture, and manufacturing (Cott, pp. 182-183). In one study of 142 Wellesley graduates of the class of 1897, less than 6 percent were married and working outside the home in 1907 or 1910 (Antler, 1980).

Leta Hollingworth was promoted to the rank of full professor in 1929, making her one of very few women academics to hold this rank. In one survey conducted during the 1920s of 13,000 faculty at 145 institutions, women held only 4 percent of the full professor positions, a figure that dropped to 3 percent if schools of home economics were excluded (Rossiter, pp. 163-164). Like the fictional New Woman, but unlike most women in the United States at that time, Leta Hollingworth managed to combine a companionate marriage, a career, and the support of women friends. Many of these friends she met in Heterodoxy, a feminist group of women that she belonged to from the mid-1910s to her death in 1939 (H. Hollingworth, 1943/1990, p. 92; Schwarz, 1986). Like her New Woman fictional counterpart, Leta Hollingworth never had children. Whether this was by choice or necessity has never been made clear (Rosenberg, 1982, pp. 85-86). Few married women professionals who continued with their careers also had children. In a sample of career women's autobiographies published in the 1920s, 70 percent were or had been married, but only 29 percent had children (Showalter, 1978, pp. 5-7).

Leta Stetter Hollingworth's publications in the 1910s and 1920s comprised a body of critical work that reflected and gave scientific voice to the major feminist ideas, particularly those of equal-rights feminists of the United States. In reviewing this work, I will describe four themes: (1) Variability for a privileged few, (2) Social construction of difference through external forces, (3) Motherhood as limitation and opportunity, and (4) Science as a double-edged sword. Each of these themes interacts and overlaps with the others, as both Hollingworth's work and feminist ideas developed as a whole. Although I will discuss each theme separately, I will also point to areas of overlap throughout the discussion. Given my thesis that any feminist critique meant to undermine the status quo can also be deflected to support it, I will focus on both progressive and reactionary consequences of each theme.

VARIABILITY FOR A PRIVILEGED FEW

The word feminism has a relatively recent history. First introduced in France in the 1880s and England in the 1890s, it was in common use in the United States by 1913 (Cott, 1987, pp. 13-16). The feminists of the 1910s emphasized each woman's right to vary from the traditional norms of womanhood and femininity in order to realize her potential. The recent access to higher education of an elite group of women and the growth of single women's employment provided highly visible examples of individual women who had successfully varied from the rigid roles assumed for women only a generation earlier. Focusing on women's membership in the human race, feminists reacted against the notion of the woman as a morally superior social force, and reinvigorated the demand for equal rights. Thus, Rheta Childe Dorr described the New Woman who wanted "to belong to the human race, not to the ladies' aid society to the human race" (Rosenberg, 1982, p. 54). Charlotte Perkins Gilman defined the feminist: "Here she comes, running, out of prison and off pedestal; chains off, crown off, halo off, just a live woman" (Cott, p. 37).

Both Rheta Dorr and Charlotte Gilman, along with Leta Hollingworth, were members of Heterodoxy, a group whose motto,

"Breaking into the Human Race" (Cott, 1987, p. 39), reflected the desire of many feminist women to reject motherhood as a point of political unity and concentrate instead on the feelings of deprivation and rebellion that arose from the limitations of motherhood. Heterodoxy was a fascinating group of feminist women founded by Unitarian minister Marie Jenney Howe in New York City in 1912 (Schwarz, 1986, pp. 1-16). Meeting every other Saturday for lunch and debate in Greenwich Village, the 35 to 50 women varied among themselves in age, political beliefs, sexual orientation, and ethnicity. Although Grace Nail Johnson was the only black woman to belong, a number of Jewish and Irish women were members, along with the expected representation of white women of Protestant background. The women of Heterodoxy experimented in their personal lives. Some were single, some lived common law, some married, and some lived with women. Some remained childless, some bore biological children, and some adopted children, including a few of the women couples (Schwarz, pp. 75-96). In 1920 the divorce rate in the U.S. was between four and eight per 1000 marriages. In contrast, by the 1920s one-third of the Heterodite marriages had ended in divorce (Schwarz, p. 76). Members supported each other's relationships, including acknowledging anniversaries, sicknesses, and deaths in lesbian as well as heterosexual couples.

What held this group of feminists together until the early 1940s was their pride in being unorthodox women who represented a diverse range of personalities and interests (Schwarz, 1986, p. 2). Most were highly educated and involved in professional occupations. They were teachers, lawyers, physicians, psychoanalysts, psychologists, press agents, social reformers, actors, playwrights, writers, editors, and journalists. They frequented theatrical performances involving Heterodites, read each other's books and articles, and discussed common professional interests. Leta Hollingworth often discussed education with Elisabeth Irwin, founder of the Greenwich Village "Little Red Schoolhouse," an experiment in progressive education (Schwarz, 1986, p. 67).

The Saturday discussions covered a range of topics including "pacifism, birth control, the Russian Revolution as seen firsthand by Heterodoxy women, health issues, infant mortality, anarchism as a political tool for social change, education of women, Black civil rights, disabled women, the Irish independence movement, free love, psychology, and so much more" (Schwarz, 1986, p. 19). Each member gave a talk about her childhood. Leta Hollingworth described her childhood on the prairies and how all her dresses were made from flour bags (p. 20). She also suggested, as a topic, that the mothers among the members describe how they were raising their children differently than they had been raised (p. 20), and in the 1930s gave a talk about a group of high IQ children she had followed for 20 years (p. 67). The flavor of support, encouragement, and affection that existed among these women is captured by a poem that Leta Hollingworth wrote for the "Heterodoxy to Marie" album that members produced and gave to club founder Marie Jenney Howe in 1920 (p. 74):

SALUTATION

Het'rodites, Yuletide greetings!
At this season of gifts.
Shall I tell you the gifts you bestow on me,
As we sit at the long tables,
And the years slip along?
Gifts intangible and imponderable,
Yet bright with reality?

For there is no subtler pleasure
Than to know minds capable
Of performing the complete act of thought.
There is no keener joy than to see
Clear-cut human faces,–
Faces like those men choose
For coins, and cameos.

Leta Hollingworth admired the women of Heterodoxy who emphasized individuality in their lives. In addition, she attacked scientific theories which proposed that women varied among themselves less than men. The theory of greater male variability began with Darwin and provided a major scientific justification for women's inferiority through the early part of this century (Feingold, 1992; Shields, 1975, 1982). Faced with the equal average intelligence of women and men, male superiority was rescued by the assumption that male intelligence ranged more widely, resulting in more males than females with the lowest and the highest intellectual abilities. The evidence for the theory of greater male variability was, on the one hand, the greater number of males in institutions for the mentally retarded, and, on the other, the greater number of men of eminence. Leta Hollingworth attacked this theory on both fronts. Turning first to the greater number of males among the mentally retarded, she conducted a study of 1000 consecutive cases from records at the Clearing House for mental retardation. She found, as others had, that males outnumbered females, 568 to 432. However, she further analyzed the data by age group and found that the predominance of males held only among those under 16 years of age. In contrast, over the age of 16, women outnumbered men by a ratio of 2:1, and over the age of 30 by 3:1. Her interpretation was that females were just as likely to be mentally deficient as males, however, females were better able to survive outside institutions until they were older because they did not need to compete mentally as much as males (Hollingworth, 1913). "The girl who cannot compete mentally is not so often recognized as definitely defective, since it is not unnatural for her to drop into the isolation of the home, where she can 'take care of' small children, peel potatoes, scrub, etc." (Hollingworth, 1914b, p. 515). As they grew older, these women were more likely to lose the protection of parents or husband and, as a consequence, come into contact with institutions where their existence became part of the public record.

Equally important for Leta Hollingworth's argument, the greater eminence of men also could be explained by environmental factors. Women were expected to expend nearly 100 percent of their energy on traditional tasks where eminence was impossible. "Eminent housekeepers and eminent mothers *as such* do not exist" (1914b, p. 526). Thus, women's traditional roles both protected them from, and handicapped them in, the competitive struggles of society. Through her scientific work on variability, Hollingworth highlighted the political problem that women had in trying to combine achievement and procreation, a problem that men had never had. Consistent with the feminists' emphasis on women's right to vary, she argued that it was socially desirable that women find a way to vary and procreate or else

". . . society must tend to lose the work of its intellectual women or else lose their children" (p. 528). Disproving the theory of greater male variability was central to the goals of equal-rights feminists. Rheta Childe Dorr, in her popularization of Leta Hollingworth's scientific work, pointed out that if greater male variability existed, then "Sex democracy is impossible, and women's vision of social and political equality an idle dream" (1915, p. 15).

Both the proponents and critics of greater male variability were not concerned with how group differences, such as race or class, might interact with gender. Rather, they were concerned with individualism. That the individual should be able to succeed to the best of his or her ability and receive the rewards based on that achievement was an unquestioned good. The goal was to remove the restrictions that kept individual women from their greatest success, as determined by their inherent intelligence. Women should be allowed to both vary and procreate as men had always done. Supporting this argument, Beatrice Hinkle (1929), a Jungian psychoanalyst and member of Heterodoxy, argued that the terms masculine and feminine were arbitrary. As a clinician she found that these sets of characteristics did not apply to the individuals she saw, and for some there were very negative consequences of trying to live up to the collective vision of their sex. She concluded that women must do more than overthrow masculine domination. Freedom would require also that all people realize their individual nature regardless of sex (Hinkle, 1920). Leta Hollingworth (1929) similarly described masculine and feminine traits as accidents of social development, as arbitrary as masculine and feminine garments.

How were women to accomplish the combination of achievement and motherhood? By the late 1920s, the advocated solutions to this dilemma were individual ones. In Leta Hollingworth's discussions of gifted girls (1926, pp. 4-17, 346-353) and vocational aptitudes of women (1929), she argued that individual rather than generalized solutions were most feasible. She most clearly advocated individual solutions in her view of the New Woman. Each New Woman had to live her "experimental life" in her own unique way. The fundamental principle that explained the history of womankind was the psychological learning experiment: "A puzzled organism will learn to do whatever happens to bring relief from its major persistent craving" (1927, p. 15). Universal laws of learning, which applied to all individuals, even animals, had become the basis of social change.

In actuality, this version of individualism meant the freedom for a very few women to succeed, while most women, as most men, had the freedom to be exploited for low wages. In the case of most women and some men these wages were not sufficient for them even to imagine economic independence. Sexual freedom was similarly limited to a small group of privileged women who were neither economically nor socially tied to traditional marriages. In the 1910s, suffrage provided a political identity that balanced the focus on individualism with a sense of female solidarity. In contrast, in the 1920s, women's groups organized on opposite sides of major social issues such as protective legislation and pacifism. Furthermore, women's attempts at solidarity were tabooed as sexual deviance or magnified into sex wars. Given the continuing oppression of women, any emphasis on difference risked reconfirming the gender hierarchy and threatened the goal of equal opportunity championed by equal-rights feminists. The prevailing atmosphere among women who chose to call themselves feminists became one of individualism at the expense of gender solidarity. Although individualism could and did provide models of achievement, such as Leta Hollingworth, it made impossible the development of a program for change of women as a group (Cott, 1987, pp. 115-142, 241-268, 271-283). Many maternalist concerns, such as protective legislation, child welfare, and peace activism, were carried forward in the 1920s and 1930s by women organizing as women (Cott, pp. 117-142, 243-267; Swerdlow, 1993, pp. 25-36). These women, however, chose not to identify as feminists. Furthermore, equal-rights feminists held gender to be the primary and only proper focus of feminist action and rejected other political causes advocated by women as either diversionary or in conflict with their goal of equal opportunity.

Even for the small class of women who were privileged enough by education and income to expect the rewards of individualism, the reality of experimentation became much more limited in the 1920s. What began as a liberating claim for heterosexual freedom in the 1910s became in the 1920s the right to a companionate marriage (Cott, 1987, pp. 156-162; Honey, 1992, pp. 17-22). Women were suspect if they chose not to marry, and deviant if they chose to love women. At a meeting of Heterodoxy in January 1927 Leta Holling-worth ". . . included in her definition of perfect feminist a woman happily married and with children . . ." (Schwarz, 1986, p. 38). Although it is not clear from this description that she excluded other women, it is significant that she highlighted the married mother in her definition. Very few of the Heterodoxy women were ". . . happily married and with children . . . ," yet all considered themselves feminists. Although the women of Heterodoxy continued to pride themselves on their individuality and unorthodoxy throughout the 1920s and 1930s, consistent with the climate of the times, very few new members joined the group in these years (Schwarz, pp. 97-106).

Furthermore, the professions, based on education and merit, which held out the promise of achievement to many educated women, continued to discriminate against the women in their midst. During the 1910s, many women protested this discrimination, but by the 1920s, the primary strategy was not organization but individual struggle as women encouraged themselves and each other to get more education, to work harder, and to struggle as individuals to earn a place through merit (Cott, 1987, pp. 213-239; Rossiter, 1982, pp. 129-159). Society did not reward the woman who truly embraced individualism and sought through her own experimental life to discover her own true self. Leta Hollingworth, who knew just how little society was prepared to greet the New Woman, closed her article on this topic with the following words: "To experiment knowingly with one's own life to find the Good Life–surely this requires a courage and a genius deserving something better than blame or jeers, deserving at least open-minded toleration and assistance" (1927, p. 20).

THE SOCIAL CONSTRUCTION OF DIFFERENCE THROUGH EXTERNAL FORCES

Scientific literature on sex differences[1] at the turn of the century had been constructed and reconstructed to demonstrate women's natural inferiority. A number of feminist social scientists, including Leta Stetter Hollingworth, sought to remove this particular restriction on women's independent activity. They believed that there was a truth to be known and that science, if well and carefully done, would reveal that truth. An important feminist task was separating the literature of opinion from the literature of fact (Hollingworth, 1929). Feminists were highly critical of the existing body of knowledge, most of which was based on opinion or very questionable empirical evidence.

Feminists were quick to point out that differences, when found, were interpreted as advantageous to males. Faced with more male idiots, greater male variability was proposed which allowed for more male geniuses as well. Had the original finding been more female idiots, then the interpretations would have been an inferior female mind (Lowie & Hollingworth, 1916). In fact, girls did score better on the emergent individual intelligence tests, but no one interpreted this to mean that girls were inherently smarter, although the reverse finding would most likely have led to the opposite conclusion (Woolley, 1914). Both Leta Hollingworth (1916a) and Helen Thompson Woolley (1914) remarked that young women's better marks in schools and universities had led male professors to change their arguments. Before women were admitted to universities, the argument was that women in the university classroom would lower the standards. Now, with women receiving better grades, they were likely to argue that young men had become discouraged with the competition and that the number of women admitted to honor societies ought to be limited. In her study of the effects of the menstrual cycle on women's behavior, Leta Hollingworth pointed out that the male theorists who assumed that women should rest for one-fifth of their time rather than pursue professional or industrial jobs never proposed that these same women should be relieved of housework or maternal duties because of a menstrual handicap (1914a, p. 97).

The central and most pervasive argument of the feminist social scientists was that observed differences between the sexes should not be considered inherent differences. Just because women had not achieved did not mean that they lacked the ability or intellect to achieve. It was just as likely that observed differences were due to historical factors and current environmental influences that held women back. Although the same argument had been made by others, notably the reformers who had fought for women's admission to universities and graduate schools (Rosenberg, 1982, pp. 1-27;

Rossiter, 1982, pp. 1-50), the feminist social scientists applied this argument to the scientific literature of sex differences. One of the earliest and most influential was Helen Thompson who published her thesis, *The Mental Traits of Sex*, in 1903. After demonstrating that there were few differences between university males and females on a number of tasks, she returned to the importance of the environment in determining sex differences that she did find. Aware that this argument was met with derision often enough, she stated that it was worthy of at least unbiased consideration. She also countered the argument that it was inherent differences that determined the differences in training by pointing out that if this were true, it would not be necessary to spend so much time and energy making boys and girls engage in the conduct proper to their sex (pp. 169-182). Leta Hollingworth and other feminist scientists consistently voiced arguments against inherent differences throughout the early years of this century (Allen, 1927; Hinkle, 1920; Hollingworth, 1914b; Hull, 1917; Lowie & Hollingworth, 1916; Woolley, 1910, 1914).

Although sharing a faith in science to reveal true differences, the flavor of much of the feminist social scientists' writing was that any sex differences would be small, and inconsistent from study to study. For example, Leta Hollingworth in her study of women's menstrual cycles included men as well as women and was thus able to show that the variation over a month was as great for males as for females who were menstruating. At several points, she reported that tests which were affected by one to two grams of caffeine showed no influence of the menstrual cycle (1914a, pp. 16, 42).

In a series of reviews of the sex differences literature by Helen Thompson Woolley (1910, 1914) and Leta Stetter Hollingworth (1916b, 1918, 1919), both women emphasized the methodological requirements for determining sex differences and the general lack of research that incorporated these requirements. These requirements included matching men and women in terms of all important background factors, using large groups of subjects, replicating findings, and using rudimentary statistical tests of significance before declaring that a difference exists. Both authors were clear that very few studies met these criteria and that the ones that did tended to find small and inconsistent sex differences. Both women remained critical of the scientific literature. In 1910 the best Helen Woolley could say was:

> The general impression produced by a survey of this motley mass of material is first, that the literature of the subject is improving in tone. There is perhaps no field aspiring to be scientific where flagrant personal bias, logic martyred in the cause of supporting a prejudice, unfounded assertions, and even sentimental rot and drivel, have run riot to such an extent as here. . . . The signs in the literature of greater moderation in tone and more respect for evidence are in the direction of a much needed reform. (pp. 340-341)

Eight years later Leta Hollingworth, after laying out the methodological requirements for good research in the area, concluded that any reviewer who was limited to such studies would ". . . automatically tend to do himself out of his review" (1918, p. 428). In 1919, she ended this series of reviews with the following statement:

> The year's work yields nothing consistent as a result of the comparison of the sexes in mental traits. In this respect it resembles the work of other years. . . . Perhaps the logical conclusion to be reached on the basis of these findings is that the custom of perpetuating this review is no longer profitable, and may as well be abandoned. (p. 373)

These academic feminists held a great hope that education would both equalize women and men in the marketplace and provide women with the knowledge to liberate themselves from outdated myths. Within the lifetime of Leta Hollingworth middle-class white women had made tremendous strides in gaining an education equivalent to men of their race and class. White women represented almost half of the undergraduate students at many coeducational universities by the turn of the century (Rosenberg, 1982, p. 44), and at the graduate level had fought successfully to gain admission and be granted degrees by almost all institutions, receiving 15.5 percent of the doctoral degrees in 1920 (Rossiter, 1982, p. 131). On an individual level, feminists were also hopeful that education and science would provide knowledge that would change women's lives. Helen Hull, a member of Heterodoxy and of the English Department at Columbia, wrote in 1917: "A *tabu* can not be forcibly extracted; it vanishes with the entrance of knowledge" (p. 442), a view that her colleague Leta Hollingworth also voiced (1916c).

The work of these feminists illustrates some of the best critical science of their time. I will discuss the extent and limits of their influence later, when I discuss science as a double-edged sword. At this point, I would like to discuss briefly two ways in which the liberating conception of sex difference as constructed through external forces also had reactionary consequences. The first involves the emphasis on external factors as the determinants of difference. In the context of the actively feminist climate of the 1910s, feminist social scientists' attacks on inherent sex differences provided a rationale to liberate women from traditional roles. With the demise of a broad-based feminist movement in the 1920s, however, too much emphasis on historical and other external forces undermined women's sense of agency and of the potential for change (Cott, 1987, pp. 273-274). Furthermore, when external forces changed from liberatory to reactionary, women were helpless to overcome them except as individuals. This emphasis on external forces at the expense of feminist agency is reflected in Leta Hollingworth's article on the New Woman. She argued that the change in women's status over the past 100 years was hastened but not caused by feminist propaganda. The change was caused by men of science, inventors, and philosophers who were as a group indifferent to the problems of women. Examples that she cited were the scientific method, inventions that took production out of the home, machines that did women's work, and birth control (Hollingworth, 1927).

The second reactionary consequence of the work of these feminists lay in their faith in good science to produce the truth about sex differences. Only myths were socially constructed; truths were revealed. In many ways the deconstruction of the theories of inherent sex differences prevalent at the turn of the century was a radical undertaking. However, Leta Hollingworth's assumption at the end of the 1910s that the study of sex differences was a thing of the past (1919), was premature because of her faith that linked science with truth. Good science as well as bad is constructed and can be used to support the status quo (Harding, 1986; Morawski, 1985). In the

1920s and 1930s, in the face of the evidence of small and inconsistent sex differences in intelligence, scientists turned to the study of personality. Beginning in the early 1920s with the assumption that masculinity and femininity were real, Lewis Terman and Catherine Cox Miles conducted an extensive empirical study of sex differences in attitudes and values. The results (Terman & Miles, 1936) consisted of a 910-item test which successfully discriminated between women and men, reproduced Victorian stereotypes, and was linked not to inherent differences, but to individual and societal mental health (Morawski, 1985).

MOTHERHOOD AS LIMITATION AND OPPORTUNITY

At the turn of the century, maternal instinct was a popular scientific concept that underlined sex difference. Women were thought biologically suited for the rearing, as well as the necessary bearing of children, and conversely, unsuited for public pursuit. For feminist scientists, who wanted to bring about women's full participation in the human race, maternal instinct was an anathema. Leta Hollingworth repeatedly attacked the concept of a maternal instinct in her writings. The most she would concede was that *if* the maternal instinct did exist, something she very much doubted, then it would vary among women like any other trait. Some women would be born with a large amount of maternal instinct, some with very little, and most women would be somewhere in the middle of the distribution (Hollingworth, 1916c, 1929). Helen Hull (1917) also emphasized that women varied in their fitness and desire for the vocation of motherhood. Both women argued that maternal instinct was not only invalid scientifically, but also was a form of social control. Childbearing was like the work of soldiers in that it was a necessary, required sacrifice, and was dangerous. Thus it was expected that societies would exert continuous social effort to ensure that it was done. Once women were enlightened about these cheap forms of social control, they would cease to be effective, and the society that needed increased population would have to compensate women adequately either in money or in fame (Hollingworth, 1916c, 1918; Hull, 1917).

Maternity was a biological handicap to women's achievement. Leta Hollingworth made this clear in a number of ways. A woman's reproductive system was likened to a cage. In a clever linguistic maneuver, she illustrated the nature of this cage by listing euphemisms for pregnancy including "caught, confined, in trouble, and tied down" (1927, p. 15). The ". . . strong, intelligent old maid. . ." (p. 17) who chose to remain childless was important in the making of the New Woman because she was free to demonstrate her abilities. In contrast, men were, and had always been, free both to procreate the species and to achieve. Leta Hollingworth illustrated this difference by proposing to her readers a thought experiment: "Imagine a man and a woman of exactly equal ability, allowed to compete intellectually for a given social prize, on the condition that each shall become the parent of two or three children. Under the prevailing economic and social order, there is no question as to which will win" (1916a, p. 933).

The solution to this dilemma was not an attack on maternity, but social changes that allowed women to procreate and to achieve as men had always done. It was the most difficult dilemma facing a modern woman. She was helped by advances in birth control, machines that made housework easier, and some changes in public expectations, but her solutions were individual ones. Each woman had to find the way to best combine her own skills and abilities with procreation (Hollingworth, 1914a; 1926, pp. 346-353; 1927). Leta Hollingworth's individualism in this area was consistent with many feminist views of society in the 1920s. One of very few attempts to go beyond individual solutions was made by Henrietta Rodman, leader of the Greenwich Village Feminist Alliance and member of Heterodoxy. In 1915, she proposed an apartment building for professional women which included centralized services. Although plans were drawn up, the building was never built (Showalter, 1978, pp. 18-19). A later attempt was made by Ethel Puffer Howes as director of the Institute for Coordination of Women's Interests at Smith College. This institute, funded by the Laura Spelman Rockefeller Memorial Foundation, had the goal of combining professional employment for women with marriage and motherhood (Cott, 1987, pp. 202-204). Ethel Howes' suggestions did not question the division of labor in the home, but concentrated on the possibilities of combining employment and motherhood through part-time work or paid work in the home.

Feminist deconstructions of the maternal instinct along with the absence of any attempt to change the sexual division of labor in the home helped pave the way for the professionalization of motherhood. This had both negative and positive consequences for women. On the one hand, if women did not instinctively know how to be mothers, then they needed to study for it and for nothing else. This ideology effectively continued to tie most mothers to the home (Cott, 1987, pp. 167-170). On the other hand, the association of motherhood and science did open up some professional jobs to women.

The vast majority of women remained unable to combine motherhood and a career. Mothers who were employed as professionals remained a rarity. In 1930, less than 12 percent of married women were in the labor force (Cott, 1987, pp. 182-183). In a study of 142 Wellesley graduates of the class of 1897, only one woman had combined motherhood with a career by 1910 (Antler, 1980). In a series of career women's autobiographies published in the mid-1920s, only 29 percent of the women had children. Most career women combined a single life or a childless marriage with a career that was independent of the office and the time clock. This strategy allowed them to bring in money, but not disturb the traditional division of labor in the home (Showalter, 1978, pp. 3-29). Although Leta Hollingworth claimed in the 1930s that most gifted girls were choosing self-development rather than reproduction (1940, p. 102), none of the studies of the gifted supported her assertion. Just how persistent women's choice of motherhood remained is illustrated by a follow-up study of eight students from Speyer School for the gifted that Leta Hollingworth directed in the late 1930s. Forty years later, the four males had attended prestigious universities, obtained advanced degrees, and were working as a business lawyer or in academic settings. All of the men had married and become parents. One woman received a PhD at the age of 43 after raising four children and becoming divorced. One obtained her BA at age 50, having held various clerical positions and raising two children. One woman obtained her BA from Stanford, delayed her career while she married and raised three children, and then became a part-time writer. The fourth woman received an MA in clinical psychology and remained employed while raising her child (White & Renzulli, 1987).

The difficulty of even imagining mothers achieving in the world outside the home is reflected in the absence of children in the fictional stories of the New Woman published between 1915 and 1930. In an anthology of these stories one heroine imagines she will have children in the future (Honey, 1992, pp. 53-70) and two are older women whose children have left home (pp. 113-124, 239-257). One grown, married daughter even pleads with her mother not to take a job because it upsets her so to think of her mother not at home (pp. 239-257). These fictional women achieved, rejected males who did not support their careers, earned their own income as single or married women, but did not raise children.

The views of scientists consistently reinforced and prescribed motherhood. Jill Morawski (1984) has described the visions of motherhood in the utopias of three famous psychologists, G. Stanley Hall (1920), William McDougall (1921), and John B. Watson (1929). All limited women's roles to procreation, and provided scientist experts to guide women in this function. In G. Stanley Hall's "The Fall of Atlantis", a woman bore children until the age of 60 and wore a star on her breast for each child born. In William McDougall's "The Island of Eugenia" women married early and had five to ten children. In John Watson's "Utopia", each couple was assigned a different three children to raise by standard scientific principles every four weeks, so that by the age of 20 each child had 260 different sets of parents. Women stayed home and raised the children, assisted by male behaviorist physicians in the community (Morawski, 1984). Joseph Collins, a prominent neurologist, commented on a series of feminist autobiographies in 1927 (Showalter, 1978, pp. 144-147). His main focus was the feminists' lack of interest in children. Although he admitted that there might be good reasons for a woman to be unwilling to have ten to 20 children, he saw many good reasons for her to have five to ten children.

In contrast to the majority of women, a few women were able to take advantage of the professional opportunities that developed in the process of making a science of motherhood. Because motherhood and women were so closely associated, women were thought appropriate for jobs that brought them into contact with children or the study of children. In 1902, Edward Thorndike hired Naomi Norsworthy, the first woman to receive her PhD in psychology from Columbia, as an instructor at Teachers College. At the time he wrote to William James that he had hired her to take over the burden of his work and free him to teach graduate courses and do research (Rosenberg, 1982, p. 90). In a letter to Dean William Russell, he also stated that he was able to hire her for half the price of a similarly qualified male (Silverman, 1992). Six years later, Thorndike won her promotion by arguing that employment of women in Teachers College would not undermine the conventional view of womanhood (Rosenberg, pp. 90-91). When Naomi Norsworthy died in 1916, Leta Hollingworth was hired to replace her as instructor in educational psychology and head of the school for exceptional children at Teachers College. In this position she was promoted to Assistant Professor in 1919, Associate Professor in 1922-23, and Professor in 1929 (H. Hollingworth, 1943/1990, p. 99).

Women's participation in the scientific study of childhood was facilitated in the 1920s when Lawrence K. Frank and Beardsley Ruml developed a vision of a series of child development research institutes (Russo, 1983). These institutes, funded by the Laura Spelman Rockefeller Memorial Foundation, were associated with, but separate from, academic departments at a number of major universities (Rossiter, 1982, pp. 203-204). Although these institutes segregated women's work and reinforced women's traditional roles, they did provide jobs and a supportive work environment for many women. As the head of the Institute at Teachers College, Helen Thompson Woolley was a colleague of Leta Hollingworth's between 1925 and 1930 (Shields & Mallory, 1987). In the 1938 edition of *American Men of Science*, 20 women were listed as faculty in the Psychology departments of the 20 major universities in the United States. Eleven of these 20 women were in education departments, institutes of child welfare, or a department of home economics. Eight of these 20 women had attained the rank of professor, and six of these eight were either in education departments or child welfare institutes (Rossiter, 1982, p. 182). Leta Stetter Hollingworth was one of the six women. Women were not welcomed into academia or the professions. If they found success at all, it was very likely to be as symbolic mothers in positions that were perceived as compatible with traditional motherhood. Most women became actual mothers and were unable to combine motherhood with professional success.

SCIENCE AS A DOUBLE-EDGED SWORD

During the 1910s, progressive female and male scientists supported feminist ideals of equality and feminists turned to science as the basis of social reform (Rosenberg, 1982, pp. 54-113; Rossiter, 1982, pp. 100-128). The connections between science and feminisms were clear in Leta Stetter Hollingworth's work and life. Much of her work, which I have discussed earlier in this chapter, applied a sophisticated scientific methodology to the critique of scientific research on sex differences. At the same time, she was active in suffrage work, serving as a poll watcher for the Woman Suffrage Party of New York City and marching with many university people in suffrage parades (H. Hollingworth, 1943/1990, pp. 91-92). Her work was published in scholarly journals and also popularized in *The New York Times* (Dorr, 1915). She was referred to as the "scientific pillar" for the cause of feminism (H. Hollingworth, p. 91). She published, with anthropologist Robert Lowie, an article titled "Science and Feminism" (Lowie & Hollingworth, 1916). Leta Hollingworth believed that science, which dealt with fact and truth, was distinct from social policy, which was concerned with the socially desirable, the good, and the expedient (1940, p. 15). She also firmly believed in progress through science (1927; Shields, 1991). She was confident that the truth would prove to be progressive: "Let us say the truth, by all means, and if we do not like to say the truth as it stands, then let us make the truth something we can like to say . . ." (H. Hollingworth, p. 66).

Although the male psychologists at Columbia were not particularly open to equal-rights feminisms, there was an aggressive spirit of skepticism and empiricism that facilitated Leta Hollingworth's work (Heidbreder, 1933, pp. 287-327; Rosenberg, 1982, pp. 84-113). Her ideas on variability were directly in conflict with those of Edward Thorndike, a main proponent of greater male variability and her thesis supervisor at Columbia. As I will argue later, there is no evidence that he changed any of his views based on her work, but he clearly was willing to engage in the debate. In the introduction to a lecture on variability that she gave to his class, Leta Hollingworth noted that if one disagreed with Professor Thorndike, sooner or later one would be called on to state one's view (1940, p. 11). Her work, and the work of other feminists, was published in main stream scholarly journals of the time. Their greatest influence on the North American social sciences of their time was in the transition away from hereditary and toward environmental theories over the first part of this century. Sex differences were, in many scientists' minds, closely linked to heredity. When this link was persuasively questioned by feminist scientists, the power of heredity was seriously undermined (Rosenberg, 1982, pp. 107-109; Rossiter, 1982, pp. 112-115; Shields, 1982). Just how important the undermining of heredity was to feminists' desires to promote social change is shown in a statement Leta Hollingworth made to Edward Thorndike's class: "For a condition due to environment could be changed by changing the environment; whereas we cannot modify a tendency if it is determined in the germ plasm" (1940, p. 13).

Even though the feminist scientists were published and had an influence on the science of their time, their faith in the power of science to change individual attitudes and social policy was not realized. Because science was so closely linked with the truth, any view associated with science would be taken as true. This included the feminist views of women like Leta Hollingworth, and the views of conservative males like Edward Thorndike. Thus, although the work of Leta Hollingworth and other feminist social scientists was published and taken seriously, it did not change the views of any male scientist who believed in greater male variability (Shields, 1982). At the same time that Leta Hollingworth published her major work criticizing greater male variability (1913, 1914b; Montague & Hollingworth, 1914), Edward Thorndike published a revised edition of his text on educational psychology. In this he argued that although average differences between the sexes were so small as to be insignificant, greater male variability assured that most high achievers would be men. He also asserted the other half of the argument of greater male variability: "It is well known that very marked intellectual weakness is commoner amongst men than amongst women" (1914, p. 189). All of this is stated without any reference to Leta Hollingworth's work (Thorndike, 1914, pp. 169-205). Although the male scientists of the day accepted feminist claims that women and men had similar average abilities, they remained reluctant to accept similar feminist arguments that women and men were equally variable. They did not view themselves as average men, but rather men of some achievement. Therefore, to admit that the average woman was as intelligent as the average man was no threat. What was a threat was competition from highly intelligent women, a threat that was reduced by theories of greater male variability.

In the same text, Edward Thorndike (1914) also undermined the feminist arguments about environmental determinism. He agreed that the sexes were subjected to differences in training, but he assumed that these differences were the *result* of inherent differences (p. 168). This led back to the importance of original or inherent differences, undermined the feminist arguments of environmental determinism, and validated differential education for the sexes. He further postulated a fighting instinct in men and a nursing instinct in women, and linked the fighting instinct to men's superior achievement (pp. 202-203). Whereas the feminists argued that one should exhaust social causes before looking to physical and instinctual causes, Edward Thorndike here argued that one should exhaust physical and instinctual causes before resorting to "the hypothetical cause" of differences in intellect (p. 203). Edward Thorndike and other male researchers, who were unable to agree on the nature of sex differences, easily agreed that differences were inherent (Woolley, 1914).

CONCLUSIONS

Leta Stetter Hollingworth combined marriage and a career at a time when very few women were able to do so. She was highly visible and successful in her profession while most educated women remained on the margins in their professions. She did not, however, escape discrimination. Leta Hollingworth did not receive any research grants in all of her later work with gifted children, even though she applied for many (H. Hollingworth, 1943/1990, pp. 99-102; Silverman, 1992). In contrast, Lewis Terman in his longitudinal study of gifted children received a total of almost $150,000 (Rossiter, 1982, p. 209). She was one of the first psychologists to become skilled at giving mental tests, yet she was not invited to join her male colleagues in World War I in developing mental tests for the army (p. 119). Lewis Terman (1944), in a review of Harry Hollingworth's biography of Leta (1943/1990), commented that comparable productivity by a man would have been rewarded by the presidency of the American Psychological Association or even membership in the National Academy of Sciences.

Feminist assaults on traditional views of sex differences did not endure beyond the 1910s. It was not until the 1970s that such views would resurface. Two factors contributed to the shift away from the scientific study of gender by Leta Hollingworth and other feminists. First, the discipline of psychology turned away from the study of the individual and individual differences. The focus of research was either on the laws governing the behavior of the universal organism, or on the statistical analysis of the artificially constructed experimental group (Danziger, 1990, pp. 68-87). Leta Hollingworth consistently resisted both of these trends and insisted on the careful study of individual children and appreciation of individual differences. She was very critical of the style of research increasingly common in psychology throughout this century. "The adding machine has tremendous advantages over the child as an object of intimate association. It has no parents; it does not lose its pockethandkerchief; it has no measles; it does not kick or yell" (1940, p. 53). Second, with the lack of a broad-based feminist politics after suffrage and a strong emphasis on individual solutions and equal opportunity, gender ceased to form a basis of political activity. Feminist scientists, like other feminists, turned to individual effort and ingenuity to try to fit into the male-dominated world.

Leta Stetter Hollingworth was an active feminist who successfully combined career and marriage. Although she worked in education, a maternal profession, she did not have children of her own. In her scientific work she used evidence and argument to directly attack Darwinian theories of inherent or biological sex differences that limited women's opportunities in the public world. She convincingly argued that greater male variability was false. She undermined maternal instinct, questioning its value as a scientific construct and urging the compatibility of maternity and individual achievement. Her goal was to prove that scientific theories of inherent sex differences were false, a result of bad science. Her published work describes her success. That her ideas had to be redis-covered in the 1970s by another generation of feminists describes the failure of science to be self-correcting. In order to break this cycle of discovery and loss we must recognize the socially constructed nature of *all* science, both good and bad.

NOTE

1. I have chosen to use the term sex differences in this chapter rather than gender differences in order to be consistent with the terminology used by Leta Hollingworth and other feminist social scientists of the early twentieth century. The distinction between sex and gender and considerable discussion of the meaning of each are products of the second wave of feminisms (Deaux, 1993; Unger & Crawford, 1993). However, Leta Hollingworth and her feminist colleagues argued that sex differences were socially constructed, a theoretical position consistent with modern feminists' use of gender differences.

Chapter 3

Female from the Start: Karen Horney and Maternal Feminisms

... I, as a woman, ask in amazement, and what about motherhood? And the blissful consciousness of bearing a new life
within oneself? And the ineffable happiness of the increasing
expectation of the appearance of this new being? And the joy
when it finally makes its appearance and one holds it for the
first time in one's arms? And the deep pleasurable feeling of
satisfaction in suckling it and the happiness of the whole period when the infant needs her care?

Karen Horney
The Flight from Womanhood, *Feminine Psychology*,
1926/1967, p. 60

That many-faceted thing called love succeeds in building
bridges from the loneliness on this shore to the loneliness on
the other one. These bridges can be of great beauty, but they
are rarely built for eternity and frequently they cannot tolerate
too heavy a burden without collapsing.

Karen Horney
The Distrust Between the Sexes, *Feminine Psychology*,
1931b/1967, p. 117

The historical antecedents of the modern differences tradition in
feminist psychology are found in psychoanalysis and Western maternal feminisms. During the 1920s and early 1930s, Karen Horney,
a German psychoanalyst, challenged Sigmund Freud's ideas about
female psychological and sexual development. In her challenge, she

reflected many of the ideas of the German maternal feminists of her time. In particular, she argued that female development, including potential and actual motherhood, was a unique process with its own inherent problems and rewards. It was complementary to male development, which included an envy of female reproductive potential. Her strategy did not involve an attack on the psychoanalytic assumptions of biological gender difference, but rather the creation of a counterdiscourse within psychoanalysis, one that created a woman-centered and woman-positive theory of female development. Similarly, German maternal feminists accepted evolutionary theories of gender difference, and created a counterdiscourse that subverted androcentric biases by emphasizing a woman-centered view of evolution which emphasized cooperation and altruism. (Allen, 1991, pp. 156-163). In this chapter I will first give a brief description of Karen Horney's life. Then I will explore rhetorical and ideological connections between her work and the work of German maternal feminists active during the first three decades of this century.

Karen Clementina Theodora Danielsen was born September 15, 1885 in a small town near Hamburg, Germany. Her mother, Clothilde Marie van Ronzelen Danielsen, was 17 years younger and from a higher class background than her father, Berndt Henrik Wackels Danielsen, a sea captain. These differences in age and class, compounded by the difficulties of integrating the children from Wackels' first marriage, led to a deteriorating relationship which Clothilde finally left in 1904. Throughout her childhood Karen and her older brother Berndt took their mother's side against their stern and religious father. Both children were wanted and loved, but the strain between their parents created a climate of tension and unhappiness (Quinn, 1987, pp. 19-35, 75-76; Rubins, 1978, pp. 5-25).

Karen Danielsen was very successful at school, enjoyed it immensely, and was ambitious at a young age. In 1899, at the age of 13, she formed the plan to become a doctor. At this time no university in Germany admitted women and there was no Gymnasium for girls in Hamburg where she could prepare for taking the Abitur, the university entrance exam (Horney, 1980, p. 9; Quinn, 1987, p. 40). But Karen Danielsen had the good fortune to formulate her plans at a time when higher education for women was becoming available.

In 1901, the first Gymnasium for women opened in Hamburg. After nine days of persuasion from her mother, her mother's friends, and her brother, Karen's father agreed to let her attend if she promised that after Gymnasium he would no longer have to support her (Horney, pp. 24-27; Quinn, pp. 49-50). In 1906 she passed the Abitur and moved to Freiburg to enter medical school. Except for a small allowance which he was always threatening to cut off, her father did not support her in medical school. Karen made some money tutoring other students and her mother took in boarders. The University of Freiburg had admitted its first women students in 1900, and by 1906 there were 34 women entering medicine and 58 women in a student body of 2350 students (Quinn, pp. 88-89, 93-115, 126-130).

Heterosexual relationships assumed an early importance for Karen Danielsen. In both Gymnasium and at medical school she often was dating more than one man at a time and tended to play them off against each other. This pattern continued while she was dating her future husband, Oskar Horney, whom she met when she first went to medical school. They married and settled in Berlin in 1909. He was a successful young lawyer with the Stinnes Corporation and she completed her medical studies in psychiatry, submitting her thesis in 1915. During this same period her father died in 1910, and her mother died unexpectedly in 1911 just weeks before the birth of Karen's first daughter, Brigitte. Her second daughter, Marianne, was born in 1913, and her third daughter, Renate, in 1916. With two incomes, the family lived well in spite of the war, moving to a house in the suburb of Zehlendorf in 1918. However, the inflation of 1923 led to financial disaster for Oskar Horney. After several years of emotional and financial difficulties, Karen Horney separated from Oskar in 1926 and moved with her three daughters from Zehlendorf to an apartment in Berlin (Horney, 1980, pp. 55-83, 119-146, 163-233; Quinn, 1987, pp. 70-89, 107-124, 153-204; Rubins, 1978, pp. 34-55, 76-89).

While finishing medical school and having a family, Karen Horney became involved in the establishment of psychoanalysis in Berlin in the 1910s. Because of the disapproval of psychoanalysis by the psychiatric establishment, she carried on her work in psychoanalysis separately from her psychiatric training. In 1908 Karl Abraham established the Berlin Psychoanalytic Society and began to develop his own practice. Two years later Karen Horney, who probably learned of psychoanalysis from one of her avant-garde circle, went to Karl Abraham for treatment of a recurring depression and problem with fatigue. Although it is not clear that psychoanalysis helped her personally, it did spark her intellectual interest. In 1911 she began attending the meetings of the Berlin Psychoanalytic Society, and beginning in 1914 she served at various times as secretary and treasurer of the society. In 1917 she presented her first psychoanalytic paper (1917/1968), and in 1919 she began a private practice as a psychoanalyst. In 1920 she was the only woman among the six founding members of the Berlin Psychoanalytic Institute. During the 1920s, she was instrumental in developing the training program for the Institute (Horney, 1980, p. 237; Quinn, 1987, pp. 135-152, 196-198; Rubins, 1978, pp. 56-75, 108-142). The Berlin Institute was, during the 1920s, the best training institute in Europe, with more candidates, greater financial success, and better quality of work than Freud's Vienna Institute (Roazen, 1975, p. 329).

In addition to her work within the Berlin Institute, she was a popular public speaker. She spoke to the National Society of Women Social Workers and to the Professional Organization of Kindergarten teachers. Her paper, "The Distrust Between the Sexes," was delivered to the Berlin-Brandenburg branch of the German Women's Medical Association and later published in their journal, *Die Arztin* (1931b/1967). She taught courses on female sexuality at the Berlin Institute and lectured to sexologists. Her public addresses were given to large audiences, composed primarily of women, and aroused lively interest and discussion. One of her talks was written up in a major Berlin newspaper. Another, about the relationship of women's lives to psychoanalysis, was given to an audience of 200 university students and was so popular that it was repeated several times and finally became a series. She was an important public figure in Weimar Germany and an accepted authority on the psychology of women. She became widely known in the 1920s as an exemplar of the new emancipated woman (Moulton, 1975; Quinn, 1987, pp. 197-198, 228; Rubins, 1978, pp. 75, 92, 111).

In 1932, Karen Horney immigrated to the United States where she lived first in Chicago and, from 1935 until her death in 1952, in New York City. She was active in several psychoanalytic societies, eventually founding her own society. Although she made major contributions to psychoanalytic theories throughout her life, her explicit work on female development was largely completed before she left Germany. I will focus in this chapter on her earlier work as an example of a gender-based rhetoric that drew upon and informed the maternal feminisms of her time.

The intellectual theme that ran throughout the life and work of Karen Horney was a resistance to and challenge of orthodoxy (Quinn, 1987, p. 15). She was interested in a wide range of ideas and, according to her daughter, Marianne Eckardt, "She was always questioning and working and debating and discussing, and that went on throughout her life" (Clemmens, 1986, p. 68). Often this interest in ideas took the form of discussion groups that met regularly. She began this in medical school, and continued it in Berlin. In 1930-1931, she held monthly meetings in her home, inviting Adlerians and existentialists as well as Freudians. In Chicago, she joined psychoanalyst Lionel Blitzsten's Monday evening seminars. In New York, she was a member of Harry Sullivan's Zodiac Club in which each member chose an animal identity, Karen Horney's being the water buffalo. Later in her life when her interests turned to Eastern philosophy and religion, she participated in a series of evening meetings on the topic (Rubins, 1978, pp. 45, 131, 169-171, 193, 296-297).

Throughout her life, she challenged orthodoxy wherever she found it. She began in childhood, disagreeing with her father and some of her teachers about religion. She challenged the psychiatric orthodoxy of her time by seeking training in psychoanalysis. In the 1920s she confronted both Karl Abraham and Sigmund Freud on the origins of female sexuality. Once in the United States, she rejected Freudian orthodoxy, especially instinct theory and the centrality of sexuality. As a result, in 1941 her status as a training analyst in the New York Institute was revoked. In response, she and four other analysts walked out of the meeting, left the Institute, and formed their own society (Quinn, 1987, pp. 30-35, 50, 138-141, 204-241, 328-350; Rubins, 1978, pp. 143-156, 232-244).

In spite of her willingness to challenge orthodoxy, Karen Horney remained apolitical throughout her life. First and foremost an individualist, she was concerned with political reality only through its effects on the individuals she knew (Clemmens, 1986; Rubins, 1978, pp. 93-94, 221-222). Although she was widely seen as an example of an emancipated woman in Weimar Germany, she never identified as a feminist (Moulton, 1975; Rubins, p. xii). Even more difficult to explain is her lack of involvement in Jewish politics in the 1930s. Although not Jewish herself, she had many Jewish friends and colleagues and all her daughters married Jewish men (Rubins, pp. 297-298). More important she was a leading member of a profession that, because of its association with Jews, was under consistent attack by the Nazis. She was very helpful to individual Jewish people who were her friends, but remained uninvolved in the political work designed to help psychoanalysts emigrate from Nazi Germany. Over the Christmas holidays in 1936, she returned to Germany and gave a paper to the German Psychoanalytic Institute, implying tacit approval for the avowedly Aryan-only institute (Horney, 1937/1967; Rubins, pp. 208-210). She refused to join the Emergency Committee on Relief and Immigration formed by the American Psychoanalytic Association and the New York Psychoanalytic Society (Rubins, pp. 221-222). When she later interviewed a young woman who had survived the Holocaust, she not only declared it was not possible, but also said "I would not have let that happen to me . . . I would have done something about it" (p. 103). That she could describe herself as "outspokenly anti-fascist" was not a political but a philosophical statement (p. 107).

Why was Karen Horney apolitical? In an article, "Can You Take a Stand?" (1939a), she described the kind of personality that was vulnerable to Nazi propaganda as a person who did not have enough self-trust to take a definite stand on personal or social issues. This person's thoughts and feelings were determined by others, and her or his ego was susceptible to the bolstering provided by extreme ideologies. Through the use of a personal story, she included herself in the category of people who cannot take a stand. The implication was that she may have avoided politics because she saw herself as vulnerable to Nazi propaganda (Rubins, 1978, pp. 232-233). This self-description, however, is unconvincing from a woman who took on Sigmund Freud and Freudian orthodoxy all of her professional life. When it was important to her, she was more than able to take a stand against the most powerful ideology of her profession.

There probably is no satisfactory answer to why she was apolitical. She may have viewed all politics as an orthodoxy that she resisted through a steadfast focus on the individual. Certainly, she believed in the power of personal growth. Although not feminist, she courted her image as an emancipated woman. She was generous to individuals and sympathetic with the socialist orientation of the Berlin Institute, which gave free treatment to a proportion of its clients who could not afford to pay the fees (Quinn, pp. 187, 196). In her private practice, she always had a sliding scale for fees and charged less than she might have, given her reputation. In New York in the 1940s she charged $10 or less depending on the client's ability to pay, while Sigmund Freud was paid $25 an hour in the 1930s (Cherry & Cherry, 1973; Roazen, 1975, p. 424).

Her own privilege may also have been a factor in her apolitical stance. As a woman she was privileged, not only by her position in society, but also by the times in which she lived. At each point in her life, opportunities opened up to her just as she was ready for them (Clemmens, 1986). By combining motherhood, heterosexuality, and a career in medicine and psychoanalysis, which were perceived as requiring special feminine skills, Karen Horney achieved the ideals of many maternal feminists of her time (Allen, 1991, pp. 149-172; Chodorow, 1989, pp. 199-218; Grossmann, 1993).

Karen Horney's life was representative of only a very small percentage of women's lives in Weimar Germany. In 1925, 35 percent of German women were in the labor force and the vast majority worked in labor intensive unskilled jobs in agriculture and industry, earning 30 percent to 40 percent less than their male peers (Bridenthal & Koonz, 1984). Given women's increasing access to higher education, a few women, Karen Horney among them, made significant gains. This included a dramatic increase in the number of women doctors. In 1907 there were 195 women doctors who represented .65 percent of all doctors in Germany. By 1925 this number had risen to 2,572 (5.4 percent), and by 1933 the 3,376 women physicians represented 6.5 percent of German doctors (Bridenthal & Koonz; Grossmann, 1993).[1] For these women doctors, Weimar Germany was a brief historical moment of bourgeois privilege which offered them the ". . . extraordinary opportunity for integrating family, career, and social activism without overwhelming guilt or exhaustion" (Grossmann, p. 79). Even among women doctors, Karen Horney occupied a privileged position. As a psychoanalyst, she chose a profession that was remarkably open to women, especially in Europe. In the 1920s and 1930s about 30 percent of the psychoanalysts were women. And although women did not often hold public positions of power, they exerted an effect proportional to their representation as training analysts. Unlike other professions, to be a psychoanalyst one had to first take the role of client and be analyzed. This structural difference gave considerable power and influence to training analysts (Chodorow, 1986). Karen Horney was active as a training analyst from the beginning of her career in psychoanalysis (Rubins, 1978, pp. 56-75, 108-142). Furthermore, when she immigrated to the United States, she did so as a single woman, a psychoanalyst, and a Gentile with no history of leftist or anti-Nazi political activity. She also had a position waiting. In contrast, two-thirds of the German women doctors who were exiled from Germany never worked as doctors again. Faced with the double prejudice against Jews and women physicians, they often sacrificed their own careers while supporting their physician husbands who could more easily re-establish their professions in America (Grossmann, 1993).

GERMAN MATERNAL FEMINISMS

Although Karen Horney did not identify as a feminist, her ideas reflected and would have been familiar to maternal feminists of her time. In order to explore the connections between her work and German maternal feminisms, I will first briefly describe the ideas of German maternal feminists, and then explore in more detail the rhetorical similarities between Karen Horney's writing and that of the maternal feminists. The dominant themes of German feminists in the nineteenth and early twentieth century included the ethical significance of the mother-child bond, the integration of individual and social responsibilities, and an ideology that emphasized gender differences. Both radical and moderate feminists used the mother-child relationship as experience and metaphor to redefine women's public and private roles. Feminists of the time did not see maternalism as an antithesis to equal rights, but rather as an ethical basis through which to claim rights and change both public and private gendered relationships (Allen, 1991, pp. 1-13, 150-151; Koven & Michel, 1993).

Three feminist organizations active in pre-war and Weimar Germany held maternal feminist ideals and attempted to implement public policy reflecting these ideals. The first group, the Federation of German Women's Associations (BDF, Bund Deutscher Frauenvereine), was founded in 1894 and was active until 1933 when it was outlawed by the Nazi government. It was an umbrella organization that had as many as 900,000 members in the 1920s. The federation emphasized the widening of women's narrow sphere within the framework of traditional values and acknowledged fundamental differences between the sexes (Kaplan, 1984). Equal-rights arguments were present but not central. Two members of the radical wing of the Federation, Lida Gustava Heymann and Anita Augspurg, left the BDF and joined the Women's International League for Peace and Freedom, a group more sympathetic to their concerns with pacifism and equal rights (Koonz, 1987, pp. 21-49).

The second group, the League of Jewish Women (JFB, Judischer Frauenbund), was founded in 1904. This group remained active in the German women's movement until 1933, and in the Jewish community until 1938. The League, which had a membership of 50,000, was a member of the Federation of German Women's Associations from 1907 to 1933. The League stressed duty and service, with an emphasis on family values and solidarity with the Jewish community (Kaplan, 1984; N. Shepherd, 1993, pp. 222-223). Bertha Pappenheim, founder and leader of the JFB, worked within the Jewish community and with international groups to stop the prostitution of Jewish women from Eastern Europe (N. Shepherd, pp. 223-242).

The third group, the League for the Protection of Mothers (Bund fur Mutterschutz), was active from 1905 to 1933 when it was outlawed and its leader, Helene Stocker, exiled (Hackett, 1984). Although this group remained relatively small in numbers, with 3,800 members in 1908 (Allen, 1991, p. 175), it was much more influential throughout the 1920s than its numbers would indicate. Some of the most radical demands were made by this League in the name of protecting mothers. These included aid to unmarried mothers, divorce reform, abortion, birth control, eugenics education, the rights of illegitimate children, and maternity benefits (Allen, pp. 173-205; Koonz, 1987, pp. 21-49).

One of the clearest links between the ideas of Karen Horney and maternal feminisms was her enthusiasm for the work of Ellen Key, a Swedish writer whose ideas influenced both German and American feminists in the early twentieth century (Cott, 1987, pp. 46-49; Key, 1903/1911, p. xv). An enthusiastic supporter of the League for the Protection of Mothers, Ellen Key was not sympathetic to equal-rights feminisms, or to the view that women were better than men (Allen, 1991, p. 185; Key, pp. 246-286). Rather, she argued for a bisexual[2] society which was based on a complementary unity of male and female principles (Key, p. 257). To this end she was not sympathetic with women who chose not to mother, or with women's participation in the labor force, but she did propose a radical critique of the family. She argued for married women's legal rights, the rights of illegitimate children, easier divorce laws, nonmonogamy, wages for housework, and the responsibilities of fathers for all their children (pp. 287-399). She believed in a new morality that validated relationships based on love rather than legal definitions, in a great love that was based on a unity of the senses and the soul, and in a eugenics that hypothesized that the best children were produced in relationships of true love (pp. 13, 74, 105, 158). If women must work outside the home, then they should find work which allowed them to express their feminine nature (p. 196).

Karen Horney's adolescent diaries reveal that she both read and admired Ellen Key. She referred to Ellen Key as ". . . *our* champion" (Horney, 1980, p. 103), and in a review of Key's ideas about love and marriage said "All I have been thinking about 'love and marriage' in recent years, all I have won for myself in ardent battles, all this she sets before the world in radiant letters. What I saw and understood in mute forebodings, I see in her in bright daylight" (p. 92). What Horney found most appealing was the importance of combining sensuality and spirituality in a great love that would heal the conflict between body and soul (pp. 105-106, 113-114). A woman who gave herself freely in love to a man stood "morally way above" the woman who married for money (p. 61). The young Karen Horney also knew of, and was considerably less favorable towards, the campaign of Lida Gustava Heymann's feminist movement to abolish prostitution (p. 73; Quinn, pp. 62-65). This difference in response was indicative of Karen Horney's early sympathy with the ideas of maternal feminisms.

In Karen Horney's later work there is evidence that the ideas of Ellen Key remained important to her. She argued for the importance of gender difference and motherhood in female development (1926/1967), defined frigidity as ". . . the incapacity for a full (that is, including both body and soul) love relationship with a heterosexual love object" (1926-27/1967, p. 74), analyzed the problems with the monogamous ideal (1928/1967), argued that the problems of marriage were not solved by appeals to duty or by unlimited freedom (1932a/1967), argued that motherhood, especially illegitimate motherhood, was not sufficiently protected by law (1931b/1967), and described as a modern type the woman who wanted a career and, at the same time, was unwilling to renounce her femininity (1934/1967). By choosing psychoanalysis as a career, she further reinforced Ellen Key's and other maternal feminists' views that women were particularly suited for careers that required maternal skills (Chodorow, 1986, 1989, pp. 199-218; Grossmann, 1993).

Karen Horney shared with Ellen Key and Helene Stocker, leader of the League for the Protection of Mothers, a passionate interest in making sexuality freer and more fulfilling for women. A very positive introduction to Ellen Key's *Love and Marriage* was written by Havelock Ellis (Key, 1903/1911, pp. vii-xvi). Although Ellen Key did not discuss female sexuality in explicit terms, she did believe that sexual fidelity should be maintained only for the right reasons, which included love and passion but not duty. Fidelity that rested on conventional duty ". . . will be in the fire like a fire-escape of straw" (p. 303). Women who would not be asked to commit crimes for the sake of their children should not be asked to prostitute themselves for their children by staying in a marriage in which there was no love. A mother's responsibility to her children did not always include maintaining a home with their father (pp. 287-295).

Helene Stocker's commitment to a freer female sexuality was as clear as her concern with making motherhood more rewarding for women (Hackett, 1984; Koonz, 1987, pp. 35-36). Like Karen Horney, she felt alienated from German equal-rights feminists who treated women as either asexual or as sexual victims of men (Hackett, p. 112; Horney, 1980, p. 73; Quinn, 1987, pp. 62-65). In her view, the morality of intercourse was determined by the intent and consequences of the act, not the legal relationship of the two people involved. Furthermore, intercourse was important not only for reproduction but also for a harmonious life. In keeping with her beliefs, she lived openly in a common-law relationship with Bruno Springer from 1910 until his death in 1931 (Hackett, p. 114). She defended abortion as ". . . the right over oneself" (Hackett, p. 117). Beginning in 1901 she worked for the repeal of a German law which forbade male homosexuality. In 1911 the League for the Protection of Mothers, led by Helene Stocker, organized a public meeting to protest the expansion of the law forbidding homosexuality to include women as well as men. This was probably the first time a feminist organization openly defended lesbians (Allen, 1991, pp. 170-171). Helene Stocker identified with the new scientific movement to study sexuality and with psychoanalysis. She edited *The New Generation*, the journal of the League, which published articles by Sigmund Freud and Havelock Ellis (Hackett, pp. 113-114). In late 1912 or early 1913 she attended a meeting of the Vienna Psychoanalytic Society in the company of Lou Andreas-Salome (Appignanesi & Forrester, 1992, p. 258). She later joined the Berlin Psychoanalytic Institute, where she and Karen Horney would have been two of a very few women members (Quinn, p. 67). In 1941, at the end of her life, Helene Stocker moved to New York City and lived in the German immigrant community, thereby sharing for a short time a North American neighborhood with Karen Horney (Hackett, p. 123).

KAREN HORNEY'S DEBATE WITH FREUD

Karen Horney's most significant and original contribution to the feminist discourses of her culture was her debate with Freud over the nature of femininity and female psychology. The major arguments on each side were first stated in the mainstream psychoanalytic forums of the International Congresses and *The International Journal of Psychoanalysis*, which was published simultaneously in German and English beginning in 1919. However, the ideas were heard outside narrow psychoanalytic circles because of a general interest in female sexuality, and because Karen Horney was a popular speaker to lay audiences (Koonz, 1987, pp. 35-36; Rubins, 1978, pp. 75, 92, 111). Later in her life Karen Horney recalled that she first questioned Sigmund Freud's theories because of his ideas about femininity. She first expressed this view in the early 1930s at a social evening in Chicago (Rubins, p. 180), and later acknowledged it in print in the introduction to *New Ways in Psychoanalysis* (1939b, p. 7). Although much of the Horney-Freud debate focused on penis envy, it was not primarily over penis envy. They agreed that both a primary, and a secondary (regressive) penis envy existed. What they disagreed on was the relative importance of each to female development (Freud, 1925/1961, 1933/1964; Horney, 1923/1967, 1926/1967). The major disagreement at the center of the debate, as I will describe it below, was over the existence of a primary femininity (Fliegel, 1973). For Freud, femininity was derived from a primary, or original, masculinity. For Horney, femininity was primary. The little girl was female from the start.

The debate over female sexuality went on for over ten years and involved several theorists besides Karen Horney and Sigmund Freud. In order to give an overview, I begin with a brief chronology of the players and events. Then, I turn in some detail to Sigmund Freud's ideas and Karen Horney's objections and her own theories of female sexuality.

Karen Horney first wrote about penis envy in 1911 when she was pregnant with her first child. In a diary entry she described how, as a child, she wanted to be a boy, and attributed her own pride in doing better than her brother in school to penis envy (1980, pp. 250-252). She was not drawn into a public debate until 1920 when Karl Abraham presented his paper, "Manifestations of the Female Castration Complex" (1922), to the Sixth International Congress in Holland. Karen Horney met Sigmund Freud at this conference and undoubtedly heard Karl Abraham's paper. Something in it troubled her and she began to compose her reply upon her return to Berlin (Quinn, 1987, pp. 208-211; Rubins, 1978, pp. 64-65). In 1922 she made her reply public in a paper entitled "On the Genesis of the Castration Complex in Women" (1923/1967) which she presented to the Seventh International Congress held in Berlin. Of the 256 people in attendance at the Congress, 112 were analysts. Karen Horney presented her paper in a session chaired by Sigmund Freud.

In this first and tentative questioning of Freud's theory, she took on not only Sigmund Freud, but also Karl Abraham, who was her first analyst and the head of the Berlin Institute (Quinn, pp. 211-214; Rubins, pp. 68-70). Tentative as it was, Sigmund Freud recognized the challenge and replied with a paper, "Some Psychical Consequences of the Anatomical Distinction Between the Sexes" (1925/1961), which Anna Freud read for him at the Ninth International Congress in Bad Hamburg. This was his first major paper on female sexuality and a direct contradiction of Karen Horney's earlier paper (Rubins, pp. 109-110). She wasted no time in forming her reply and this time she was much less tentative. Between September 1925 and April 1926 she wrote her paper, "The Flight from Womanhood: The Masculinity-Complex in Women as Viewed by Men and by Women" (Horney, 1926/1967). It was originally to be included in a Festschrift for Sigmund Freud's seventieth birthday, but as the Festschrift was never published, her paper first appeared in *The International Journal of Psychoanalysis* later in 1926. The paper was a stinging critique of Sigmund Freud's views, which Karen Horney claimed she had softened by wrapping "my stone in a little cotton-wool" (Quinn, p. 220). If "Flight from Womanhood" is a softened version, one wonders what the original version was like (Quinn, pp. 220-225; Rubins, pp. 111-113). At this point several other analysts entered the debate, including Ernst Jones, Jeanne Lampl de Groot, Helene Deutsch, and Otto Fenichel, all of whom were later cited more systematically than Karen Horney (Fliegel, 1973). By 1928 Karen Horney had removed Sigmund Freud's picture from her living room (Rubins, p. 121). Although the major terms of the debate were set by 1930, both Sigmund Freud and Karen Horney published two more papers which basically reiterated and hardened their former views (Freud, 1931/1961, 1933/1964; Horney, 1932b/1967, 1933c/1967).

This was a debate which Karen Horney lost in two ways. First, Sigmund Freud so dominated the psychoanalytic scene by the 1920s that no one could successfully challenge him. Furthermore, in 1923, the year in which Karen Horney's first paper challenging his theory was published, Sigmund Freud was first diagnosed with cancer, an event that led to the desire on the part of many of his followers not to cause schisms (Fliegel, 1973; Roazen, 1975, pp. xxxi-xxxii, 298-303). Second, citations of Karen Horney's work were systematically eliminated from the literature on female sexuality and replaced by citations of those more acceptable in orthodox circles, who used ideas that were originally hers (Fliegel).

Karen Horney's strategy in this debate was to create a counterdiscouse within the Freudian instinct framework. She did not question the existence of differences between women and men, nor did she attack the notion of instinctual sexual drives. Rather, she stood difference on its head. Sigmund Freud's ideas were not wrong as much as they were perverted. She exposed the bias of a masculine vision of female sexuality, and argued for a unique female sexuality with its own strengths and problems that was complementary to a unique male sexuality which also had problems as well as strengths. In many ways her strategy was similar to that of maternal feminists who created a counterdiscourse within evolutionary theory. Rather than attack the notion of difference, or the biological basis of evolution, German maternal feminists adapted Reform Darwinism to their own uses. These included the elevation of cooperation over competition, and location of the progress of the species in the qualities of the mother-child bond. Through this strategy of counterdiscourse they were able to subvert androcentric biases and create feminist interpretations (Allen, 1991, pp. 159-163).

Although Sigmund Freud did discuss bisexuality, he never applied the idea seriously to sexual development, especially the development of the girl. The lack of seriousness with which he explored bisexuality is illustrated by his use of it as a cop-out. In one swift move, he dismissed any feminist assertions of masculine prejudice by ". . . standing on the ground of bisexuality" (1933/1964, p. 116). He dismissed feminists' protests by using bisexuality to label them more masculine than feminine. In contrast, his most consistent view of the little girl was that she was a little man (1933/1964, p. 118). This theoretical position had a number of consequences. The most important was that early female sexuality was masculine. Thus, the little girl was active in her orientation to the world, loved her phallic mother, masturbated with her phallic clitoris, and was devastated when she discovered the fact of her castration, i.e., she did not have a penis but only a vastly inferior clitoris. This beginning influenced all her later development. Normal femininity required that she replace her active orientation to the world with a passive one, that she give up the love for her mother and transfer it to her father, and that she transfer her sexual energy from her phallic clitoris to her feminine vagina, which remained undiscovered until puberty. Feminine sexuality and motherhood became compensations for a lost masculinity, i.e., a lost penis. A baby, especially a baby boy who brought with him the longed-for penis, was a penis substitute (1925/1961, 1931/1961, 1933/1964). This wish for a penis was ". . . *par excellence* a feminine one" (1933/1964, p. 129).

Abnormal femininity was also based in masculinity. In this case, the girl either gave up sexuality altogether because she was so repulsed by her inferior clitoris and her castrated state, or she continued to strive to obtain the prized penis. This latter stance could take the form of homosexuality, or, more commonly, the masculinity complex, in which the woman strove to emulate men in the public sphere (Freud, 1925/1961, 1931/1961, 1933/1964).

Femininity became a castrated masculinity. There was no independent female sexuality. At best, femininity was a consolation prize for the lost penis. At worst, it was a frustrated striving after the impossible. To protest this view was to demonstrate penis envy. To accept it also demonstrated penis envy. As Karen Horney later commented: "In fact, there is scarcely any character trait in woman which is not assumed to have an essential root in penis-envy" (1939b, p. 104). For Sigmund Freud, all femininity was rooted in frustrated masculinity.

Karen Horney always tested theory against her own experience. When she examined Sigmund Freud's theory of femininity against her experiences as a heterosexual woman, mother, and therapist, she found them wanting. What she knew from her own life and heard from her patients led her to develop a theory of primary femininity. Her early heterosexual experience included satisfying clitoral orgasms. This awareness was shaken by her early contact with psychoanalysis. She wrote shortly after her marriage that now she felt shame at such pleasure and that she would not admit it gave her more satisfaction than a normal, i.e., vaginal, orgasm (Quinn, 1987, pp. 162-163). However, she remained aware of sexual pleasure originating in the clitoris and defended this pleasure in her later writing: "And I do not see why, in spite of its past evolution, it should not be conceded that the clitoris legitimately belongs to and forms an integral part of the female genital apparatus" (Horney,

1926/1967, p. 65). She also used her own experience to validate women's experience of motherhood. Her awareness of the importance of motherhood may have been heightened when her own mother died just weeks before her first daughter was born. In her diary at the time she wondered about possible unconscious feelings of hostility she might have toward the baby. On a conscious level, however, she was aware of much more positive feelings: "And the feeling of carrying in me a small, becoming human being invests one with higher dignity and importance that makes me very happy and proud" (1980, p. 262). Certainly the power of the experience of motherhood for female psychology and for male envy is evident in many of her later writings (e.g., 1926/1967, 1931a/1967, 1931b/1967, 1932b/1967, 1933a/1967, 1933b/1967). Her experience as a therapist also informed her theory. She once said that although her theoretical convictions changed, her technique as an analyst never altered (Roazen, 1975, p. 400). This technique gave her information she could trust, more than one could trust abstract theory. One of her main arguments against the importance of penis envy was that it clouded the real issues in therapy because the patient herself found this an acceptable and relatively harmless explanation compared to her more painful conflicts (Horney, 1939b, pp. 106-110).

Based on her own experience, her knowledge of psychoanalytic theory, and the cultural discourses available to her, Karen Horney proposed the existence of an innate or instinctual heterosexuality. The boy was born male and the girl was born female. Each sex had its own distinctive developmental pattern. Her view of male development was much as Sigmund Freud had described it, with the important addition of male envy of female reproductive powers. The girl early in life discovered not only her clitoris, but also her vagina. This occurred with or without explicit experiences of masturbation, because knowledge of the sexual organs was instinctive. She envied the boy his penis because it allowed easier masturbation, the fantasy of omnipotence through producing a jet of urine, and the visual reassurance that no damage had been done. In due course, her innate heterosexuality led her to seek her father's love. At this point she instinctively fantasized that her father's large penis in her small vagina would wound her and cause pain. If these fantasies were not too frightening and if the disappointment of not being able to win her father was not too great, then she would go on to develop as a normal woman who would value her reproductive abilities and her heterosexuality. However, if the fantasies evoked too much guilt, she would flee from them and from her femininity, seeking safety in a masculine identification. The feelings of inferiority elicited by this regression were less disturbing than her earlier guilt. This flight from femininity revived her earlier penis envy, only this time it was not simple envy but much more strongly motivated and much more damaging to her development as a woman. The masculinity complex arose out of a disappointed femininity, not as Sigmund Freud would have it, from a frustrated desire for masculinity (Horney, 1923/1967, 1926/1967, 1933c/1967).

To modern readers, the most painful aspect of Karen Horney's theory is her willingness to reinforce the Freudian orthodoxy that all childhood seduction was fantasy. She acknowledged her patients' insistence that their fantasies were real, but used this as evidence of the centrality of the ". . . basic fantasy of having suffered castration through the love relation with the father" (1923/1967, p. 51). In other writing she was equally insistent on the instinctive fantasy life of the girl that led to specific fantasies of rape, or of a large penis wounding her small vagina (1926/1967, 1932b/1967, 1933c/1967). Sometimes Karen Horney emphasized a more general disappointment in the love relation with the father rather than specific wounding fantasies (1931b/1967, 1932a/1967). After she came to the United States, she mentioned for the first time the reality of premature and intense sexual experiences that frighten or overwhelm the young girl. Although she did not label these as incest, she was clear that they were problematic for female development (1933a/1967, 1933b/1967, 1934/1967).

If there is a complementary, unique, and equally important instinctive female sexuality that balances male sexuality, the possibility of male envy as well as female envy arises. Sigmund Freud was unable even to imagine womb envy, and he remained silent on the issue. If femininity was compensated masculinity, then there was no possibility of womb envy. As Eva Kittay has pointed out: "It is incoherent to speak of an envy for the *compensation* for something that one *already* has" (1984, p. 98). However, for Karen

Horney, the existence of a primary femininity as well as a primary masculinity made male envy a logical and necessary possibility. Influenced by George Groddeck, who first put the idea of male envy to her, Karen Horney first mentioned men's envy of women in her paper, "The Flight from Womanhood." She noted that she had observed this envy in her male patients, and she hypothesized that male cultural achievements might be an overcompensation for such envy (1926/1967; Quinn, 1987, pp. 214-217).

By the early 1930s her views of male envy had strengthened. What began as a parallel developmental process to primary penis envy had become an essential and powerful part of male development. The boy instinctively judged that his penis was much too small compared to his mother's vagina, and reacted with a fear of ridicule, dread of his own inadequacy, and injury to his self-respect. She demoted castration anxiety in men to a neurotic phenomenon, but found traces of this dread of the vagina in all men. Thus, men's dread of women was not due to the woman's lack of a penis as Sigmund Freud had argued, but rather to the instinctual heterosexual fantasies of the boy's small and inadequate penis being engulfed by his mother's large vagina and her resulting ridicule (Horney, 1932b/1967).

It is in her writing about male envy that one most clearly feels Karen Horney's anger. Articles with egalitarian titles like "The Distrust Between the Sexes" (1931b/1967) and "The Dread of Woman: Observations on a Specific Difference in the Dread felt by Men and by Women Respectively for the Opposite Sex" (1932b/1967) focused on male problems, with only minor references to female patterns. Primary penis envy in women was demoted to a minor role in female development, while primary womb envy in men became prominent in the development of all men and male culture. Male inadequacy was front and center. She expressed amazement that so little attention had been directed to man's dread of woman (1932b/1967). Sigmund Freud's intransigence in the debate must have fueled her anger. The more he, and most of the psychoanalytic community, insisted on penis envy as the primary determinant of female development, the stronger became her desire to reveal how frightened the unclothed emperor really was.

Karen Horney argued for an instinctual sexuality that fit the biological reproductive requirements of the species. At the same time, she recognized the importance of culture in determining development. In her earlier work, which I am focusing on here, there was a ". . . curious mutation in which she crossed Freudian-like biological determinism with her own recognition of sociological causation" (Garrison, 1981, p. 681). These early arguments for cultural determinism took two forms. In one, she presented the view that the sex of the observer influenced what is observed, created, and thought. She argued that what men have called culture or theory is in reality a masculine, not an objective, culture or theory. This is most clearly developed in her paper, "The Flight from Womanhood" (1926/1967). She used the work of Georg Simmel to support her argument that what was considered culture was, in reality, masculine culture. Because women had adapted to this masculine culture did not change the fact that it did not reflect their true nature (Oakes, 1984, pp. 65-132). From here she moved to the parallel argument that what was considered theory was, in reality, masculine-biased theory. In a statement that must have infuriated Sigmund Freud, she likened the male theorist's view of female development to the little boy's view of the little girl (1926/1967, pp. 57-58). She acknowledged that her feminine view might also be one-sided, but that she offered it as a contribution to the goal ". . . to get beyond the subjectivity of the masculine or the feminine standpoint and to obtain a picture of the mental development of woman that will be more true to the facts of her nature – with its specific qualities and its differences from that of man – than any we have hitherto achieved" (p. 70). She understood that the creation of an ideology was a tool of power. She described how the more powerful group creates an ideology to maintain its own position, to make its position acceptable to the weaker group, and to deny the existence of a struggle (1931b/1967, p. 116). She saw power in the parallel of female envy of male privilege ". . . to the concealed hostility of the worker against his employer" (1926-27/1967, p. 75).

Karen Horney also used culture was as a facilitator of the individual's developmental patterns. Women's flight from womanhood was reinforced by the actual disadvantage women faced in social life, a disadvantage that was much greater than most women acknowledged (1926/1967). As her work progressed, she developed this argument into a theoretical position that culture determined the observed frequency of developmental patterns. Thus, individual factors caused an individual's development, but cultural factors determined the frequency with which the pattern was seen in society. She used this to explain the differing rates of male and female unfaithfulness (1928/1967), the frequency of the feminine type who overvalued love (1934/1967), and the differential frequency of male and female masochism (1935/1967).

After Karen Horney immigrated to the United States in 1932, her emphasis on cultural determinism became increasingly dominant in her work. By 1939, when she published *New Ways in Psychoanalysis*, she had completely rejected Freud's instinct theory and adopted a thorough-going cultural determinism (Westkott, 1986, pp. 57-65). Her move from Germany to the United States facilitated this shift in two ways. First, her experience with a different culture illustrated how powerful culture was in shaping psychological development. Second, her professional association and close personal relationship with Erich Fromm and other members of the cultural school served to reinforce and develop her earlier ideas about the importance of culture (Quinn, 1987, pp. 245-274, 277-294).

EVALUATIONS AND CONCLUSIONS

After the early 1930s, Karen Horney did not continue to write about female sexual development, but shifted her emphasis to explorations of the etiology of neurosis in gender-neutral terms. This shift coincided with her immigration to the United States, and is reflected in a shift in her own writing from a rhetoric reflective of German maternal feminisms to one more consistent with the equal-rights feminisms of the U.S. In her application to immigrate she stated her scientific interest as concentrating on female psychology, a task she was particularly suited for because she was a woman: "As psychology has been until now mostly worked from the side of men, it seems to me to be the given task for a woman psychologist–or at least I think it to be mine–to work out a fuller understanding for specifically female trends and attitudes in life" (Paris, 1994, p. 55) Three years later, in 1935, she gave a paper "Women's Fear of Action" to the National Federation of Professional and Business Women's Clubs

(Horney, 1994). In this paper she argues that masculinity and femininity are artificial and that the most important task for women is to develop their full potential as human beings. She equates a cultural focus on the development of full human potential for both sexes with progress, and a cultural interest in sex differences with danger for women in a patriarchal society. Although at neither time did Karen Horney declare herself a feminist, her words at each time reflect the dominant feminisms of the culture in which she was living.

Dee Garrison (1981) has explored possible personal reasons for her shift away from her focus on female sexuality. In Chicago Franz Alexander accused her of only tearing Freud down and offering nothing original of her own. This criticism may have encouraged her to turn away from her former work. She lacked a political analysis that would have explained the hostile response her ideas had received in Freudian circles and she may have wanted to leave this hostility behind. She may have sought a wider base in order to secure herself financially in a new country.

Another reason is suggested by the work of Nancy Chodorow who interviewed a number of early women psychoanalysts who were contemporaries of Karen Horney. She found that gender was not a salient category for these women. They focused on theories of the unconscious rather than theories of female sexuality, accepted gender differences as natural, expected equality in the public sphere and traditional roles in the domestic sphere, and were not very aware of the 1920s debate over femininity. Their experience was one of relatively little gender discrimination within psychoanalysis compared to what many had experienced in medical school. Finally, they shared more central and important identities with male analysts, such as being Jewish and being psychoanalysts in a hostile world of medicine (Chodorow, 1989, pp. 199-218). Thus, the intellectual climate within psychoanalysis did not encourage a concern with gender. Perhaps what is remarkable is not that Karen Horney gave up a focus on gender, but that she focused on it as long as she did.

Furthermore, Maria Westkott (1986) has proposed a feminist interpretation of Karen Horney's later gender-neutral theories of the development of neurosis. She has developed the theory that although Karen Horney did not specifically address gender in these theories, they were nonetheless informed by her work with female patients and her own development as a woman.

In evaluating the politics of maternal feminisms and of Karen Horney's work, it is important to engage in a dialogue between the past and the present, where we listen as well as judge, and do not equate any single perspective with true feminism (Allen, 1991, pp. 4-7). To assume that a concern with motherhood is not feminist, as Claudia Koonz did when she said ". . . concern with sexuality and motherhood enjoyed greater support than pacifism and feminist reform" (1987, p. 36), is to discredit those maternal feminists who were concerned with sexuality and motherhood. Both German maternal feminisms and the work of Karen Horney had radical and conservative consequences that are predictable when the political goal is the creation of a counterdiscourse that values the feminine.

Maternal feminists advocated goals that included a radical critique of both the family and the state. Furthermore, they envisioned a state that embodied maternal values and included real women as active participants (Allen, 1991, pp. 1-13; Koven & Michel, 1993). This ideal vision was difficult for maternal feminists to carry out in specific political situations because of differences among women and because they lacked the political power to control discourses and carry out political change. Male politicians adopted the maternal feminist rhetoric, but not in a way that promoted women's public participation or their strength in the family (Koven & Michel). Maternal feminisms, like equal-rights feminisms, both opened up and constrained possibilities for women (Allen, pp. 229-230). German maternal feminisms formed the basis of some very radical feminist demands. At the 1908 annual convention of the Federation of German Women's Associations a motion to legalize abortion was introduced and debated, action that would have not been thought of at the time within equal-rights feminisms (Allen, pp. 190-197). These same maternal values were distorted and used by the Nazis several decades later (Koonz, 1987, pp. 21-49). This distortion was not an inevitable consequence of maternal feminism, but one historical perversion of maternal feminist ideals (Allen, pp. 229-244).

Similarly, Karen Horney's attempt to revalue the feminine within the dominant discourse of Freudian psychoanalysis had both radical and conservative consequences. Her argument for a primary femininity that does not depend on a comparison to masculinity and does not define women in relationship to men constituted a powerful rejection of masculine culture and theory. Furthermore, her emphasis on male envy revealed the powerful to be wanting, and provided a point of strength and pride for women. The degree to which she was silenced at the time and in later discussions is evidence of the power of her argument (Fliegel, 1973). On the other hand, she mandated heterosexuality and made child sexual assault invisible with her theories of innate heterosexuality. Furthermore, to give women an equality of instincts within a theory that equates instinct with femininity is problematic. For Sigmund Freud instinct, nature, music, religion, and femininity were irrational and inferior; whereas ego, civilization, science, and masculinity were rational and superior (Roazen, 1975, p. 471; Westkott, 1986, pp. 53-65). Thus, to give women an equality of instincts did not eliminate the misogyny of a theory in which instinct was symbolically feminine.

The strengths and weakness of both maternal feminisms and Karen Horney's primary femininity were similar. Both provided important alternative visions. Both also lacked the power to change discourses and politics. Both the male-dominated public sphere and the male-dominated theoretical discourses perverted visions of bisexual complementarity into hierarchies of dominance and submission. Yet these bisexual visions were important and valuable. What Karen Horney and the maternal feminists illustrate is the possibility of gender differences that do not conflate with dominance.

NOTES

1. Although these two texts agree on the number of women doctors in 1925, they differ in the number of women doctors they report for 1933. Bridenthal and Koonz (1984, p. 64) state that 4,395 of the 51,527 doctors in Germany were women (8.5 percent). Grossmann (1993, p. 67) states that 3,376 of the 51,527 doctors were women (6.5 percent). I have chosen to use Atina Grossmann's figures here because they are more recent and because her work is specifically on women doctors in Germany, whereas Renate Bridenthal and Claudia Koonz's work includes doctors in an overview of women in the German labor force.

2. I use bisexual in this context to mean the advocation of the complementarity of feminine and masculine characteristics as the basis for a full and healthy society. The closest equivalent in contemporary language would probably be androgynous. I have chosen to use bisexual because it is the word Ellen Key used in

her writing. When I discuss Freud's work later in this chapter, I also use the term bisexual. His use is closer to the contemporary meaning of sexual attraction to both women and men. However, in the contexts in which he uses bisexual in discussing the development of female sexuality, one can also read it to mean a complementarity of feminine and masculine traits in an individual.

SECTION 2:
CONTEMPORARY FEMINIST RESEARCH

In the next two chapters I focus on two examples of feminist research, each of which illustrates one of the two traditions. For the similarities tradition, I have chosen to explore the extensive literature on gender and mathematics performance in Chapter 4. In an attempt to reduce, undermine, or destroy the belief that males are better at math and therefore are suited to scientific professions, feminist researchers have produced strong and consistent data which demonstrate that females and males achieve very similar mathematics skills. In spite of this work, the myth that men are better at math persists. In order to explore why these data have had such a small impact on belief systems, I examine the symbolization of mathematics as masculine.

In Chapter 5 I turn to the debate around moralities of care and justice, which is a topic that is rooted in the differences tradition. In this chapter I examine the empirical evidence for gender similarities and differences, and the political concerns feminist philosophers have expressed about ethics of care. Finally, I explore the interrelatedness of ethics of justice and care, and the necessity of both for full moral visions.

Although these are very different topics, there are two convergences that illuminate the importance of considering both similarities and differences in order to understand the complexity of the situations involved. The first convergence appears in the empirical results. Feminist researchers in gender and math began looking for similarities, whereas feminist researchers in moral theory began by looking for differences. In spite of this, their results are quite similar. Whether similarities or differences are found depends on the construction of the questions asked. In math, the largest differences favoring males are found using white, middle-class precocious adolescents and testing them on one particular standardized test (SAT-M). If you change any aspect of this construction, gender differences become smaller, disappear, or reverse. Thus, if Asian rather than white precocious adolescents are tested in the same situation, the gender difference is smaller. If classroom grades instead of standardized tests are chosen as the measure of math achievement, then a small difference emerges favoring females. If instead of a precocious sample, a representative sample is used, differences between females and males disappear. Furthermore, race, class, and nationality differences in mathematics achievement are usually larger than gender differences within each subgroup.

In moral reasoning research, the construction of the questions is equally important. If white, middle-class North Americans are asked to reason about abstract moral dilemmas, very few differences are found. If these same people are asked to reason about a dilemma from their own life, more gender differences are found, particularly in the kind of dilemma reported. Differences in moral reasoning across class, race, and cultures are often more compelling than gender differences within each of these groups.

The second convergence appears in the symbolization of each of these areas. In both mathematics and moral theory, the symbolization of gender differences is strong and persistent, and continues in the face of contradictory evidence. The symbolization of mathematics as masculine is reflected in children's views of math as a male domain, teacher's beliefs about their students' math achievement, the valuing of different mathematics skills, and the language of mathematics. It is vital not only to produce the evidence to contradict these cultural beliefs, but also to engage in a direct analysis of how the assumptions are expressed and supported in the cultural and linguistic institutions of mathematics.

In moral theory gender symbolization appears in two forms. One is a moral division of labor in which women are supposed to care about and for others in the private world, and men are supposed to be concerned with abstract justice issues in the public world. Regulated to this moral division of labor, care and justice moral concerns are themselves symbolized in gender terms. Thus justice is seen as masculine and care as feminine, independently of how actual women and men express their moral concerns. Again, as with mathematics, empirical evidence of gender similarities or other important group differences does not change the cultural symbolization. In order to change cultural symbols, a very complex cultural analysis is required in which caregiving is untied from gender and other forms of subordination, and theories of morality are contextualized in ways which emphasize the inter-relatedness of both care and justice.

Chapter 4

Gender and Math:
What Makes a Difference?

THE ONE GIRL AT THE BOYS' PARTY

When I take my girl to the swimming party
I set her down among the boys. They tower and
bristle, she stands there smooth and sleek,
her math scores unfolding in the air around her.
They will strip to their suits, her body hard and
indivisible as a prime number,
they'll plunge in the deep end, she'll subtract
her height from ten feet, divide it into
hundreds of gallons of water, the numbers
bounding in her mind like molecules of chlorine
in the bright blue pool. When they climb out,
her ponytail will hang its pencil lead
down her back, her narrow silk suit
with hamburgers and french fries printed on it
will glisten in the brilliant air, and they will
see her sweet face, solemn and
sealed, a factor of one, and she will
see their eyes, two each,
their legs, two each, and the curves of their sexes,
one each, and in her head she'll be doing her
wild multiplying, as the drops
sparkle and fall to the power of a thousand from her body.

Sharon Olds
The Dead and the Living, 1992, p. 79

Debates about gender similarities and differences in mathematics achievement have been central for many feminist researchers. Women's alleged lower ability in mathematics has been used to explain and justify their low participation in the physical sciences and engineering. Consistent with the similarities tradition, feminist psychologists and educators have focused on the overlap in male and female scores on mathematics achievement measures; the specific contexts in which differences occur; the relationship of girls' mathematics achievement to internal factors such as attitudes and to external factors such as parents' attitudes or teachers' behavior; and the development of intervention programs (Fennema, 1993; Linn & Hyde, 1989). Gender as an analytical tool is applied to understanding and changing the development of individual women and men. In keeping with this tradition, in the first section of this chapter I will focus on the definition and measurement of mathematics achievement and the search for ever more precise information that either destroys, or sharply limits, the myth of women's inferiority in mathematics. However, after 20 years of excellent research the myth remains alive and well. In order to explore why the empirical evidence generated by feminist researchers should be so ineffective in changing beliefs, I turn in my second section to an examination of cultural beliefs that symbolize mathematics as masculine, including the belief that men should be better at math. In my concluding section, I attempt to outline how each of these visions can contribute to the development of equality and equity in mathematics training and education.

GENDER AND MATHEMATICS ACHIEVEMENT

In the empirical studies of mathematics achievement, two definitions of achievement have been used: (1) standardized tests, and (2) classroom grades. By far the greatest bulk of work has been and continues to be concerned with the examination of performance on standardized tests of mathematics achievement. Janet Hyde and her colleagues provide the most thorough review of these studies in a meta-analysis of gender differences. By calculating effect sizes they were able to examine the magnitude of the difference between male and female means expressed in standard deviation units. Their examination of over 250 effect sizes yielded an average effect size of .2. In

Gender and Math 85

other words, this is an average mean difference equivalent to 20 percent of the combined standard deviation. Of much more interest than this small overall difference is the way in which effect sizes are distributed across different contexts. In summary, differences favoring males increase with the age of the sample, the selectivity of the sample, and the kind of mathematics problem that is studied. Specifically, in tests of computation, differences favor females up to the age of 15 (5-10 years, $d = -.20$, and 11-14 years, $d = -.22$) with no difference appearing in older samples. In tests of mathematical concepts there is no systematic male or female advantage at any age. In tests of problem solving there is no difference until the age of 15 after which males have an advantage (15-18 years, $d = .29$ and, 19-25 years, $d = .32$). If only samples representative of the general population are included, there is a negligible difference favoring females ($d = -.05$) (Hyde, Fennema, & Lamon, 1990). In another meta-analysis, Lynn Friedman (1989) found a similarly small difference favoring females ($d = -.024$) in representative samples. In highly select samples of mathematically precocious youth, small to medium differences appear favoring males ($d = .54$ and .41). Furthermore, the average effect size is smaller for studies published after 1974 ($d = .14$) than before ($d = .31$) (Hyde, Fennema, & Lamon, 1990).

A disproportionate amount of research and media attention in the U.S. has been focused on studies involving mathematically precocious youth, often without acknowledging the highly restricted nature of the samples (Hyde, Fennema, & Lamon, 1990). These samples are obtained by inviting Grade 7 and 8 students who score at or above the ninety-seventh percentile on national normative tests to take the Scholastic Aptitudes Test-Quantitative Subtest (SAT-M) (Benbow & Stanley, 1980; Benbow & Lubinski, 1993). Similarly selected younger students (Grades 2-6) are invited to take the Preliminary Scholastic Aptitudes Test-Quantitative Subscale (PSAT-M) (Mills, Ablard, & Stumpf, 1993). Across the samples of highly select students who do take these timed, multiple-choice tests, which are designed for older students, males consistently perform better than females with effect sizes around .4, and these differences have remained consistent over time (Benbow & Lubinski, 1993). Larger differences favoring males also have been found among the top students in Singapore (Kaur, 1990) and Australia (Willis, 1989, pp. 10-11).

One problem with the studies of precocious youth that may exaggerate gender differences is the process of sample selection. Students scoring above the ninety-seventh percentile are notified by school personnel that they are eligible to take the SAT-M. Those who choose to participate take the SAT-M at a regular sitting of the exam which takes place outside of school hours, in an unfamiliar setting, and includes many older students who are taking the exam as a university admission requirement. The authors of these studies do not report what proportion of those eligible are notified by school officials or what proportion of those notified actually take the SAT-M (B. Becker, 1990). To the extent that the very best girls may be less likely than the very best boys to be notified by school personnel and/or may be more reluctant to take the SAT-M, the observed gender differences would be exaggerated. Because it is possible to prepare for the SAT-M with published practice tests, it would also be interesting to know if the students invited to take the SAT-M practice beforehand and if there is a gender difference in the tendency to practice (S. Chipman, personal communication, October 10, 1993).

Although there may be selection processes in the study of precocious youth that tend to exaggerate gender differences, the phenomenon of more males than females at the very highest levels of mathematics achievement appears to be empirically valid. Given even a small mean difference, the distribution of males and females will be more unbalanced at the extremes of the distribution than in the middle. If, in addition to a mean difference favoring males, there is also a larger male variability, as appears to be the case for the PSAT-M and SAT-M, then males will comprise an even larger proportion of the students with very high scores (Feingold, 1992). However, a focus on such select samples is problematic for the study of gender differences in mathematics achievement. It is highly inaccurate to generalize from samples of precocious youth to gender differences in high school and university populations from which mathematics-related professions draw their future members. One does not have to be in the top one to three percent of the population in mathematics achievement to be a successful mathematician, scientist, or engineer. For example, the average SAT-M scores of entering engineering students in the United States was 558 for females and 549 for males (McIlwee & Robinson, 1992, p. 47). It is interesting to note the slightly higher scores of the females, however, the most important point here is that these scores would mean that the vast majority of engineering students' mathematics achievement would not place them close to the achievement levels of the precocious samples.

If one shifts the definition of mathematics achievement from scores on standardized tests to grades in mathematics classrooms, then females rather than males appear to have a small advantage. The pattern of girls' higher grades and boys' higher standardized scores has been found for the U.S. and Canada (Kimball, 1989), Sweden (Grevholm & Nilsson, 1993), Spain, England, and Wales (Burton, 1994). This is consistent with the finding that girls tend to get higher grades than boys in all academic areas (Marsh, 1989; Stockard & Wood, 1984), although girls' advantage in high school mathematics classes is less than in their other classes (Bridgeman & Wendler, 1991; Felson & Trudeau, 1991). Furthermore, this female advantage in grades is found in samples of precocious youth, where the largest male advantage is found on standardized tests (Benbow, 1992; Benbow & Arjmand, 1990). At the university level, among students taking the same mathematics courses, females achieve the same or higher grades than males whose SAT-M scores are higher (Bridgeman & Wendler, 1991). Even among students in the same mathematics course who receive the same letter grade, females' SAT-M scores are 21 to 55 points lower than males (Wainer & Steinberg, 1992). A similar pattern is found in high school mathematics courses where girls and boys with the same grade in algebra and geometry classes differ in their scores on the PSAT-M with males scoring higher (Fry, 1990). Clearly, in their mathematics classrooms girls achieve as much or more than do their male peers who achieve more on standardized tests.

In contrast to small gender differences in mathematics achievement, differences among ethnic groups, countries, or schools are much larger. Sandra Marshall (1984) found small gender differences among Grade 6 students in California on a statewide test with girls performing better on computation problems and boys on problem solving. These gender differences were consistent across social class and ethnic groups; however, the gender differences were dwarfed by class and ethnic differences. Students from a higher social class background performed better, and Asian students scored higher than whites who scored higher than Hispanics. When Janet Hyde and her colleagues (1990) looked at different ethnic groups in the United States they found a small difference favoring males among white ($d = .13$) students, a small difference favoring females among Asian ($d = -.09$) students, and no gender difference for either black or Hispanic students. Interestingly, if the SAT-M data are included, then a difference favoring males appears for each ethnic group (from $d = .23$ for blacks to $d = .41$ for whites). In each comparison the largest male advantage is for white students (Hyde, Fennema, & Lamon, 1990). It is also important to note that although Asian students and white students receive almost equivalent SAT scores, American Indians, Hispanics, and blacks receive much lower scores (Carson, Huelskamp, & Woodall, 1993) and that these ethnic differences are larger than the gender differences within each group. Gender differences in high achieving samples also vary by ethnicity. In one talent search in the U.S., 27 percent of the white and 47 percent of the Asian winners were female (Willis, 1989, p. 16).

Cross-cultural comparisons of mathematics achievement consistently show small or nonexistent gender differences within cultures and large differences across cultures. Harold Stevenson and his colleagues studied elementary school children from the United States, Japan, and China. Although within each country girls and boys performed equally well, there were striking differences among the countries with Japanese children receiving the highest scores and children in the U.S. the lowest. By Grade 5 the lowest classroom average in Japan was higher than the highest classroom average in the United States (Stevenson, Lee, & Stigler, 1986). Similarly, Corinna Ethington (1990) found that differences among countries in mathematics achievement of Grade 8 students were much larger than gender differences. Using a sample of Grade 12 students from 15 countries, Gila Hanna and her colleagues found a significant country by sex interaction. Specifically, students from countries with a small gender difference experienced more parental encouragement to study math than students from countries with a large gender difference (Hanna, Kundiger, & Larouche, 1990). The mean effect size for studies in Canada ($d = .09$) and Australia ($d = .11$) indicate a very small male advantage (Hyde, Fennema, & Lamon, 1990).

Within countries, it is common to find larger differences among schools than between girls and boys within any particular school. Looking at differences across four high schools in Shanghai, Jinni Xu and Edwin Farrell (1992) found larger school than gender differences. In an examination of mathematics education and achievement in England, Valerie Walkerdine (1989) consistently found school and social class differences in achievement that dwarfed gender differences. In Australia, the percent of students from different mainland states in Year 8 who went on to complete Year 12 math ranged between 16 percent and 55 percent for females and 21 percent and 50 percent for males (Willis, 1989, pp. 11-13). Similarly, a study of high school calculus course completion in the United States found much larger differences across schools than between women and men, with figures ranging from 7 percent to 42 percent for females and 5 percent to 41 percent for males (Dick and Rallis, 1991). The correlation between social class and mathematics achievement is considerably smaller ($r = .20$) when the individual student is the unit of analysis than when the school is the unit of analysis ($r = .70$). This difference is accounted for by curriculum differences. In schools serving higher socioeconomic populations, more higher level mathematics courses are offered, whereas in those in lower socioeconomic neighborhoods, more remedial and lower level courses are offered (Matthews, 1984; Reyes & Stanic, 1988). Thus, achievement differences among schools most likely reflect both ethnic and social class differences among individual students and curriculum differences among schools.

In summary, gender differences often are not found. When they are found, typically they are small, and, if anything, have been getting smaller over time (Friedman, 1989; Hyde, Fennema, & Lamon, 1990; Linn & Hyde 1989). School, ethnic, class, and cultural differences in mathematics achievement are consistently much larger than gender differences.[1] So why all the fuss about gender? Why is the amount of research attention on gender out of proportion to the magnitude of the observed differences? Part of the answer to these questions lies in the bias toward studying largely white, middle-class, urban or suburban samples from the United States. Thus gender is the most obvious group difference to draw the researchers' attention. Clearly an important direction for future research on mathematics achievement is a change in focus from gender as a unitary variable to the interaction of gender with race, ethnicity, class, and cultural diversity.

In addition to this bias in the choice of research samples, I would argue that the focus on gender differences in mathematics achievement reflects the persistent symbolization of mathematics as masculine. In an attempt to reduce, undermine, or destroy this belief, feminist researchers have produced strong and consistent data which demonstrate that females and males achieve very similar mathematical skills. However, these data have had a relatively small impact on the belief predominant in North America that men are better at math than women. In order to understand why this is so, it is important to understand the cultural viability of the symbolic gender system which is largely independent of the individual gender system. Both systems have their own realities and it is to the reality of the masculine symbolism of mathematics that I now wish to turn.

GENDER AND THE SYMBOLIZATION OF MATHEMATICS

In spite of the fact that on many achievement tests and in mathematics classrooms girls and boys have similar achievement patterns, there remains in Eurocentric cultures a persistent belief that mathematics belongs to the realm of the masculine. I am speaking here of what Evelyn Fox Keller calls "the symbolic work of gender" (1992b, p. 17) and Sandra Harding describes as the symbolic sex-gender system (1986, pp. 52-57). In this analysis, gender is an analytical tool that can be applied to all culturally constructed human endeavors including mathematics. Although in certain contexts a cultural analysis may overlap partially with an analysis of individual gender systems, the two systems are also logically, and to a large extent empirically, independent. Thus it is possible for mathematics to be gendered symbolically even though women and men may do equally well at mathematics. What I want to do here is explore, on several different levels, from obvious to more subtle, the results of mathematics as a masculine symbol system.

On the most obvious or conscious level is the stereotype of mathematics as a male domain. This is one of the scales on the Fennema-Sherman Mathematics Attitudes Scale which has been widely used (Fennema & Sherman, 1976). The 12 items on this scale are quite transparent, e.g., "It's hard to believe a female could be a genius in mathematics" and "Females are just as good as males in geometry." Thus one can assume that most children answering these questions are aware of the purpose of the scale. Therefore it is not surprising that both girls and boys tend to express disagreement with the stereo-typed view that women are not as good at math as men. In spite of this general tendency to reject or disagree with the stereotype, large gender differences have been found on this scale with girls being much more extreme in their rejection of the stereotype. In a meta-analysis of gender differences in mathematics attitudes, Janet Hyde and her colleagues found that the average gender difference for math as a male domain ($d = .90$) was larger than any of the other attitude scales (Hyde, Fennema, Ryan, Frost, & Hopp, 1990). Furthermore, this gender difference was much larger than the largest gender differ-ences in mathematics achievement ($d = .40$), which are found only with highly select samples and with a single achievement measure, the SAT-M. In an area of investigation where gender differences are so small, this difference in stereotyping stands out. What are the girls trying to say in their almost total rejection of the stereotype of math as a male domain? I would suggest that they are expressing a strong objection to their possible exclusion from a culturally masculine endeavor. On the other hand, boys, by not rejecting this stereotype as strongly as girls, may be expressing a reluctance to give up mathe-matics as a male territory. Given their male peers' significantly greater willingness to endorse the stereotype of math as a male domain, girls will be exposed to a number of subtle or not-so-subtle comments over the years, the cumulative effect of which will be to reinforce their sense of not belonging. In math intervention pro-grams, drawing girls' attention to the sexist nature of math increased their anxiety (Fennema, 1993).

Individual girls and women consistently express the belief that they are not very good in mathematics in spite of their equal or superior performance in classrooms and on tests. This pattern begins with ele-mentary school children. Deborah Stipek and Heidi Gralinski (1991) found that elementary and junior high school girls were less confident than boys that they would do well on a mathematics test they were just about to take. In a study of Australian students in Grades 3-10, Gilah Leder (1990) found that 65 percent of the boys and 20 percent of the girls thought they had above average math ability. This pattern contin-ues through professional training. Women in graduate programs in science, engineering, and medicine at Stanford consistently assessed themselves as less competent in mathematics than did the men in similar programs (Zappert & Stansbury, 1984, cited in Gottheil, 1987).

Both male and female teachers express their belief that males are better at math in their judgments of students who are particularly successful or unsuccessful at math. These judgments often do not match the students' performance on achievement tests. It is interesting that this bias exists cross-culturally and across an age range of students. Israeli elementary teachers were significantly more likely to name males when asked to nominate the three most eminent math students they had taught (BenTsvi-Mayer, Hertz-Lazarowitz, & Safir, 1989). In England in a study of students nominated to take the O levels in mathematics, Valerie Walkerdine found that fewer females than males were nominated from a group of students who did not differ by gender on a mathematics achievement test. In contrast, almost all students were encouraged to take O levels in English, even though girls are perceived to do better in this subject (Walkerdine, 1989, pp. 165-186). In the United States, Elizabeth Fennema and her colleagues found that Grade 1 teachers were significantly more likely to nominate boys than girls as their most successful students in math. Boys were 79 percent of the teachers' first choices and 58 percent of their second choices. They were also more likely to be nominated as the least successful student although not to such an extreme degree, indicating perhaps that when these teachers thought about mathematics they thought about boys. When the teachers' nominations were compared to the students' achievement scores, the largest group of students inaccurately assigned were boys described as most successful, indicating an overestimation of males' mathematics achievement (Fennema, Peterson, Carpenter, & Lubinski, 1990). Consistent with this overestimation of male achievement, Barry Kissane (1986) found an underestimation of female achievement. Australian teachers were much less accurate in nominating girls who would do well on the SAT-M than they were in nominating similarly achieving boys.

At a more subtle level, I want to examine the persistent bias in the achievement literature that the kind of math men do is better, higher level mathematics. In order to do this I want to return to the distinction between computation and problem solving. Janet Hyde and her colleagues report a gender difference that favors young girls in computation, an advantage that disappears with age. On the other hand, a lack of gender difference in problem solving in young children changes to a male advantage after the age of 15. Tests of mathematical concepts show no gender difference at any age (Hyde, Fennema, and Lamon, 1990).

Examples of the assumption that girls prefer routine math whereas boys prefer complex problem solving abound. Girls studying for A levels in Ireland reported liking math that was straightforward and disliking difficult problems where procedures were not so obvious, whereas boys reported liking variety in math and disliking what was boring. Teachers of these girls also described them as liking routine, perhaps generating a self-fulfilling prophecy (Rodgers, 1990). In her studies, Valerie Walkerdine (1989) found that girls' good performance in math was constantly played down by teachers as rule-following and passive learning, whereas boys' poor performance and disobedience were seen as an indication of active learning, set breaking, and real understanding. Typically, females' lesser performance on standardized tests of problem solving is seen as a lesser ability to do higher level mathematics critical for autonomous learning of mathematics (Fennema & Peterson, 1985) and for success in engineering and physical sciences (Hyde, Fennema, & Lamon, 1990).

I would argue that privileging problem solving is correlated with the symbolizing of mathematics as masculine. I want to explore this assumption through the consideration of four questions. First, how clear is the distinction between girls' better performance on computation items and boys' better problem solving? Like all dichotomies, a closer look reveals complexities that blur an easy linking of gender with different mathematical skills. For *both* sexes computation items are easier than word problems and the differences across kinds of items are larger than gender differences (Marshall, 1984; Marshall & Smith, 1987). Girls do better than boys on some kinds of word problems. For example, among mathematically gifted junior high students, girls performed better than boys on problems that required them to determine if there was sufficient information to solve a problem, and on problems that required solving logical puzzles (B. Becker, 1990). In a representative sample of younger children, girls did better than boys on noncomputational verbal problems which required them to identify relevant and irrelevant information (Marshall & Smith, 1987). Thus an easy linking of males with higher level or complex math skills and girls with lower level or computational skills is consistent with the cultural norm of math as a masculine domain but much less consistent with the complexity of girls' and boys' skill patterns.

My second question is closely related to my first one. Why do girls perform less well, when they do, on problem-solving tests? Frequently, the assumption is made that girls lack problem-solving skills. Specifically, girls' skills at computation, memorization, and rule following may not be the skills that are the most useful for problem solving. Therefore, when girls behave in an appropriately feminine way, they may not get experience and confidence in working out alternative solutions on their own (Barnes, personal communication, January 17, 1994; Fennema & Peterson, 1985; Willis, 1989, pp. 20-24).

Another reason girls sometimes do less well on tests of problem solving is a lack of good test-taking strategies. In particular, they tend more than boys to omit items, especially difficult ones (B. Becker, 1990; Chipman, Marshall, & Scott, 1991). Thus it may be that boys in some situations have better strategies for taking timed tests rather than better problem-solving skills. For example on the SAT-M there is a correction or penalty for guessing in which the number of wrong items is divided by four and subtracted from the number of correct items (B. Becker). The advice given to students preparing to take the SAT-M by the Education Testing Service is not to guess (Jackson, 1990). However, guessing is a bad strategy only if all four multiple choice alternatives seem equally likely. If even one of the possibilities can be eliminated as incorrect, then guessing among the remaining three alternatives is a better strategy than leaving the item blank. That rapid intelligent guessing is a better strategy than applying and solving the correct formulas is emphasized by special courses that train students to increase their overall SAT performance by as much as 150 points (Jackson, 1990; Linn & Hyde, 1989). Thus girls' greater tendency to omit items they are not sure of may contribute to gender differences on the SAT-M.

My third question centers on the use of math in mathematics-related professions. Clearly, mathematicians engage directly in mathematical problem solving. To what extent, however, is the use of math by professional scientists a mathematical problem-solving activity and to what extent is it an application of algorithms or rules to a specific situation? Engineers report that they use very little of the higher level math that they are required to take in university in their daily work. Most of the mathematics they use involves basic algebra (McIlwee & Robinson, 1992, p. 27). As a psychologist, I have a fair amount of training in statistics and use math in order to analyze data. However, I would describe what I do as requiring the right or best application of an existing formula to my data. There *are* problems to be solved, i.e., which is the best analysis to use and whether the data meet the criteria of the test, but these are analytical not mathematical problems. Once I make the decision, the formula is available for my use, usually in the form of a computer program.

My fourth question involves a thought experiment: How could a reversed pattern of performance be interpreted to the advantage of males? Imagine that males do better as young students on computations but there is no difference among older students, and that females do better on tests of problem solving after they become teenagers. Furthermore, imagine that boys get better classroom grades although they do more poorly on standardized tests. It is possible to imagine that educators and researchers would worry about why males lose their early advantage in computation and explore what happens in classrooms that might relate to this loss. Furthermore, accuracy in computation would be seen as a "concern with, attention to, and appreciation of numerical detail or competence in handling numerical systems and their operators" (Damarin, 1993, p. 8), whereas a relative advantage on problem solving would be seen as fooling around or playing with math instead of really doing it. Much would be made of boys' better grades as more realistic measures of mathematics achievement and girls would be labeled underachievers with their pattern of higher scores on standardized tests and lower classroom performance. I am not seriously advocating that problem solving is less important or lower level than computation. But I agree with Valerie Walkerdine that both applying and understanding rules are important skills and that we may overvalue one partly because of its association with the male in a symbolically masculine field (1989, pp. 116-134).

Another aspect of the symbolization of mathematics as masculine is the underlying assumption in much of the research that men should do better in math. Involvement with this assumption can be expressed as either strong acceptance of the assumption or angry rejection (Gottheil, 1987). Given the socially unacceptable nature of such a belief, one needs to look for indirect evidence of this assumption. I will consider three kinds of evidence that point to this underlying assumption. First is the evidence from women mathematicians of active discouragement of their career choice that increases as they reach higher levels of study (J. Becker, 1990; Luchins, 1979). Some women mathematicians continue to experience hostility when they identify themselves as mathematicians (Damarin, 1993; Selvin, 1992). In contrast, men almost never report active discouragement or hostility when they choose mathematics as a career. Women are much less welcome as colleagues than men at the top universities. Although they received 22 percent of the PhDs in mathematics, they made up only 6 percent of the tenure-track assistant professors at the top ten universities in the U.S. in 1992 (Selvin).

Second, the disproportionate emphasis on standardized tests, especially the SAT-M, exists partly because these are the measures of achievement that reinforce the view that men are better at mathematics. The status of the SAT-M and its association with the largest gender differences is telling. When Janet Hyde and her colleagues removed the SAT-M studies from the total sample of effect sizes, the overall difference favoring males was reduced from $d = .20$ to $d = .15$. And, as I pointed out earlier, this gender difference favoring males is smaller or nonexistent in all ethnic groups in the United States if the SAT-M data are excluded (Hyde, Fennema, and Lamon, 1990). The controversy around the changing of items in the early 1970s on the verbal subtest of the SAT (SAT-V) to eliminate the male disadvantage and even create a small advantage, while, at the same time, not working to eliminate the male advantage on the SAT-M also can be read to indicate an underlying assumption that men should be better at math (Goldberg, 1990; Jackson, 1990; Mandula, 1990). It has been shown clearly that the SAT in general underpredicts women's and overpredicts men's average course grades (Striker, Rock, & Burton, 1991), and their grades in specific mathematics courses (Bridgeman & Wendler, 1991; Wainer & Steinberg, 1992). The solution to this problem is usually seen as including both SAT and high school grades in scholarship and selection procedures but not changing the SAT-M to include more of the kinds of items on which women do better. On the contrary, data sufficiency items which favor females are no longer used on the SAT-M (Chipman, 1988).

Third, the overemphasis, especially in the popular media, on the studies of mathematically precocious youth occurs partly because these are the samples in which the male advantage on standardized tests (almost exclusively the SAT-M) is the largest. Even in these highly select samples, girls get higher grades in math and science courses (Benbow, 1992; Benbow & Arjmand, 1990), a fact discrepant with the assumption that men should be better in math and therefore seldom reported in the popular press. Furthermore, the popular press reports do not always accurately report the highly select nature of these samples leaving open the possibility that the results are misinterpreted as applying to males and females in general, and the further implication that the differences are due to biology (Hyde, Fennema, & Lamon, 1990).

Of course the belief that men should do better in math does not include all men. In addition to the gender symbolization of math there is also a clear hierarchical symbolization that only the elite can truly understand math (Willis, 1989, pp. 26-28). Mathematics is hard and to understand math is to gain a superiority over those who do not. Thus there are unspoken racial and class assumptions in the hierarchical symbolization of mathematics; it is the privileged white male who should be better in math. And just as the small or nonexistent gender differences do not destroy the belief of masculine superiority, the high achievement of Asians (Marshall, 1984; Stevenson, Lee, & Stigler, 1986; Willis, 1989, pp. 16-17) does little to destroy the belief that superior math ability belongs to those who are white. The symbolization of math as belonging to an elite also reinforces the status of and overgeneralization from the studies of mathematically precocious youth.

The final level at which I wish to examine mathematics as masculine is in the language of mathematics. In our technological culture, mathematics is described as rational, detached (Gottheil, 1987), and aggressive (Luchins, 1979; Damarin, 1990). Mathematics has been described as involving the manipulation, dissection, and destruction of figures (Luchins, 1979). Goals of mastery include mathematical power in which the learner attacks problems by applying strategies, using drills, and engaging in competition. Misconceptions are torpedoed, and concepts are arranged in hierarchies. In contrast, feminine symbolic language such as beautiful or elegant proofs or nice solutions often refer to completed processes rather than the activity of doing mathematics (Damarin, 1990). The overwhelmingly masculine nature of the military language used to describe the process of doing mathematics is clearly illustrated by the contrast of possible alternative descriptions. As Suzanne Damarin (1990) suggests, one could speak of internalization of knowledge rather than mastery, instead of attacking a problem one could interact with it, hierarchies could become networks, and one could resolve instead of torpedo a misconception. Sexist remarks and humor convey the message that mathematics is masculine in an even more direct and hurtful way. Claudie Solar (1995) reports a joke told among French mathematicians which states that the worst thing that can happen to a mathematician is to spend the night with an unknown and not find the solution. In French, the unknown is feminine and what makes this a joke is the assumption that the mathematician is male, the unknown female, and the solution is intercourse.

It is easy as feminists to get caught up in attacking the assumption that men should be better in math or that mathematics is a male domain. Consequently much of our energy as feminist researchers has been spent producing empirical evidence that contradicts these assumptions. Valuable as this task is, it is not sufficient in itself to destroy the cultural assumptions of mathematics as masculine, because they were never based on data in the first place. It is my contention that in addition to exposing these assumptions indirectly through the production of empirical evidence that contradicts them, it is vital for feminists to engage in a direct analysis of how the assumptions are expressed and supported in the cultural and linguistic institution of mathematics.

GENDER AND MATHEMATICS: WHERE TO GO FROM HERE?

Given the discrepancy between the nonexistent or very small and very limited gender differences in mathematics achievement and the belief that mathematics is a male domain, what will bring about effective social change? Clearly a demonstration of empirical similarity is not enough. One must also work to change the symbolic masculinization of mathematics and reflect this change in the classroom. Effective social change requires both equality and equity of mathematics education. Walter Secada (1989) describes equality as a quantitative concept and equity as a qualitative one. Thus equality is determined by the absence of a difference among demographic groups, or a search for the null hypothesis. One can measure equality as opportunity to learn, access to educational resources, or educational outcomes (Fennema, 1990). An example of an inequality that affects both women and minorities is the practice of assigning beginning or disfavored teachers to general math classes and the best teachers to advanced classes (Secada, 1990).

Clearly, an educational context that results in inequality is inequitable. However, equity includes and goes beyond measurable inequalities. Equality within a system that is symbolically masculine is both difficult to achieve and insufficient to ensure equity. Equity involves fairness and requires a focus not only on the distribution of existing resources, but also on the inclusiveness of what is being taught. Important questions include: is what is being distributed worth having? (Secada, 1990); are measures of what is being learned culture-fair? It is important to notice that in these questions there is a shift from an exclusive focus on empirical inequalities to include questions of the subjective meaningfulness of mathematics for all learners (Jungwirth, 1993).

Most children learn most of the mathematics they know in the classroom. Thus the process, and content in mathematics classrooms become important equality and equity concerns. In focusing on classroom process, researchers have examined both the amount of the teacher's time and attention devoted to females and males and what kinds of classroom structures lead to equivalent outcomes for girls and boys. Girls' treatment in the classroom tends to be one of relative deprivation, particularly in having fewer interactions with mathematics teachers (Eccles, 1989; Kimball, 1989; Leder, 1990). Although girls receive fewer interactions, it is not clear how this relates to their performance as they often receive higher grades and only some of the time perform more poorly on standardized tests.

In an attempt to specify the qualitative aspects of classrooms that support females' mathematics learning, researchers have examined specific classes where girls' performance, mathematics confidence, or interactions with the teacher are similar to or greater than boys', and compared them to classrooms where girls are more disadvantaged. Jacquelynne Eccles and her colleagues identified girl-friendly classrooms, i.e., ones in which girls and boys had similar confidence levels, as involving less social comparison, less competition, more teacher stress on the importance of math, and a warmer, fairer teacher (Eccles-Parsons, Kaczala, & Meece, 1982; Eccles & Blumenfeld, 1985; Eccles, 1989). Within the girl-friendly classroom, a challenging atmosphere may be an important facilitator of girls' learning. Mary Koehler (1990) found that girls' performance in a beginning algebra class increased more in a classroom in which they were encouraged to solve problems on their own than in a classroom in which all their questions were answered. Pat Rogers (1990) chose to study the mathematics department at SUNY Potsdam because of the high percentage of graduating math majors (60 percent) who were women. What she found was a department dominated by male faculty who challenged their students to think precisely and were often described by students as scary but excellent teachers. It is important to distinguish between challenge and competition. It may be that sufficient challenge to think and work on problems on one's own is important for learning math. However, challenge does not have to occur in a highly public and competitive context.

An important related variable may be whether the classroom is teacher-centered or student-centered with the teacher facilitating learning. In a study of Grade 4 and 6 mathematics teachers, Karen Karp (1991) found that teachers with negative attitudes toward math constructed their classrooms in a very teacher-dependent manner which involved students in very little interaction in contrast to teachers with positive attitudes towards math who encouraged interaction with their students. Furthermore, teachers can learn to focus on the individual cognitive styles of each of their students, resulting in better learning for all students. Thomas Carpenter and his colleagues found that a four-week training program in Cognitively Guided Instruction for Grade 1 teachers made a significant difference in the way they taught math and resulted in consistent modest improvement in their students' mathematics performance over students in the control teachers' classrooms (Carpenter et al., 1989). As more is learned about the match between teaching styles and learning styles, it may well be that a focus on styles that are student friendly in the sense of encouraging all students to achieve mathematics competence and excellence are the styles that ensure both equality and equity for minority students and females.

In addition to their interactions and teaching styles, teachers have an opportunity to make a difference in the content they present to their students. Unfortunately, it appears that few of them do so, often reinforcing sex-differentiated and hierarchical values, if not directly, then by their silence (Eccles, 1989). For example, in 400 hours of classroom observations in one study, teachers mentioned fewer than a dozen instances of the value of math in everyday life, math as personally meaningful, or the value of math for careers (Meece, Wigfield, & Eccles, 1990). Furthermore, elementary texts seldom illustrate mathematics careers and even when they represent girls and boys in equal numbers they tend to show girls in helping and subservient roles (Garcia, Harrison, & Torres, 1990; Walkerdine, 1989, pp. 187-197). Most students experience math as rule-bound, involving operations, and lacking in creativity and imagination (Isaacson, 1990; Schoenfeld, 1989; Stodolsky, Salk, & Glaessner, 1991). For example, in one survey high school students reported spending an average of two minutes on a typical homework problem and that they would spend an average of 12 minutes on a problem before deciding it was impossible (Schoenfeld, 1989). In another study, Grade 5 children saw math as a subject that they liked or disliked based on how hard it was, as a subject one could not learn on one's own, and as very unchangeable. All of these views were held in contrast to social studies which one liked or disliked based on how interesting the material was, that one could learn on one's own, and that was open to student input and influence (Stodolsky, Salk, & Glaessner, 1991).

A number of innovative attempts have been made to make the content of mathematics courses gender inclusive. Sometimes this involves the adaptation of traditional feminine activities to the classroom such as the use of embroidery to teach border symmetry (Verhage, 1990). In other cases this is done by including examples familiar and interesting to a wide range of students including women. Thus, in a calculus course, problems of population growth, radioactive waste, spread of disease, the absorption of drugs and alcohol into the blood stream (Barnes & Copeland, 1990), the rate of temperature change in a dead body, or measuring the area of deforestation from an aerial map (Barnes, 1994) can be used instead of the typical abstract problems that are of very little interest to the majority of students, both male and female. The inclusion of many examples of the use of mathematics in careers and in everyday life, and an active advertisement campaign to promote mathematics courses are also important (Blum-Anderson, 1992). One could even make issues of equality directly relevant to learning by bringing in sets of data that examine gender or ethnicity differences on various achievement measures, and use them to illustrate statistical and mathematical concepts, including a critique of how they may be distorted (Damarin, 1990). For example, in a mathematics class for mature women in Australia, Vicky Webber focused a series of classes around an article attacking single mothers' welfare payments as a burden to the Australian taxpayer. Fueled by anger, the women developed a sophisticated mathematical analysis of the misuse of numerical data in the article (Webber, 1987/88). Marilyn Frankenstein (1990) has developed a critical mathematical literacy curriculum that presents mathematical problems in a context that emphasizes existing race, gender, and class inequalities in income and resources.

In addition to inclusive content the students' emotional responses to mathematics are important and should be acknowledged. Women mathematics teachers write about the importance of acknowledging mathematics anxiety, emphasizing that frustration is a normal part of problem solving and teaching how to cope with it, recognizing that mathematics confidence is unstable, and developing teaching styles to maintain or build confidence (Blum-Anderson, 1992; Damarin, 1990; Willis, 1989, pp. 20-24).

Finally, it is important to consider how mathematics achievement is assessed. That girls do better in classroom assessment and boys on standardized tests raises important questions (Burton, 1994; Grevholm & Nilsson, 1993; Kimball, 1989). In the United States the exclusive reliance on standardized test results such as the SAT in determining college admissions and scholarships clearly discriminates against females (Mandula, 1990) and as a result many colleges use both SAT results and high school grades, a procedure which reduces the overprediction of male and the underprediction of female performance in university (Striker, Rock, & Burton, 1991). The issue of balancing assessment between classroom performance and standardized exams has been raised as well in Europe (Burton, 1994) and Australia (H. Forgasz, personal communication,

October 11, 1993; Willis, 1989, pp. 34-37). The inclusion of course work as a component of the national or provincial assessment for high school students has had the result of raising all students' scores, especially those of girls, who did as well or better than boys on the course work component, but less well on the standardized exams. Interestingly, there also has been a significant political opposition to the inclusion of course work based on charges of lowered standards and cheating. Assumptions underlying this debate include a symbolization of standardized tests as tough, detached, hard, objective, i.e., masculine and elite; and classroom grades as soft, easy, subjective, deceptive, i.e., feminine and mediocre. Contrast these arguments with the existence of tutoring programs that coach white privileged U.S. students on the SAT raising scores by as much as 150 points (Jackson, 1990; Linn & Hyde, 1989). This is not seen as cheating, although it gives an unfair advantage to a small group of students.

In establishing more equitable methods of assessment based on different patterns of achievement by females and males, a benefit may also accrue to minority students who are disadvantaged by traditional assessment procedures. What is important is that assessment measures are sought that reflect fairly the mathematical knowledge of all students.

A problem with much of the research that has focused on gender equality and equity in mathematics is that the samples studied have been largely limited to U.S. white middle-class elementary and high school students. In these populations gender is highlighted as a marker of disadvantage. However, it is clear that when other ethnic groups and cultures are included, these differences are usually larger than gender. Therefore, if the goal is a truly equitable mathematics education, it must be equitable not only for white middle-class females, but for all students. The establishment of gender-inclusive curricula and gender-fair assessment is one place to begin and such changes may benefit many male students as well. Conversely, teaching styles, content and assessment patterns that work for most students will of necessity benefit female learners. Both of these attempts are worthy of feminist attention.

NOTE

1. It is not always easy to compare the size of various differences. The ideal way would be to have effect sizes for gender and other differences so the size of the difference could be directly compared. Unfortunately, the data necessary to calculate effect sizes are not always presented. However, some comparison is usually possible. For example Harold Stevenson, Shin-Ying Lee, and James Stigler (1986) reported that sex differences in all three countries at all three grades were nonsignificant, but data are not given separately for each gender making it impossible to calculate effect sizes for gender. The effect sizes for differences between countries range from a low of .05 to a high of 1.29. The largest country differences at each grade level are .88 (Kindergarten), .76 (Grade 1), and 1.29 (Grade 5). Although effect sizes for gender cannot be calculated, given that they are statistically nonsignificant and that the number of subjects are large (over 200 students in each country at each grade level), the effect sizes should be smaller than all but one of the nine comparisons between countries. Jinni Xu and Edwin Farrell (1992) present some of the most complete data comparing mathematics achievement across schools in China. The smallest effect sizes for gender are .004 and .046. The largest effect sizes for gender are .34 and .43. The smallest effect size differences between schools are .05 and .49. The largest effect sizes are 2.16 and 3.03.

Two other studies make size of difference comparisons using statistics other than effect sizes. In a comparison of mathematics achievement across eight countries, Corrina Ethington (1990) used a median polish analysis and found gender effects in all cases to be smaller than county effects. For example for the whole test the gender effect was .16. The smallest country effect was 1.41 (France) and the largest country effect was 13.07 (Japan). Sandra Marshall (1984) compared students' mathematics achievement in California ethnic groups (Hispanic, Oriental, and Caucasian), social class (unskilled, semi-skilled, semi-professional, and professional), kind of problem (computation and story problems), and gender. Comparing the probability of a current response across groups, she found that average gender differences ranged from zero to 5 percent. Social class differences ranged from 6 percent to 27 percent. Ethnic differences ranged from 8 percent to 30 percent.

Chapter 5

Moralities of Care and Justice

VARIATION ON THE WORD SLEEP

I would like to watch you sleeping,
which may not happen.
I would like to watch you,
sleeping. I would like to sleep
with you, to enter
your sleep as its smooth dark wave
slides over my head

and walk with you through that lucent
wavering forest of bluegreen leaves
with its watery sun & three moons
towards the cave where you must descend,
towards your worst fear

I would like to give you the silver
branch, the small white flower, the one
word that will protect you
from the grief at the center
of your dream, from the grief
at the center. I would like to follow
you up the long stairway
again & become
the boat that would row you back
carefully, a flame
in two cupped hands
to where your body lies
beside me, and you enter
it as easily as breathing in

I would like to be the air
that inhabits you for a moment
only. I would like to be that unnoticed
& that necessary.

Margaret Atwood
Selected Poems II: Poems Selected & New 1976-1986
1986, p. 87

One of the most significant and controversial issues in feminist academic dialogue has been the idea of a woman's different moral voice, one that speaks of cares and responsibilities rather than rights and obligations. Although, as I will discuss below, any simple linking of ethics of care with women and ethics of justice with men is empirically unsupported and politically problematic; moral theories remain deeply gendered in ways that are important to understand. In this chapter, I will examine three aspects of the dialectics of care and justice: (1) the empirical debate around gender differences in moral reasoning; (2) the political concerns about ethics of care; and (3) the importance of both care and justice in defining adequate moral theories.

THE EMPIRICAL DEBATE

The debate around gender differences in moral reasoning is well known to feminist psychologists and philosophers. This debate is focused on gender as an attribute of individuals, and arguments are based on empirical results of studies which examine female and male moral reasoning. Lawrence Kohlberg (1981) proposed a theory of moral development consisting of six stages based on an increasingly complex understanding of principles of justice and fairness. The original theory and scoring system was developed using an all male sample.[1] One of his students, Carol Gilligan (1982), put forth both a critique of Kohlberg's theory and an alternative theory of moral development based on her work with female subjects who, she argued, spontaneously included issues of care and responsibility in their exploration of moral dilemmas.

Her critique has inspired a great deal of empirical work on gender similarities and differences in moral reasoning, most of it centering on the question: Do women score at a lower stage than men on Kohlberg's abstract dilemmas of moral reasoning? Two years after Gilligan published her book, *In a Different Voice* (1982), Lawrence Walker (1984) published a meta-analysis which showed very

---

Portions of this chapter have been adapted from "The Worlds We Live In: Gender Similarities and Differences," *Canadian Psychology*, 35, 1994, pp. 388-404. Reprinted here with permission.

few gender differences in level of moral reasoning using Kohlberg's system. In the few studies where women did less well, they also tended to have less formal education and lower occupational status. More recent studies have continued to find that women and men achieve similar stages of moral reasoning (Pratt, Golding, & Hunter, 1984; Walker, 1986a, 1989). Furthermore, in an overview of cross-cultural research using Kohlberg's system, John Snarey (1985) found clear gender differences in only one study out of 17 from a wide range of cultures. Despite the continued debate over appropriate statistics and specific samples (Baumrind, 1986; Walker, 1986b), gender differences in performance on the Kohlberg dilemmas are small or nonexistent.

From these data the conclusion is often drawn that there are no gender differences in moral reasoning and that it is only the myth of differences that persists (Walker, 1984; Mednick, 1989). This is a massive leap in logic that ignores that gender similarities as well as differences are constructed. A common critique made by similarities theorists is that gender differences are constructed, not given in reality (Hare-Mustin & Marecek, 1990). This is an important argument and has been very useful in developing critiques of how differences are created by our theories, methodologies, and political values. As I pointed out in Chapter 1, it is equally important to apply these critiques to gender similarities, which are also constructed.

In the empirical research on moral reasoning, the similarities are constructed by studying a relatively restricted group of volunteers, asking them to reason about highly abstract dilemmas for which they have only minimal information, and scoring their responses for stage of moral reasoning using Kohlberg's justice system. There are a number of alternative possible constructions, which variously emphasize gender similarities and differences.

One possible shift in construction involves asking people to generate a moral dilemma from their own lives, and scoring their reasoning for both justice and care themes. Using this construction, Carol Gilligan and her colleagues found that most women and men expressed both care and justice reasoning; however, among those who focused on either theme, gender differences emerged. Of the men who focused on one theme, the vast majority focused on justice, whereas among the women, there was an almost equal division between those focusing on either justice or care (Gilligan, 1987a, 1987b; Gilligan & Attanucci, 1988; Lyons 1983). Overall gender similarities in justice and care reasoning on real-life dilemmas also have been found by other authors (Walker, 1989; Wark, 1992). Clearly, both gender similarities and differences emerge from this construction.

Important to the construction of gender similarities and differences in moral reasoning is the emphasis on different levels of analysis. Sometimes overview statistics reveal gender similarities, whereas more subtle analyses reveal differences. Although there may be gender similarities in the average stage of moral reasoning used by women and men, often finer analyses reveal gender differences. For example, Lawrence Walker (1986a) found that education was a better predictor of moral development for men than for women even though there was no gender difference in educational level. For women, but not for men, household decision making predicted moral development. He also found that among adults, but not among children, females more than males used response (care-based) reasoning on real-life dilemmas (Walker, 1989). Gillian Wark (1992) reported that although men and women were equally likely to use justice and care reasoning on hypothetical and impersonal real-life dilemmas, women were more likely than men to use care reasoning on personal real-life dilemmas, largely because they generated more care-oriented dilemmas.

All of these research settings are constructed to examine individuals' thoughts about their own or other individuals' moral dilemmas. These constructions limit considerations of moralities in two ways. First, to present moralities as a matter of individual choice does not call into question the problems of justice and care in a larger institutional context. For example, the health care delivery system, the old-age pension, and relative government spending on military and social services frame individual dilemmas, limiting the possibilities of moral thought in ways that are not visible given the construction of these moral dilemmas (Friedman, 1993, pp. 112-114).

Second, these constructions fail to bridge the gap between moral reasoning and moral behaviors. People can and do make moral judgments on which they do not act. Furthermore, bad moral conduct cannot challenge a stage-based theory of moral reasoning (Friedman,

1993, pp. 108-109; Tronto, 1993, p. 95). By shifting our constructions of moralities to behaviors in the world, some gender differences
become obvious. Physical assault both violates the rights of the
victim and is uncaring in the extreme. Gender differences in physical
assault are clear in many contexts. Even in situations where women
may engage in physical assault, the contexts differ by gender. For
example, in households where violence occurs women and men
direct a similar number of violent acts toward each other. These data
are misconstructed as a gender similarity if they are presented without the further information that men are more likely to initiate violence and to inflict more serious injury (Jayaratne & Stewart, 1991).
As I discuss in Chapter 7, hands-on caregiving is one expression of
ethics of care and one that is disproportionately women's work in
both the private and the public worlds.

By constructing the research around gender differences in white
privileged samples, other socially constructed differences are made
invisible. Differences that are ascribed to gender may describe as
accurately other differences of privilege. Thus racial minority and
working class children often score lower in Kohlberg's system than
white middle-class children. Gender similarities may be more evident in less privileged samples than are used in most research studies. Ethics of care may be as characteristic of African-American
voices as of white female voices (Collins, 1990; Stack, 1986, 1990;
Tronto, 1993, pp. 82-85).

In addition to acknowledging the importance of the construction
of empirical gender differences and similarities in moral reasoning,
it is also important to realize that empirical gender similarities are
neither necessary nor sufficient to prove a lack of bias in any system. The assumption is sometimes made by those working in the
similarities tradition that if gender differences are not found, then a
system is not sex biased (e.g., Mednick, 1989; Walker, 1986b). This
assumption is not necessarily true. Because women do just as well
as men within any system does not mean the system is free of bias.
Women may, indeed probably do, reason as well as men using
abstract justice systems. And moralities of justice represent biased,
i.e., partial samples of moral concerns (Gilligan, 1986). Given the
importance of the symbolic as well as the individual gender systems, values as well as data are important in deciding the relative

bias or lack of bias in any system. Thus, given that justice is seen as symbolically masculine and care as symbolically feminine (Ford & Lowery, 1986), justice-based moralities remain gender biased even if women and men use justice reasoning with equal skill.

Furthermore, Kohlberg's stage theory is hierarchical in privileging the concerns of those with the most power in society. By privileging justice, which is associated with the public sphere, and ignoring care, which is associated with the private sphere, the system reinforces and draws on the greater prestige of the public sphere (Friedman, 1993, p. 98; Held, 1993, pp. 68-73). Consistent with this, Kohlberg's system also defines a moral elite who are those with the most role-taking opportunities in positions of power and prestige in the public sphere. Although there are many role-taking opportunities and experiences in the private sphere and in positions of lesser power in the public sphere they do not correlate with stage of moral reasoning. As a result, the most moral in Kohlberg's system are the most successful (Tronto, 1993, p. 93). To reduce gender, race, and class differences in moral reasoning in adults to differences in occupation and education does not eliminate these differences (Tronto, 1993, pp. 68-72; Walker, 1984) but merely deconstructs them into two of their most salient constituents (Friedman, 1993, p. 121). This hierarchy ranks not only individuals in different social groups, but also cultures. In a review of cross-cultural research, John Snarey (1985) found that collective or communal principled reasoning was more common in folk and working class cultures. It was also missing or misunderstood at the highest stage levels of Kohlberg's system, with the result that people from working class and folk cultures were underrepresented at the highest stages of moral reasoning.

The privileging of the moral reasoning of a social elite is not accidental, but rather is inherent in the structuring of the stages in Kohlberg's system. Group loyalty is central to the conventional stages, in particular stage four. At post-conventional stages five and six, the moral thinker reincorporates others who, although previously excluded as different, are now assumed to be the same as the self. This assumption of the similarity of the other is a very different requirement for those who have benefited from social inequalities than for those who have been harmed. The assumption that morally mature people forget the harms of social inequality in order to see the equal moral worth of all, requires that the oppressed forget wrongs done to them and allows the privileged to ignore the harms they have done. If group loyalty is undesirable and irrelevant to the highest forms of moral thought, oppressions become invisible in moral theories (Tronto, 1993, pp. 72-75).

POLITICAL CONCERNS ABOUT MORALITIES OF CARE

In addition to empirical concerns about linking women to care-based moralities, significant political concerns about such a link have been raised by feminist psychologists and philosophers. These political concerns center around the relationship of care with subordination and oppression.

One concern is reflected in the argument that women's caring has nothing to do with gender per se. Rather, women care for others because they are subordinate and must care for others to get their needs met. This argument also predicts that other oppressed people would show more care because they have to in order to survive. This link is supported by evidence that people in subordinate positions do express more care-based moral reasoning (Collins, 1990; Stack, 1986; Tronto, 1993, pp. 82-85), and that in some cases the same person will use justice arguments when in a dominant position and care reasoning in a subordinate position (Hare-Mustin & Marecek, 1990, pp. 38-39). If the only reason women value care is because they are oppressed, then feminists are in the very awkward political position of glorifying women's oppression if women's caring is valued. In an analysis of her own research on women Holocaust survivors, Joan Ringelheim (1985) examined this link. She argued that it is dangerous to glorify the caring and support in the stories of women survivors because it detracts from the horror and oppression of the Holocaust, which was a loss–not a gain–no matter how heroic some individuals may have been. As she says: "Oppression does not make people better; oppression makes people oppressed" (p. 757).

The second concern about the relationship of care and subordination expressed by several feminist philosophers is that care, especially thought of as a female virtue, fails to acknowledge that violence and harm are possible, indeed frequent, in intimate human relationships (Friedman, 1993, pp. 149-150). Ethics of care can valorize exploitative relationships (Card, 1990) and encourage women to stay in abusive relationships out of a sense of moral responsibility for those who abuse them (Houston, 1990). Staying in a destructive relationship is ethically diminishing, not enhancing, and ethics of care are problematic to the extent they do not enable women to reject bad relationships (Hoagland, 1990).

The third concern around the relationship between care and oppression is that care and other womanly virtues may help women survive oppressive situations without offering most women the resources to fight the enemy and resist oppression (Houston, 1987; Ringelheim, 1985). The assumption is that if caring makes women not only better people but also more likely to survive oppression, then there may be little incentive to risk survival or a positive view of one's self through resistance.

All of these political concerns arise out of valid fears that if the relationship between women and caring is glorified, the relationship between women and oppression is supported and made invisible. One useful way to address these concerns without giving up the value of care for women is to be aware of and resist all forms of essentialisms. Any essentialist argument involves a generalization to all members of a group or to all situations without consideration of variability and difference. An essentialist argument is statistically analogous to looking for main effects and ignoring interactions of these effects with other variables. The most familiar are gender essentialisms, which associate all women with caring or assume that women are more caring than men without specifying: which women? which men? under what conditions? Also problematic are moral essentialisms which assume that care is a moral value and caring a moral act without specifying the context of caring. For example, care is a very different moral act for a woman who cares for an abusive man, or even for one who does not return her care, than it is for the same woman who cares for her child.

Furthermore, there is also the problem of political essentialisms which assume that oppression and resistance are always and everywhere the same. Although I would argue that all oppression is bad, it is not the same in every context. Beyond asserting that ". . . oppression makes people oppressed" (Ringelheim, 1985, p. 757) it is important to examine how oppression works in specific cultural historical contexts and what opportunities for resistance are possible. Resistance also cannot be understood without a context. For example, to ask "Is survival resistance?" is not a very useful question without knowing who is surviving, what conditions of oppression they are surviving, and what they must do to survive (p. 760).

Another political essentialism that is dangerous is the assumption that oppression totally determines behavior and eliminates individual choice and agency. There is no question that oppression limits choice and in some contexts more than in others. However, as the survivors of the Holocaust show, no matter how severe an oppressive situation is, some limited choice is possible. It is important to hear survivors' stories and to validate their sense of agency in these stories (Linden, 1993, pp. 95-102) as well as to be critical of glorifying oppression (Ringelheim, 1985). This balance is difficult to achieve. Joan Ringelheim asks, "Did anyone really survive the Holocaust?" (p. 760). I am sympathetic with her concerns that the horror of the Holocaust should never be forgotten or underestimated; certainly no one should ever have to survive at such a cost. However, in a situation where six million died, perhaps half a million Jews survived (Linden, p. 87). Given the extreme oppression where one's chances of being gassed or dying from starvation or illness were so high, ". . . we need not ask why so many people died. Rather, the question is how so many managed to survive" (p. 102). Surviving was often a matter of luck. At the same time, surviving oppression requires agency. All people in the concentration camps were ". . . engaged in an active struggle *not to die*," (p. 95). No one will ever know if the survivors did anything differently than those who were killed. But we can know the meaning that the survivors construct to make sense of their lives. In addition to luck, survivors have also emphasized the importance of knowledge and information, practical skills, affiliations, and attitudes (Linden, 1993, pp. 95-102; Ringelheim, 1985). It is important to honor these stories *and* to guard against glorifying the oppression that made them necessary.

Although there is a relationship between caring and subordination, it is not absolute. Women do choose to care when it is possible not to, in a range of situations with equals, subordinates, and those in dominant positions. Women also choose *not* to care in an equally wide range of situations. Individual women may resort to pleas for relatedness and compassion when in a subordinate position and to rules and logic when in a dominant position (Hare-Mustin & Marecek, 1990, pp. 38-39). We all have the capacity to be dominated or dominating (hooks, 1990) and the relative power we have in any particular situation will influence our behavior. But it does not absolutely determine our behavior. Thus, people in subordinate positions will sometimes express care and relatedness, and other times demand justice for themselves and at others like them. Likewise, in a position of dominance, they will sometimes use rules and sometimes will make decisions based on compassion and care. Children's well-known objection, "That's not fair!" illustrates that they use justice as well as pleas for care e.g., "If you loved me, you'd let me do it," in negotiating with adults whom they depend on and are subordinate to.

The causal relationship between care and subordination is not simple. The assumption is often made that women and other subordinate groups care because they are oppressed and only by being nice and helpful can they expect to have any of their needs met. It is also possible, however, that powerless groups are devalued because they care.[2] Or, as Joan Tronto said: "It is difficult to know whether the least well off are less well off because they care and care is devalued, or because in order to devalue people they are forced to do the caring work" (1993, p. 113). It makes sense that the powerful will construct ethics of care as a response to subordination because this allows them to avoid devalued caregiving work and preserves their privilege. If they can also mystify care as saintly, so much the better. The situation of the powerless who give care is more complex. Sometimes they view care from the viewpoint of the powerful and devalue themselves or what they do. On the other hand, they can and do resist this view by insisting that care is important. Seeing an essential truth, that care is valuable and necessary to human continuity, does not eliminate their subordination, but it is an important part of resisting subordination (Friedman, 1993, p. 151; Tronto, 1993, pp. 89-90, 111-117).

CARE AND JUSTICE IN MORAL THEORIES

In spite of the empirical and political concerns about attaching ethics of care to women, the importance of including care with justice to form adequate moralities is widely acknowledged by feminist philosophers (Baier, 1987; Benhabib, 1987; Card, 1990; Friedman, 1993; Houston, 1987; Tronto, 1993). Even Nel Noddings who has argued for the sufficiency of ethics of care, has acknowledged the possible need for justice in some contexts (1990a). In order to explore the theoretical dialectics of care and justice, I will first explore the applications and limits of each and then describe one developmental theory that includes the roots of both care and justice in human development.

In a traditional justice system, I have the right to pursue my own interests and desires as long as they do not interfere with or infringe on your rights to do the same. When our interests and goals conflict, the rules of fairness, which assume the equal rights of the individuals concerned, are used to resolve the conflict. Individuals are connected to each other through individual choice and social contract. Justice has always been a demand of oppressed people fighting for their rights, and feminists have always been clear that women deserve the same rights as men. At the same time they have identified justice, as traditionally defined, as problematic (Code et al., 1991). From a position of oppression, they have been able to see some of the faults of dominant theories (Baier, 1987).

The limits of justice include both the moralities of unequal or unchosen relationships and emotional impoverishment. As these two concerns are interrelated, I will discuss them together. Feminists have pointed out that traditional justice theories focus on equal participants who enter a contractual relationship with each other, either on a one-to-one basis or as individuals in a larger social contract. Yet some of our most personal relationships are not chosen, and in some very important situations they are unequal. The primary unchosen,[3] unequal relationship that has been the focus of feminist ethics is the parent-child relationship, especially the very young child in the care of her or his parents and the elderly frail or ill parent in the care of her or his adult child (e.g., Held, 1993; Ruddick, 1989). In these relationships the justice rules of equal rights and noninterference do little to protect the powerless, young or dying from neglect, or to teach them responsibility (Baier, 1987).

Although children need to be treated justly, they also need love and emotional engagement from those who care for them. They are not equal participants who can reciprocate in kind. They do interfere with parents' self-directed goals and desires. Most important, they require more from parents than respect, fairness, and the space to develop their own interests. For growth, they require both love and care, and this requirement highlights the problem of emotional impoverishment in justice theories. The emotions of concern in ethics of justice are nasty ones like jealously and greed, that might, if acted on, lead an individual to steal or to take more than his or her fair share of resources. The law, based on justice theory, contains but does not transform negative emotions (Benhabib, 1987). By focusing on the control of passion, ethics of justice miss the importance of a parent's active and positive love for her or his child (Baier, 1987). Even in equal relationships between intimates, strict adherence to rules of noninterference can lead to isolation and alienation. This emotional impoverishment is captured by Annette Baier who describes traditional justice theories as "traffic rules for self-asserters" (cited by Houston, 1987, p. 252), and by Lawrence Kohlberg who conceptualizes the highest level of justice reasoning as "moral musical chairs" (Kohlberg, Levine, & Hewer, 1984, p. 310).

Intimate relationships are morally different from relationships with strangers. Marilyn Friedman illustrated this by changing Lawrence Kohlberg's moral dilemma of Heinz and the druggist. In the original version Heinz's wife was dying of cancer. The druggist was charging $2000 for a drug that might save her life. Heinz tried to borrow the money and was able to get only half of it. The druggist refused to sell him the drug cheaper or to let him pay the balance later. The problem posed to the person participating in studies of moral reasoning is: Should Heinz steal the drug? Why or why not? Marilyn Friedman asked her reader to consider the difference it makes if we assume Heinz might steal the drug for his wife or for a stranger. The rules of fairness make no distinction between the two, yet most people would be more willing to take such a risk for a spouse or partner than for a stranger, or for their own child than for a stranger's child (Friedman, 1993, pp. 105-107). Each of us needs a few people who recognize and cherish our own particularity and uniqueness, and the moralities of these relationships require ethics of care that emphasize our responsibility to respond to those who need us, and to sustain and develop particular human connections (pp. 134-141).

This point, in turn, brings me face to face with the limits of care. Ethics of care render insignificant our relationships with most people in the world and risk valorization of exploitative relationships. Because we do not care for most people in the world, we need ethics that apply to relationships of cause and effect as well as to those based on affect and caring (Card, 1990). The danger of care-based ethics is their conservatism (Tronto, 1987). In preserving our relationships and our social networks, we risk excluding and ignoring others who are not part of our community, sustaining racism, and discriminating against those who do not belong. Thus, care without justice in the public world can degenerate into patronage and xenophobia (Friedman, 1987). Although I do not believe in the usefulness of context-free universal moral principles, Lawrence Kohlberg was right in choosing justice over care as a potential universal because it prescribes moralities that apply equally to those we do not know as well as to those with whom we form community and family.

Care unmodified by justice is problematic in relations with intimates as well. If the sustaining and development of relationships and connections is important, then in intimate chosen relationships among equals, there must be a reciprocity of care. Without this reciprocity, intimate relationships can degenerate into exploitation (Friedman, 1993, pp. 155-163). As I mentioned earlier, the most obvious example of this is the abusive relationship. However, in any intimate relationship between equals where one person cares and the other is cared for, imbalance and exploitation exist. Ethics of care that stress the continuation of connections are limited if they fail to help women demand equal caring and, if necessary, to end bad relationships.

In conclusion, it is clear that both care and justice are basic and raise critical moral questions in all contexts. Claudia Card says this well:

> In one sense caring is more basic to human life than justice: we can *survive* without justice more easily than without caring. However, this is part of the human tragedy because, in another sense, justice is also basic: life can be *worth* living despite the absence of caring from most people in the world, but in a densely populated high-tech world, life is not apt to be *worth*

living without justice from a great many people, including many whom we will never know. (1990, p. 107)

If both justice and care are important how might we integrate them? Carol Gilligan has argued the need to move away from a single moral perspective to a model of justice and care as two interconnected aspects of moralities. The relationship between the two is not simply one of opposites, nor can we reduce one to the other without losing important ambiguities and missing the point of the interconnection. The metaphor she has used is one of a reversing figure-ground picture. For any individual one figure may predominate at any one or even most times. However, both can be seen, and a single-minded attention to either care or justice leaves one with moral blind spots because the ambiguity arising from the awareness of both images is missing (Gilligan, 1987a; Gilligan & Wiggins, 1988). This image of a reversible figure is useful in symbolizing two perspectives which cannot converge but, at the same time, are not diametrically opposed (Tong, 1993, p. 93). An interesting example is the different definitions of human rights by Western and revolutionary governments. Western governments define human rights in terms of freedom of expression, a justice-based view. Revolutionary governments are more likely to define human rights as having enough to eat, employment, and adequate housing, a care-based view. Both are important human rights and not necessarily mutually exclusive, however, by focusing on one to the relative exclusion of the other very different discourses and policies emerge.

In a developmental model, Carol Gilligan and her colleagues have proposed that the early childhood experiences of inequality and attachment form the bases for moralities of justice and care, respectively. All children begin life in a vastly unequal relationship and grow into greater equality with parents and other adults. This experience provides the basis for the development of justice-based moralities. However, the whole experience of childhood is not one of inequality. Attachment, the experience of loving and being loved, provides the basis for the development of ethics of care (Gilligan, 1987a, 1988; Gilligan & Wiggins, 1988). The differences between these two experiences lead to two different sets of interrelated practices of morality with different aims, goals, and standards of success.[4] The practices of attachment/

care focus on love with the goals of establishing connection and preventing abandonment. These practices are distorted when care becomes self-sacrifice. The practices of inequality/justice focus on fairness with the goals of establishing equality and autonomy and preventing oppression. These practices are distorted when the masculine is equated with the human.

Although useful in expanding a unidimensional view of moralities, this model is limited in several important ways. I would agree with Carol Gilligan and Grant Wiggins (1988) that all children begin life in a relationship of inequality and form attachments to other people. However, the inequality between children and adults is not the only form of inequality. Children's and adults' experiences with gender, race, class, and other inequalities in the family and in society also critically affect the development of ethics of care and justice in ways that remain invisible in this model. Furthermore, childhood socialization experiences are not the only, or necessarily the primary, determinants of the practices of justice and care in Eurocentric or other cultures. The practices of justice and care derive from many cultural institutions, among which culturally specific socialization patterns are only one. Carol Gilligan's model reflects a psychoanalytic object relations view of human development, one that has developed out of a particularly Eurocentric view of the relationship between self and other. Viewed as a correction to a developmental model that idealizes autonomy and justice, the addition of attachment and care is valuable. However, it is important to realize that if such an inclusion does not question the universalizing assumptions of white liberal models of morality, it will fail to include more than a few privileged women and men (Tronto, 1993, pp. 82-91)

What might it mean to expand theories of morality to include the practices of care and justice? First, it increases moral ambiguity as conflicts arise not only within each practice but through the interdependent nature of the two. Second, it calls for major changes in concepts and methodologies. It becomes necessary to examine a range of moral experiences dependent on different kinds of relationships, different cognitive and emotional maturation levels, and different social and cultural contexts. The domain of the moral becomes more complex. Third, it reduces the possibility of describing moral development in a stage theory. With the increase in complexity, simple linear stage theory will probably not be possible or desirable. Rather there may be developmental moments that promote or threaten moral progress which occurs as a complex interaction between the two systems (Gilligan & Wiggins, 1988).

One of these moments that Carol Gilligan has explored is adolescence. She has discussed the adolescent dilemma in Eurocentric cultures as a conflict between voice and exit. Voice involves speaking out and being heard, attempting to change the system by including the self. Exit involves leaving the system; in the case of the adolescent, this is the family. Ultimately adolescents do leave and this has been viewed as a milestone in the development of independence. Carol Gilligan (1988) has enriched this picture by emphasizing the importance of issues of attachment and voice as well as exit and independence. Her particular vision of maturity involves connection as well as separation. As a result, the conflict and change involved in voice is important as a precursor to, or part of, the necessary exit. Silence becomes a form of exit in which integrity is protected in the face of disconfirmation, but only at the cost of isolation (p. 154).

If both justice and care are important moral concerns, how do they relate to gender similarities and differences? The justice and care debate, in all its complexity, illustrates the importance of including both the individual and the symbolic gender systems and of being clear when each is being discussed and when the issue is overlap. I think much of the fire around the moralities debate comes because people are not clear about this distinction. Thus, Carol Gilligan has said that she is not talking about gender difference but about different moral voices, yet often has illustrated the different moral voices in ways that associate women with care and men with justice, confusing the two systems (Gilligan, 1982, 1988). In order to demonstrate individual gender differences, it is necessary to demonstrate quantifiable differences between women and men, at least in some situations (Greeno & Maccoby, 1986). On the other hand, the study of symbolic gender differences relies more on beliefs about what women and men should do, sanctions for violating these rules, and images from popular culture (Friedman, 1993, pp. 122-126, 163-173).

In order to understand gender in all its forms and interactions, we must, as I argued earlier, reject all kinds of essentialisms–gender, moral, and political–and take seriously the idea that all moral acts and thoughts have a complicated context that makes the simple application of universal principles, whether care or justice, impossible. We must realize that even in seemingly simple situations we supply context, sometimes stereotypic. Returning to Heinz, Marilyn Friedman has asked what would our moral decision be if the druggist were a single mother with three children and barely able to survive financially on her drugstore business? What if Heinz's wife were so ill that although the drug would keep her alive, her life had been reduced to one of constant pain and physical degradation? (1993, pp. 111-112). I think these are interesting examples because they are so different from the context I, and I think many others, provide when considering Heinz's dilemma–a rich, selfish male druggist and a terminally ill wife who is still able to enjoy life. By looking at and attempting to describe and study the complex contexts of moral problems we will begin to understand gender differences and similarities in new and interesting ways.

CONCLUSIONS

Moralities are gendered, raced, and classed not so much through the different reasoning of individuals as through the symbols and myths that create moral divisions of labor. In these divisions, care becomes what women and other subordinate people should do in private spaces with particular others. And this is devalued. Justice is what men and other privileged people should do in public spaces applying universal principles to distant others. And this is valued. Although moral divisions of labor are symbolized in these dichotomies, in everyday practice justice and care are more intermingled and compatible than these symbols would suggest. This compatibility can be offered as one possible explanation of why individuals' moral reasoning does not consistently follow the gender, class, and race lines so clearly outlined in the symbolic dichotomies (Friedman, 1993, pp. 119-126).

Pointing out that individuals of different social groups use both care and justice to reason about moral dilemmas will not break down symbolic dichotomies. These empirical findings are necessary but not sufficient. The symbols must also change. Ethics of care and justice are both important in public and in private settings, in equal and unequal relationships, and with distant, unknown as well as particular, intimate others. Although they have aspects in common, for example the importance of resolving conflicts among people, neither can be fully reduced to the other without losing important perspectives. Both bring principled considerations to bear in particular contexts. Considerations important to both perspectives are present in any moral context. Although in any specific situation they may conflict, the concerns of justice and care are fundamentally compatible.

Adequate ethics of justice and care have to be able to deal with both equal and unequal relationships. No single relationship can serve as a paradigm for all moral relationships. Equality is an important political ideal and moral considerations, such as fairness and reciprocity of care, are important in evaluating chosen relationships among adults. However, not all relationships are equal. The acceptance of disability means the acceptance of nonreciprocal, unequal, and uneven relationships (Hillyer, 1993, p. 248), as does raising children and caring for the frail elderly. Ethics of care and justice are important for evaluating these relationships, and for evaluating the larger social structure which can support or undermine the justice and care of individual relationships.

NOTES

1. Since the original development of Kohlberg's system, the scoring manuals have been revised and female as well as male samples included. Thus the current system applies equally well to both genders, and, as I show below, gender differences are rare using the current system. Although the current system is equally applicable to both genders, much of the literature until recently used all male samples. For example, John Snarey found that only 56 percent of the cultures studied and 38 percent of the individual studies included both males and females. Of the single sex samples, 93 percent were male only (1985).

2. I wish to thank Janet Dahr for this insight which she made as a contribution to a class I was teaching in November, 1990.

3. Obviously, many people choose to have children. However, one is unable to choose an infant with specific personality characteristics, attitudes, or interests in the way that we choose peers. Furthermore, once entered into, the parent-child

relationship is ethically much more difficult to end. And, of course, no one chooses their parents.

4. In Carol Gilligan's model care and justice are static ideals of moral thought. I prefer to think of them as human practices that involve both thought and activity. Human practices are defined by socially constructed aims and goals by which people evaluate their own and other's thoughts and actions (Held, 1993, p. 155; Ruddick, 1989, pp. 13-16; Tronto, 1993, pp. 108-109).

SECTION 3:
POLITICAL APPLICATIONS

In the final two chapters I turn to applications of each of the traditions to political concerns of feminists. In Chapter 6, I extend my earlier discussion of gender and math from Chapter 4 to an examination of the participation of women in science. I review evidence concerning discrimination against women scientists and their subjective experiences of practicing science. I also explore the ways in which science is symbolized as masculine by analyzing cultures of science.

In the final section of this chapter, I propose that the revisioning of science is central to feminist political projects. I do not see this revisioning as either replacing the masculine symbols with feminine ones or adding on feminine qualities. Rather, I argue that what is important is revisioning science as a human practice that is similar in fundamental ways to other human creative activities. All human visions, including scientific ones, are partial. All must be believable to some human community and open to criticism. Science is created, understood, and evaluated in specific historical and social contexts.

In Chapter 7, I extend my earlier discussion of moral theory in Chapter 5 to an examination of caregiving and the use of care as a basis of political resistance. In the first section I focus on hands-on caregiving that has been the traditional role of women and other subordinate groups and consequently devalued. In the second section I look at three examples of the use of a care-based maternalist rhetoric for political resistance. The examples I have chosen for this section are the Maternalist movements in Latin America, political organization of the urban poor in Mexico, and Women Strike for Peace from the United States.

There is always the problem of choice in constructing a text, particularly so in these sections. In the first section I have not dealt with all kinds of caregiving. Most notable is the absence of mentoring or generativity that occurs in the public sphere and is often the work of privileged men. I have chosen instead to focus on caregiving that is socially devalued, because feminists have been most concerned with changing the institutions and belief systems that relegate care to subordinates and, in turn, devalue them because they care. In the second section, I could have chosen other examples of the use of care as a basis of resistance, most notably ecofeminists or feminist health activists, in particular the political work of midwives. For two reasons I have chosen instead to illustrate my point with groups of women who often do not identify as feminists and who use a distinctly maternalist rhetoric. First, their ideas echo those of Karen Horney and thus provide a link with the discussion in Chapter 3. Second, they are most useful for questioning and expanding definitions of feminisms. Because these women usually do not identify as feminists and yet do political work as women that challenges dominant institutions, they raise important questions about the boundaries of feminisms.

In the final section of Chapter 7, I discuss the interrelatedness of care with both dominance and subordination. If we wish to untie care from gender and other forms of subordination, then we must see how caregiving and carereceiving are involved in the perpetuation of dominance as well as subordination.

As examples in both of these chapters show, all political visions, like all human creations, are partial. All have both strengths and limitations. Feminist scientists have sought to increase the participation of women in science through the elimination of discrimination and through educational programs to encourage young women to enter science. On the other hand, feminist critics of science have emphasized the importance of the social reconstruction of science to eliminate its masculine and hierarchical symbolic aspects, in order to increase women's participation and success in science. Both of these views have strengths and limitations. By attempting to choose one or the other, we are left on the horns of an impossible dilemma. Neither encouraging women to contribute to a masculine science that is hierarchical and antiliberatory, nor alienating women from entering science is a useful feminist goal. A better solution is to match specific strategies to specific situations, remembering always how any political vision can both promote change and be distorted to support the status quo.

The political uses of the maternalist ideologies that I discuss in Chapter 7 are similarly partial, with both strengths and weaknesses. On the one hand, women using these strategies have been able to successfully challenge regressive political regimes in contexts where other forms of resistance were impossible. These movements have empowered individual women and opened possibilities for a politics of care. On the other hand, these groups often do not continue to exist after the single issue around which they were organized disappears, and they seldom serve to challenge or question existing gender roles. The main point of these two chapters is that politics, like science and all other human visions, is partial. There is no one politically correct strategy, although there are better and worse strategies in specific contexts. It is important to consider a range of possible effective strategies, choosing not to apply automatically any single strategy to a situation because it matches some idealized vision of resistance.

Chapter 6

Partial Visions: Changing Science from Within and Without

THERE IS ONLY ONE OF EVERYTHING

Not a tree but the tree
we saw, it will never exist, split by the wind
    and bending down
like that again. What will push out of the earth

later, making it summer, will not be
grass, leaves, repetition, there will
have to be other words. When my

eyes close language vanishes. The cat
with the divided face, half black half orange
nests in my scruffy fur coat, I drink tea,

fingers curved around the cup, impossible
to duplicate these flavours. The table
and freak plates glow softly, consuming themselves,

I look out at you and you occur
in this winter kitchen, random as trees or sentences,
entering me, fading like them, in time you will disappear

but the way you dance by yourself
on the tile floor to a worn song, flat and mournful,
so delighted, spoon waved in one hand, wisps of
    roughened hair

sticking up from your head, it's your surprised
body, pleasure I like. I can even say it,
though only once and it won't

last: I want this. I want
this.

Margaret Atwood
Selected Poems, 1976, p. 236

The major political focus of equal-rights feminisms has been the increased participation of women in the male-dominated public institutions. Science has been, and remains, one of the most male-dominated of academic disciplines. Thus, for feminist researchers and educators working within the similarities tradition, encouraging and supporting women's participation in science has been central. In this chapter I will first examine the participation and experiences of women who have chosen science. The puzzle remains as to why more women who have the qualifications and abilities do not choose science. In exploring possible reasons for this, I will compare and contrast the critiques of science made by women scientists and by feminist theorists from outside science. Both views are partial, and both useful. Feminist scientists tend to emphasize similar abilities of women and men to practice science, and factors external to science, primarily discrimination, as the primary problems for women. Feminist theorists focus on the gendered nature of the scientific enterprise as a deterrent to women's choice of and participation in the cultures of science.

WOMEN'S PARTICIPATION IN SCIENCE

During the past few decades in the United States women have entered science and engineering in increasing numbers. Recently, however, this increase has leveled off or slowed down (Brush, 1991). In 1989 women earned 27.8 percent of doctorates in science and engineering compared to 8 percent in 1966 (Holloway, 1993). These percentages vary across disciplines within science. In 1985 women earned almost 30 percent of the doctorates in the life sciences, 10 percent to 12 percent in the physical sciences, math, and computer sciences, and less than 5 percent in engineering (Windall, 1988). In engineering at the bachelor's level there was a large increase during the 1970s and 1980s with a leveling off at about 15 percent by 1989 (McIlwee & Robinson, 1992, pp. 2-4). This pattern varies considerably across countries. Using physics as an example, the percent of bachelor's degrees earned by women varied from a low of about 7 percent in Japan to a high of 50 percent in Hungary in a recent survey. In only six of the 20 countries did women earn more than 20 percent of the bachelor's degrees. At the doctoral level, women in Japan and the Netherlands earned 4-5 percent of the PhDs in physics, compared to the Philippines where women earned 60 percent of the PhDs. In half of the countries women earned between 20 and 30 percent of the PhDs, in contrast to the U.S. where women represented under 10 percent of the PhDs (Holloway, 1993).

Information about minority participation in science is scarce. Most often information is either categorized by gender, collapsing across racial and ethnic groups or by race, collapsing across gender. When women's participation is compared to minority representation in the United States, there is a varying pattern. In the natural and applied sciences the participation in 1991 of Asians (women and men) was higher than the participation of women. The most extreme case was engineering where Asians accounted for 19.5 percent of those employed and women for 3.1 percent. The reverse was found in the social and biological sciences with the most extreme case being psychology, where women accounted for 36 percent of the employed scientists and Asians for only 1.5 percent. In all fields the participation of women was higher than that of blacks or Hispanics (Brush, 1991). In 1989 minority women represented 1 percent or less of employed PhD scientists in all fields, including the life sciences where white women accounted for almost 20 percent of those employed (Holloway, 1993). In computing science, where approximately 30 percent of the work force is female, less than 5 percent of the women earning bachelor's degrees are black or Hispanic (Kramer & Lehman, 1990).

Based on these statistics one would expect to find very few white female or visible minority faces in any lab. This expectation, however, reflects a bias in the reported statistics. In most studies, scientists are defined as those having PhDs, not lower degrees, and those who work in academic settings rather than in industry and government (Zuckerman, 1991). White women and minorities are working in science, but primarily as scientific support staff. For example, in Sharon Traweek's (1988, pp. 18-45) ethnographic study of the high energy physics community at the Stanford Linear Accelerator Center (SLAC), women comprised 15 percent and minorities 25 percent of the more than 1300 employees. The physicists were overwhelmingly white and male. Women and minorities held some of the support jobs. The clerical staff were all female, and with the exception of one black woman, all were white. The cafeteria staff were mostly Hispanic, the head of the staff a Hispanic woman. The engineers and craftspeople were all male, and many of the younger workers were black or Hispanic. The head librarian was male, all the other librarians were female, one of whom was black. Three support jobs were held by white and minority men and women. Illustrators who developed the graphs and other illustrations for the physicists' publications were both women and men, all of whom were white or Asian. Scanners analyzed the films produced by some of the high energy particle detectors. This job used to be done by graduate students until the physicists realized that it could be done equally well by lay people. At SLAC nine of the 13 scanners were women, six were black, and one was Asian. A particularly interesting example was the job of accelerator operator. This is an important and well-paying job which involves delivering the high energy beam to different detectors. Because the physicists must have beamtime to conduct their experiments, the accelerator operators often are under pressure from the physicists who compete with each other for beamtime. This job was held by both women and men, largely because the male director established a policy of promoting some women from clerical jobs to this higher paying one.

In conclusion, although women, including minority women, are in science, they are largely invisible because they do not appear in the statistics or in academic studies. Thus the scientists I will speak of are almost all white, have PhDs, and reside in the United States. Only engineers differ in usually having bachelor's degrees rather than doctorates.

Why are there so few women at the upper levels of science? The rest of this chapter will focus on a range of partial explanations. However, before I do this, I want to put to rest the common argument that women are not in science because they avoid mathematics. I am convinced that this argument cannot account for the underrepresentation of women in science for the following reasons. First, many women study math at a level that qualifies them to enter science programs, yet few enter and stay in these programs. In the United States women earn half of the bachelor's degrees in math (J. Becker, 1990; Rogers, 1990). In Italy this percentage is much higher at 75 percent (Fenaroli, Furinghetti, Garibaldi, & Somaglia, 1990). Even where it is lower, for example in Canada (37 percent) (Statistics Canada, 1993) or New Zealand (34 percent) (Thornley, 1993), it is high enough to permit many more women to go into science. In the U.S. women and men take the same number of mathematics courses in high school (Marsh, 1989) and in most European countries math is required throughout high school in academic programs. Second, as I discussed in Chapter 4, when women take math courses they do as well or better than males. Third, among those students with the most math background, fewer women than men choose science. In one study, of the 280 men and 220 women who finished high school with sufficient mathematics to enter a university science program, 140 men and 44 women did so (Windall, 1988). In another study of graduating high school students who had taken both calculus and physics, 64 percent of the males and 18 percent of the females planned to study engineering or science programs in university (Dick & Rallis, 1991). Finally, many young women who choose to go into engineering do so because of their strong math skills and report enjoying the math and theory required in their university programs, often getting better grades than their male peers (Dench, 1990; McIlwee & Robinson, 1992, pp. 23-26, 47-50).

For individual female students who do not have a mathematics background, science is not an option. However, in terms of numbers, enough women take sufficient math to allow them to enter science careers, yet choose not to do so. Although an adequate mathematics background may be necessary, it is not sufficient to encourage women to enter science. The explanations of why there are so few women in science are partial, multiple, and complex. Throughout the rest of this chapter I want to look at the experiences of women scientists and the cultures of science in order to begin the process of understanding women's lack of participation at the highest levels of science.

EXPERIENCES OF WOMEN SCIENTISTS

I want to tell two stories here, one more commonly told than the other. The first is the story of the discrimination and barriers women scientists face. The second is the story of what it is about science that they love.

The story of discrimination is clear and compelling and has been told by many researchers and by women scientists themselves. The statistics, which are consistent and dramatic, are similar in pattern to those for women in other professions and in the labor force generally. Women graduate students in science are about 15 percent less likely to finish their degrees (Holloway, 1993) and three times as likely as men to report experiences of discrimination in graduate school (Windall, 1988). For those who do survive and earn their doctorates, women among the most recent cohorts are more likely than women in the past to begin their careers in positions equivalent to their male peers (Jagacinski, 1987; McIlwee & Robinson, 1992, p. 3; Zuckerman, 1991). However, as careers progress, the gap between women and men increases. This gap is not explained by number of publications (Zuckerman), initial supervisory level, taking time out to have children (Jagacinski), the amount of time on the job, or technical self-confidence and assertiveness (McIlwee & Robinson, pp. 84-93). Thus, it appears easier to eliminate biases in recruiting than to remove structural barriers once women are on the job (Bielby, 1991). Women scientists typically earn about 25 percent less than men and are twice as likely to be unemployed (Holloway; Zuckerman). In both North America and Europe, women are most underrepresented in higher status and leadership positions within science. For example, women constitute only 2.2 percent of the Nobel Laureates and 3.4 percent of the membership of the National Academy of Sciences in the United States (Stolte-Heiskanen, 1991, pp. 1-8; Zuckerman).

A small sample of anecdotes from women scientists themselves creates a more vivid picture. Maria Goeppert-Mayer who later received the Nobel prize in physics, immigrated to the U.S. from Germany in 1930. Her first paid job, indeed her first job of any substance in science, came in 1942 working on the atomic bomb project for the government. She felt quite conflicted about this position, and might not have taken it had university positions been available to her (Dash, 1991, pp. 8-19). When Rosalind Franklin went to King's College in 1951 she could not eat with her fellow scientists in the male-only dining room. This, however, pales beside the story of how her work on the x-ray diffraction of DNA was used without her permission and without citation by James Watson and Frances Crick in the development of their model of DNA, for which they later won the Nobel Prize (Sayre, 1975, pp. 96-98, 137-167). These are older stories, but more recent ones reveal a similar picture. Evelyn Fox Keller (1977) describes the undermining and isolating environment of graduate physics at Harvard in the late 1950s. Naomi Weisstein (1977) describes similar frustrations as an experimental psychologist in the 1960s, including the ever-present antinepotism rules and an editor who tried to take her research idea and use it as his own. Andrea Dupree, an astrophysicist who received her doctorate from Harvard in 1968, currently holds a position at the Harvard-Smithsonian Center for Astrophysics. When all salaries at the Center were published in the 1970s, she was shocked at how low hers was in comparison to her colleagues'. When she sought an explanation, she was told that of course it was so low because she had a husband who was supporting her (Zuckerman & Cole, 1991a).

These are women who went on to be successful scientists. Much less is heard of those who drop out because they are not given much opportunity to tell their stories. In the most extreme example, the 14 young women at Ecole Polytechnique (13 students of engineering and one staff member) who were gunned down in Montreal on December 6, 1989 by an antifeminist killer, will never be heard from again (Malette & Chalouh, 1991).

There are two legal definitions of discrimination. Both are important in order to describe the experiences of women scientists as well as to begin to understand why women do not enter science. The first is a procedural definition in which the goal is equal treatment, and the second is a substantive definition in which the goal is equality of outcome (Fiss, 1991). Using a procedural definition women in science have certainly suffered discrimination. A substantive definition also is important because it points to the possibility that even equal treatment can be discriminatory and lead to unequal outcomes. For example, if male faculty are equally intimidating and unavailable to male and female engineering students, women are more disadvantaged because this field is nontraditional for women. If university engineering programs provide equally little practical mechanical experience for all students, young women, with their lack of background in tinkering, are at more of a disadvantage because of their lack of confidence and experience in this area (McIlwee & Robinson, 1992, pp. 47-50, 54-56). If engineering programs require equally heavy workloads of all their students, and women have more hours of housework and part-time work per week, the women are at a disadvantage in their studies (Dench, 1990). If science teachers let both male and female students cope on their own with peer interactions, and male science students boo when females give the wrong answers, sigh when they ask questions (Staberg, 1994), pick on females, or treat them as inferior (McLaren & Gaskell, 1995), female students will experience more conflict around science.

Equal expectations of female and male scientists also work to the disadvantage of women scientists, who experience more problems combining work and family than do male scientists. If they marry, more than half of women scientists and engineers marry men in the same field (Cole & Zuckerman, 1991; Jagacinski, 1987; McIlwee & Robinson, 1992, p. 50). In most of these dual career marriages the husband's job is still given priority with the result that women scientists and engineers are less geographically mobile (Gornick, 1983, pp. 86-93; Holloway, 1993; McIlwee & Robinson, pp. 151-154). If women scientists have children, they do not fall behind in publications, but almost all have hired help, assume responsibility for the children, and eliminate all activities except work and childrearing from their lives (Cole & Zuckerman, 1991; Dash, 1991, pp. 15-16, 51-52; Zuckerman & Cole, 1991a, 1991b).

In contrast to this rather bleak and discouraging story, there is a second one that is much less commonly told. It is based in subjectivity and focuses on the intellectual excitement of practicing science. My story here focuses on women. This is not because I think men's stories would be different. Indeed, I am quite sure many would tell similar stories. I choose to focus on women's stories to provide a contrast to their experiences of discrimination, and to give some of the flavor of what keeps some women participating in science.

This is the story of the subjective delight in discovery, of seeing something new, of knowing how a part of the physical world works. When Vivian Gornick (1983) interviewed over 100 women scientists, she found that they reported not only problems but also the pleasures of discovery, which for most of them nothing else could match. All reported a transforming perception of the physical world as whole and knowable. Many described moments of insight when a problem they had been working on suddenly became clear. These moments, which were rare, became the reward for years of hard work and the motivation for enduring more frustration, uncertainty, and doubt (1983, pp. 37-66). As one scientist said, "It's that you've got this secret. You know something about the universe no one else knows" (p. 128). Barbara McClintock, a geneticist, described the delight and excitement of problem solving, of seeing the solution whole before doing the experimental work necessary to prove the correctness of her solution (Keller, 1983, pp. 65-68, 96-105, 113-118). Anna Brito, a pseudonym for the biochemist whose story June Goodfield (1981) has told, described the power of the experience of seeing something new and then testing whether it matches the physical world, ". . . it was true in your mind before it was true in your microscope" (p. 144).

As I said above, I believe that these stories of the excitement of discovery would not be told by all female scientists, and equally important, would be told by many male scientists. Women scientists by inclination and certainly by training, learn to practice and think about science in ways similar to men. One aspect of the ideology of science that most women scientists share with their male colleagues is an uncritical and unreflective attitude toward the process of doing science (Leavitt & Gordon, 1988; Longino & Hammonds, 1990). The social studies of science, including feminist critiques, have largely developed outside of science and are viewed by scientists as, at best, irrelevant to what they do and, at worst, dangerous and wrong (Harding, 1986, pp. 36-52; 1991, pp. 77-102).

This lack of a critical analysis of the ideology of science has led many women scientists who are sympathetic to feminism or who are active feminists (Dagg & Beauchamp, 1991; Gornick, 1983, pp. 16, 144-156) to develop certain political strategies. The assumptions underlying these strategies include primary identification as scientists, a belief in the gender neutrality of science, and a desire to be judged as scientists not as women scientists (Leavitt & Gordon, 1988; Sayre, 1975, pp. 52-55). Critical to these strategies is the intellectual position of the similarity of women and men, especially in the cognitive skills necessary to become scientists and to be good at science. Women scientists have worked to encourage more women to enter science, to fight discrimination within science, and to destroy stereotypes of women as unable to perform science. From their point of view both stereotypes and discrimination are irrational and unnecessary, and more importantly, not an integral part of science itself (Brush, 1991; Holloway, 1993; Kistiakowsky, 1980; Windall, 1988). They also have portrayed a more human side of science which includes intuition, insight, and hunch (Longino & Hammonds, 1990; L. Shepherd, 1993, pp. 203-224) as well as doubt, uncertainty, and struggle (Goodfield, 1981, pp. 58-59). Science is seen as a part of humanity and as Naomi Weisstein says, "To deny us the right to do science is to deny us our humanity. We shall not have our humanity denied" (1977, p. 250).

Women scientists have also recognized the importance of women's organizations within their own professions. These groups of women physicists, chemists, or mathematicians have formed political pressure groups to study and improve the situations of women in science. They strive to eliminate procedural discrimination by challenging unfair treatment, and substantive discrimination by encouraging women to enter science (Kistiakowsky, 1981; Sadosky, 1993). Women scientists have also joined together with other women in the scientific workplace to study and improve the conditions of women within the organization. One example is SLACWO, the women's organization at SLAC, which included women working at all levels of the organization; they met regularly to discuss issues of concern to women at SLAC as well as in the larger community (Traweek, 1988, pp. 27-28, 32-33).

Many women scientists are committed politically to the view that men and women are equally capable of practicing science and to the correlated view that only irrational factors such as discrimination and stereotypes keep women out of a science which is gender neutral. An alternative view, held by most feminist theorists of science, is that the very structure of science is symbolically masculine and that science itself, not only irrational discrimination, is responsible for the underrepresentation of women (Harding, 1986, pp. 136-162; 1991, pp. 51-76; Keller, 1985, pp. 69-126; 1991, 1992a, 1992b, pp. 15-36).

The views of the feminist theorists make so little sense to many women scientists that they are heard only as arguments that women's nature is alien to science or that women practice a different kind of science. These reductions do make sense to women scientists because, although feared, they are also falsifiable (Keller, 1987). Thus, feminist theorists' arguments about symbolic gender are reduced inappropriately to ones of individual development. The assertion that science is masculine is seen as dangerous because it reinforces stereotypes of women as unable to do science, essentializes all women scientists as the same, and further discourages women from entering science. Furthermore, if science is masculine, then women who are scientists will be perceived as inferior scientists or inferior women, further justifying exclusions, especially at the higher levels of science and in more prestigious positions.

I see much that is valuable in the similarities position adopted by women scientists; at the same time, I would argue that, like all political analyses, it is partial, with both strengths and weaknesses. The view that the problems of women in science are due primarily or only to the intrusion of irrational discrimination and stereotypes into a gender-neutral science coupled with a denial of difference has failed in two ways. First, it has not worked to bring women into science in significant numbers, and second, it is inadequate in principle in not taking into account the importance of internalized beliefs and the scope and importance of gender in our society (Keller, 1991). Gender norms are a factor in individual development but also become the ". . . silent organizers of the mental and discursive maps of the social and natural worlds we simultaneously inhabit and construct–*even those worlds that women never enter*" (Keller, 1992b, p. 17). Although beliefs do not act, people who believe them do (p. 25). Although language does not determine social institutions, it does act in a transformative way to constrain the questions we ask, the concepts we form, and our view of what is real, right, and possible (Cohn, 1987).

On the other hand, the view that the most important barrier to women's participation and success in science is ". . . derived from the pervasive belief in the intrinsic masculinity of scientific thought" (Keller, 1992b, p. 23) is also partial. It overemphasizes the cultural construction of science and tends to underemphasize the limits that logical proofs and empirical evidence put on cultural constructions. In short, science works, or as Mary Hawkesworth says, "The world is more than a text" (1989, p. 555). Metaphoric language is also problematic in that it can be read too simply as indicative of individual motivation when it originates not in individuals but in the broader social context (Cohn, 1987). Furthermore, it can contribute to essentializing women and men as doing science differently with the consequence that women scientists will continue to be devalued and excluded.

Both of these views are partial in that each has something to contribute to our understanding of why women are excluded from science, and problematic as single or exclusive explanations. Both can be used to create change for women and both are vulnerable to being used by regressive political interests. By attempting to choose one or the other, we are left on the horns of an impossible dilemma. On the one hand, seeking equality through the rejection of difference has not worked; on the other, the acknowledgment of difference is employed to justify exclusion (Keller, 1991). Neither encouraging women to contribute to a masculine science that is hierarchical and antiliberatory, nor alienating women from entering science are useful feminist goals (Harding, 1991, pp. 53-60). My view is that rather than rejecting either of these views because they are partial, we should use both for their strengths and guard against their misuses. As I will argue in the conclusion to this chapter, partial knowledge is worth striving for. All human knowledge, including scientific knowledge, is partial. Before I do this, I want to expand first on what I mean by science as masculine by examining the cultures of science.

CULTURES OF SCIENCE

In discussing the cultures of science I emphasize the plural because there is no uniform or essential culture of science. Rather there are elements that symbolically link to some concepts of masculinity. In different cultural contexts, some elements are emphasized more, some less. For example, the academic culture of engineering emphasizes the importance of mathematics and abstract theory, whereas the workplace culture places more emphasis on mechanical knowledge, tinkering, and an aggressive style of self-presentation (Hacker, 1983; McIlwee & Robinson, 1992, pp. 109-143). The aspects that I describe below reflect a specific range of masculinities in a Eurocentric culture and therefore incorporate racial and class perspectives as well as gendered ones. Many of the elements are overlapping and also interact with each other. The examples I describe here are meant to be illustrative but not exhaustive.

One aspect of the cultures of science is the objectivity/neutrality/arrogance complex. The assumption here is that not only is science capable of revealing universal truths, but also as an intellectual process, it is culture free and better than other kinds of human knowledge. Thus the power and force of language is seen to be irrelevant to the gathering and reporting of scientific facts, and the development of models of nature. Because science is pure, scientists bear no responsibility for how their findings are applied or used by the culture they live in. Science becomes independent of and privileged over other kinds of knowledge. A related belief is that science is self-correcting and should be free of outside intervention. Thus, the scientists testifying at the 1981 U.S. Congressional hearings on fraud in science argued that the problem was not with science but rather one of a few crazy individuals that science in its self-correcting way would deal with. Basically they argued that science was coping with the problem of fraud, that there really was no problem, and that they were wasting their time even talking about it (Broad & Wade, 1982, pp. 11-21).

Closely related to the ideals of neutrality are the working concepts of meritocracy and hierarchy. These are believed to apply to science in contrast to other kinds of knowledge, and also within science. Science is objective and true and, therefore, more meritorious than other kinds of knowledge. Within science a hierarchy of people, ideas, and methodologies is possible, accurate, and desirable. The assumption that science is better than other kinds of knowledge is reflected in the attitude of one-way communication. Scientists assume they have much to tell other scientists lower on the hierarchy or nonscientists, but that they have nothing important to learn in reverse. Carol Cohn (1987) in her study of the culture of defense intellectuals found that they did not believe that there was anything of interest they could learn from her. Furthermore, they dismissed her attempts to use normal English, for example to speak of peace, as ignorant and simple-minded.

Within science there is a ranking of different kinds of knowledge. Thus, in physics, theorists rank higher than experimentalists and even among theorists, those the furthest removed from data have the most status (Traweek, 1988, pp. 111-113). Andrea Dupree commented that theorists in astrophysics love to rank all other theorists in their field (Zuckerman & Cole, 1991a). In computing science, styles of mastery which may be equally effective for learning are defined as acceptable or unacceptable by the dominant culture. As a result, people using a nondominant style will sometimes downplay their style or fake using the more dominant style. In contrast, those comfortable with the dominant style see no reason to hide or fake their style (Turkle & Papert, 1990). Another consequence of the assumptions of meritocracy and hierarchy is the belief that those who fail or who are not present either do not deserve to be or do not want to be scientists. Therefore, there is often an outright rejection of affirmative action as both unnecessary and dangerous because it threatens to disrupt a natural and objective hierarchy (Traweek, pp. 28, 74-105). Disciplines commonly have an internal hierarchy and an ideology that includes the superior aspects of their knowledge. The ideology of science is more extreme in two ways. First, science is assumed to be at the top of the knowledge hierarchy. Second, the ideology of objectivity contributes to a rigidity of ranking both within science and across disciplines.

Another aspect of some scientific cultures is tinkering. This includes mechanical expertise, technological know-how, experimenting, and manipulating physical objects. The association of tinkering with men, but not women, begins early. In a study of Swedish science classrooms in Grades 7 to 9, Else-Marie Staberg (1994) found that girls rejected boys' interest in technology as childish and immature in contrast to their own maturity. Margaret Benston (1992) described how her interest in science went along with an avoidance of labs and technology whenever possible. She earned a PhD in theoretical chemistry partly as an avoidance of lab work. The women engineers in Judith McIlwee and Gregg Robinson's study (1992, pp. 47-54, 176) felt most insecure and inadequate with the tinkering aspects of engineering culture and, like Margaret Benston, were much more confident and at home with the mathematics and theory they were required to take in university.

Another cultural element that incorporates a symbolic masculinity is the common metaphor of the masculine knower and the feminine known. Implied in this metaphor is an image of practicing science as a love affair. The object of the scientist's love is a female nature. The scientist seeks to woo, unveil, know, or, in more extreme forms, to force or rape nature in order to gain her secrets (e.g., Harding, 1986, pp. 112-126; Keller, 1985, pp. 33-42; Traweek, 1988, pp. 102-105). The result of these symbolic love affairs or marriages is progeny which prove the scientist is virile and the master of nature (Traweek, p. 159). Ironically these views coexist with views of science as independent of human agency, the irony invisible to scientists because of the belief that metaphors are not real or important. Women scientists also use love metaphors to describe science. In my reading, the rape and conquest metaphors were largely absent; however, the gentler metaphors were no less gendered. Anna Brito rejected Kant's idea of putting nature on the rack to force her to yield her secrets. In its place she offered the metaphor of attraction between a country girl and boy who fall in love, "The boy keeps giving the girl flowers. I keep inventing more refined concepts" (Goodfield, 1981, p. 229). Love metaphors also reflect a desire to possess. One of the scientists interviewed by Vivian Gornick described why she worked with the organism she did: "I really *love* my organism. . . . I love it because I've come to know it. Because I work *well* with it. . . . It's mine as nothing else is mine. And what happens when I'm possessing what is mine cannot happen anywhere else in life. Not for me anyway" (1983, p. 140). What varies in these metaphors is not the gender of the knower and known, but rather the amount of force used by the masculine knower. This ranges from a tough, macho, violent, and uncaring seducer to a gentler, more respectful, kinder wooer. Symbolic gender relations, however, remain constant.

The final element of some science cultures is the presentation style of the competitive workaholic. This includes the views that there is never enough time, and that there is a race for each discovery. Therefore, one must work day and night not only to make a discovery, but also to be first. Sometimes this message is presented as part of a double bind, the official message being that cooperation and contribution to the lab are most important, the unspoken one that competition and risk taking are required to demonstrate merit and earn a place in the community (Traweek, 1988, pp. 85-94; L. Shepherd, 1993, pp. 183-188). The race is sometimes even invented where it does not exist to justify ethically questionable practices. Anne Sayre (1975, pp. 108-119) deconstructs the race to discover DNA presented by James Watson in *The Double Helix* (1968). She argues that the race was not perceived as a race by the other competitors at the time. Rather James Watson constructed it partly to justify his use of Rosalind Franklin's data without her knowledge or proper citation. In an atmosphere where one is supposed to take risks, and be right, and be there first, speculative exploration is not encouraged. To be wrong is to be left behind, to be cast out, to lose merit and privilege of place. Anna Brito described this well when she metaphorically linked the danger of having cancer to the danger of having a wrong idea, which, in a competitive culture of science, is equivalent to death (Goodfield, 1981, p. 178). Ruth Hubbard described as ridiculous the ". . . notion that if you don't work 24 hours a day, nature is going to run away. It won't. It will still be there next year, unless we louse it up" (Holloway, 1993, p. 103).

All of these elements are not present in all science workplaces. However, where these cultures of science are the strongest, women tend to be absent, and when present are most likely to be perceived as not belonging and inferior. In extreme cases, women are seen as a threat to a male retreat (Keller, 1977). I want to discuss two examples that illustrate the importance of, as well as the variability in, cultures of science.

For my first example, I turn to a discussion of variations in engineering workplace cultures and their effects on women engineers as described by Judith McIlwee and Gregg Robinson (1992, pp. 109-143). Specifically, they contrasted a large government aerospace workplace with a smaller high-tech private company. Although there was more overt sexism in aerospace, and it was seen by both female and male engineers as a worse place for women, women who worked there were more likely to survive and advance. In analyzing this puzzle, the authors emphasized the workplace cultures of the two settings. The high-tech company was founded and run by engineers. As a consequence, the workplace culture was very gendered in the sense that the image of an aggressive competitive person obsessed with technology was necessary for success. This presented two problems for women. Often they were not comfortable engaging in the behaviors of this culture. Furthermore, even when they did engage, their male colleagues perceived them to be unsuccessful. In contrast, the aerospace setting was a large bureaucracy which engineers were a part of but did not run. As a government bureaucracy, this workplace was often frustrating to both women and men engineers, but because the rules were formal, clear, and combined with a strong affirmative action program, women performed well and advanced.

My second example focuses on Sharon Traweek's (1988) study of the high energy physics community as an extreme example of a culture that combines an ideology of neutrality and objectivity with a highly masculine culture of science, making it a setting where women are virtually absent. Physicists in this culture had a clear sense of being the best, and above social structures and requirements. This was combined with a strong emphasis on technology where research groups built their own detectors, and a highly competitive culture where equipment was not shared, even equipment no longer in use. An aggressive presentation of ideas was critical to survival for the younger members and to success for the more senior ones. These physicists viewed science as a calling and prided themselves on spending long hours in the lab, viewing their science as the most important part of their lives, and seeing themselves as superior to other scientists (pp. 106-125). Sharon Traweek summarizes the culture of the particle physics community as ". . . an extreme culture of objectivity: a culture of no culture, which longs passionately for a world without loose ends, without temperament, gender, nationalism, or other sources of disorder–for a world outside human space and time" (p. 162).

CONCLUSIONS

Science, like all other human creations, consists of partial visions which are limited by empirical and logical constraints, open to critical assessment, and socially constructed. "Vision is *always* a question of the power to see . . ." (Haraway, 1991, p. 192) and all visions, even if partial, are not equal. Evidence, critical assessment, and social analysis can help to distinguish among partial visions and this is as applicable to science as it is to art, history, psychoanalysis, or literary criticism.

It is important that science be conceptualized as similar to other human creations in two major ways. First, all scientific visions, like all human visions, are politically, historically, and culturally located. No vision is value free. Each is created within the confines of specific methodological and disciplinary procedures. Each reflects the personal values of the creator including, among others, gender, racial, age, and ethnic values. Each is embedded in the often unspoken background beliefs of a time and culture. These ideas have been proposed frequently by feminist critics of science, and follow from Sandra Harding's ideas of strong objectivity (1991, pp. 138-163) and Donna Haraway's situated knowledges (1991, pp. 183-201).

Second, science shares with other human creations a process of construction. Here I will draw on the experiences of some women in science to describe one process of creativity that is similar to the process described for many other human endeavors. I do not assume that this process is a universal description of how science or any other creative activity is accomplished. I most definitely do not think it is in any way specific to women. Like any partial vision, it is historically and culturally limited. However, my point is that, within these limits, science is no different from other human endeavors. Science does not generate superior knowledge, and the process of creating science is not qualitatively different from other human creations. For a description of one process of human creativity, I draw on the Jungian idea of intuition as described by Linda Shepherd (1993). There are four stages to this process. The first involves preparation, including a period of study, a focus on a problem, and a formulation of questions. This period can often be years in length and provides the necessary knowledge base for what is to follow. Second is a period of incubation. This is most likely a time without processing, perhaps a vacation, a walk in the woods, or an involvement in a daily activity. The third is the illumination when the solution to the problem becomes clear. This is sometimes experienced as a vision, sometimes as a thought, but it is whole, compelling, and carries with it a subjective sense of being both right and necessary. These moments are often quite short, even momentary, but emotionally powerful. I described a few of these moments earlier in this chapter when I spoke of some of the experiences of women scientists. Fourth is a process of verification. Here the illumination or understanding is tested and refined, sometimes even rejected through thought and experimentation (Shepherd, 1993, pp. 211-214). As a part of this process, the results of thought and experimentation are communicated to others, as it is necessary that the creation is accepted by a human community, however broad or narrow, before it counts as a partial vision.

Although not a universal or necessary process, this description of intuition is useful and certainly describes the experience of some women who are scientists. Both Barbara McClintock (Keller, 1983, pp. 121-138) and Maria Goeppert-Mayer (Dash, 1991, pp. 21-33) described the discoveries that eventually brought them Nobel Prizes in this way. Both saw the solution to a problem they had been working on for a number of years as a moment of insight and then did the calculations or the experiments to communicate their ideas to the wider scientific community. Maria Goeppert-Mayer's theory of spin-orbit coupling was accepted quickly. In contrast, Barbara McClintock's theory of the transposition of genes took many years before it found acceptance (Keller, pp. 139-151, 171-195), but for both of them the rightness of their visions was compelling. One of the scientists interviewed by Vivian Gornick (1983) put it well when she said, "It's like any intellectual with an insight. You think you've got a piece of the truth. You want them to see not only that *you've* got it, but that it *exists*" (p. 59).

There are two important points here. The first is that the insight or vision is always partial. The details of the understanding are never totally grasped in the moment of insight. Through the process of constructing the evidence and logic to communicate the idea and exposing it to criticism, the original insight is modified and changed. Another, somewhat different, partial vision is the result of these processes. The second is that the subjective feeling that accompanies the insight into the partial vision is one of wholeness. I am arguing that it is as important to empower this subjective feeling as it is to stand back from it and examine its partiality.

Most central to the project of revisioning science is that this process is similar in fundamental ways to other human creative activities. Vivian Gornick describes the process of writing a novel in a very similar way. The author has a sudden and compelling vision about the relationship between two characters and then tests, validates, changes, and ultimately communicates this as a partial vision in the form of a written novel. The novel is constrained by the empirical and social worlds that the novelist and her readers live in. Indeed, it must be believable to some readers at least or it is not a novel (1983, pp. 38-41). It is also open to critical assessment. Most likely it will not be believed by all readers. Flaws and inconsistencies will be pointed out in much the same way a community of scientists will find flaws and inconsistencies in scientific studies, models, and theories. It is difficult but crucial to see science as having no special privilege, as being in no way different from other forms of human knowledge. To illustrate this, I want to consider an interesting and fairly compelling argument for science as different. Anna Brito argued that if Beethoven had never lived we would not have the symphonies of Beethoven, although of course there would be other symphonies generated with the same musical rules and relationships. However, without Watson and Crick we would still have the structure of DNA (Goodfield, 1981, pp. 231-232). Yes, there would have been the discovery of the molecular structure of DNA, but with different people, or in a different culture of science, we might not have had the theory of the master molecule which privileges DNA as primary and causal, the single secret that explains life (Keller, 1983, pp. 153-170; 1992b, pp. 39-55). Instead, DNA might have been seen as one link, of more or less importance, in a complex and interactive picture of the structure of life. This theory would have looked as different from the master molecule theory as a symphony written by someone sharing Beethoven's time, talent, training, and culture would have been different from a Beethoven symphony.

I want to be clear that I do not think that the process of creativity I have outlined above is the only way science or any other creative activity is accomplished. It is not necessarily more common to women or to men. As its origins are Western, it is probably more compatible with Eurocentric visions of creativity. All of these are empirical questions that as yet have not been studied and so are unanswerable at this time. I assume there are other ways of constructing both science and other creative visions. What I am claiming, and this is critical to my argument, is that however science is constructed, it is not in any fundamental way different from other human creative activities. To reiterate, science is like other human creative activities in two ways. First, it comes into being within a certain historical, social, and cultural context. Second, the process of construction shares with other human constructions fundamental cognitive and emotional similarities. As a human practice, science has specific aims, goals, assumptions, and criteria of success. These specific characteristics which define the practice of science may be different from the aims, goals, and criteria of success that define other human practices. Thus, astronomy, which uses empirical criteria to judge success, is a different practice from astrology which uses human subjectivity as a criterion of success. What they share is the process of social construction common to all human practices.

It is important to demystify science thoroughly in order to break down the existing hierarchy within the cultures of science and to validate many different ways of practicing science. Multiplicity already exists within science, but multiplicity can support either pluralism or competition (Turkle & Papert, 1990). As long as science is believed to produce a vision of reality that is superior to other forms of constructed knowledge, then some methods within science will be seen as better, i.e., as producing knowledge that is more objective, closer to reality. Some metaphors, such as cooperation, mutualism, and interdependence will be projected onto women and dismissed as romantic, whereas others such as competition, conflict, and individualism will be presented as reality, even though they represent a romantic view of masculinity (Keller, 1992a). The goal is neither a gender neutral nor a feminist science. Rather it is a range of sciences which are not built on, but are inclusive of, differences–differences that exist within as well as between social groups.

These changes are necessary to create inclusive visions of science, but they are not sufficient. There is a clear danger that science can incorporate different values and remain male dominated. Sharon Traweek (1988) describes the physics culture in Japan as valuing interdependence, teamwork, consultation, and the capacity to nurture new members. These values are believed those most necessary to do physics and they are masculine virtues. As a result, physics in Japan, although stressing different values, is at least as male dominated as physics in North America (pp. 102-105, 115-117, 145-156). Theories, such as the chaos theory and quantum mechanics, emphasize uncertainty and relationships between the observer and the observed. These qualities are sometimes held up as alternative visions of science that incorporate more of the feminine (L. Shepherd, 1993, pp. 89-95, 112-116, 242-246). However, these fields are highly male dominated. In addition to changes in science, it is also necessary to continue to engage in the political work advocated by women scientists. Women and minorities need to be encouraged to enter science, supported within science, and not subjected to any unfair or discriminatory treatment.

The complexity of nature is beyond any human story. Consensus will always be partial and it is valuable to recognize rather than suppress this partiality. In recognition of partiality it is useful to shift our metaphors of nature from a passive woman whom scientists mirror, court, or conquer to that of the Coyote or trickster (Haraway, 1991, pp. 199-201). This shift encourages and prepares scientists for surprise and irony as they open their eyes, match wits with nature, tell stories, present evidence and reason to support stories, engage with others who collaborate and challenge these stories, revise these stories, and create new ones. As one woman scientist said, "The design will change but there will always be a design" (Gornick, 1983, p. 138).

Chapter 7

Care and the Paradox of Resistance

Here are our albums,
these are the photographs
of their faces.
Come closer, do not be
afraid.
Isn't it true they're very young?
She is my daughter.
Look at this one.
She is Andrea and this
is my daughter Paola.
We are the mothers of the
disappeared.
We collect
their faces
in these photographs
and we often talk with them
and ask ourselves
Who will caress
Graciela's hair?
What have they done with Andres'
little body?
Notice that they had names,
they liked to read,
they were very young.
None of them ever got to celebrate
their eighteenth birthday.
Here are their photographs,
these immense albums.
Come close,
help me.
Maybe you
have seen him,
and when you travel
take one of these photographs with you.

Marjorie Agosin
Circles of Madness: Mothers of the Plaza de Mayo, 1992

A major concern within the differences tradition has been the reconstruction of care. This reconstruction involves both revaluing of the caring that women have traditionally done, and disconnecting care from gender in order that it might become valuable human labor, central to the political and social institutions of society (Tronto, 1993, pp. 157-180). In this chapter I will examine the role of gender in the social construction of care, and the use of care by women as a strategy of political resistance. I will emphasize both the subordination of caregivers and care-receivers and the radical possibilities of a gendered care.

THE SOCIAL CONSTRUCTION OF CARE

Feminist theorists have drawn attention to issues of care. Women have raised the issue of care and responded to it with recognition (Held, 1993, pp. 88-89; Noddings, 1990b). Recognizing both the importance of the caregiving and the lesser value of care in our society, feminists have examined the role care should have in moral theories and in feminist actions (Friedman, 1993; Held, 1993; Tronto, 1993). Historically, care has not been exclusively associated with women. In the eighteenth century a number of social and economic changes occurred which prompted male philosophers to move away from the centrality of moral sentiments to universal moral principles. In this transition, moral sentiments, such as care, moved from the public to the private sphere and were assigned to women (Tronto, pp. 25-59). Although there is no necessary connection between women and care, this gendered moral division of labor in modern Eurocentric society has meant that women have often brought care to the forefront of the public debate. An interesting example is the issue of countertransference in psychoanalytic therapy. Countertransference, or the therapist's feelings that are evoked by the client, provides the basis for therapeutic empathy and resonates with feminist discourses of care. Sigmund Freud, who was well aware of countertransference as early as 1910, considered it an error that the therapist should strive to overcome lest it interfere with the rationality of the analytic process (Roazen, 1975, pp. 153-154). Diana Relke (1993) has described how women psychoanalysts were central in bringing countertransference to theoretical center stage in the late 1940s and 1950s.

What is care? Care involves both an emotional disposition and caring labor (Graham, 1983). Care is a practice in which both thought and action are integrated around central aims or goals. People engaged in the practice of care do not always meet the goals; indeed, sometimes goals are violated. However, the aims and goals define the practice. Those who engage in any human practice, for example science, care, or political theory, must evaluate their behavior in terms of the goals of the practice and share their knowledge with a human community (Held, 1993, p. 155; Ruddick, 1989, pp. 13-16; Tronto, 1993, pp. 108-109).

Joan Tronto has defined care as "... *a species activity that includes everything that we do to maintain, continue, and repair our 'world' so that we can live in it as well as possible*" (1993, p. 103). In the practice of care she has included four phases: (1) caring about, or the recognition that care is necessary; (2) taking care of, by assuming the responsibility for need and responding to it; (3) caregiving, through a direct hands-on meeting of needs; and (4) care-receiving, through a reciprocity that includes the care-receiver (pp. 106-108). Specific contexts influence the way care is practiced. Patricia Collins (1994) has emphasized that for minority women, motherwork involves a focus on physical survival, power as a struggle against dominant socialization, and fostering a meaningful racial identity. In contrast, middle-class white women can assume economic security and foster the development of individual autonomy in their motherwork. Nancy Scheper-Hughes (1992) has described the effects of extreme poverty and high infant mortality on maternal love in Brazil. Here, where keeping an infant alive can require almost superhuman effort and mothers must make choices no one should have to make, mothers do fail to care for some infants who are perceived as hopeless, or not wanting to live (pp. 353-364). Maternal attachments are selective and "... mother love grows slowly, tentatively, and fearfully" (p. 359).

Who cares? Everyone gives and receives care in some form throughout her or his life. In spite of the ubiquity of care, patterns of care are gendered in important and complex ways that interact with age, class, race, ability, and sexual orientation. One way to imagine the complexity of care is to consider the metaphor of a symphony in which gender, although seldom silent, appears in different variations, sometimes a main theme, sometimes changing to a minor theme, harmony, or counterpoint.[1]

Families provide the bulk of caregiving to both able-bodied and disabled people in North American society. Almost all children are raised in families, two-thirds of severely mentally handicapped children live with their parents, and 70 percent to 80 percent of the long-term care of the elderly is provided in homes (Abel & Nelson, 1990). Because most of this care is provided by women, feminist researchers have focused on the economic, social, and emotional costs to women of providing this care. The most thoroughly studied aspect of caregiving has been the work of white, middle-class, middle-aged daughters and elderly spouses caring for elderly family members with dementia. Within this population gender interacts strongly with age. In middle age, caregiving is almost exclusively a woman's issue, whereas in old age, given the need arises, women and men are equally likely to engage in the care of a disabled partner.

Although middle-aged sons and daughters have reported equal feelings of obligation to care for elderly parents (Finley, 1989; Storm, Storm, & Strike-Schurman, 1985), daughters or daughters-in-law have been much more likely to give care to elderly parents. Across a number of studies, between 77 percent and 90 percent of adult children caring for their elderly parents were women (Abel, 1990; Miller & Cafasso, 1992). In one study in England, residents in nursing homes with surviving children were much more likely to have sons than daughters (Wright, 1983). Sons care mainly when a daughter is not available. Amy Horowitz (1985) found that 88 percent of sons giving primary care were only children, had all male siblings, or were geographically closer than any of their sisters.

Not only do more middle-aged daughters than sons care for elderly parents, women are more likely to experience negative consequences that result from caregiving. One of the most significant consequences is disruption of paid employment. Information from the early 1980s in the United States showed that middle-aged female caregivers were much more likely than male caregivers to give up paid employment (11.6 percent vs. 5 percent), rearrange their work schedules (34.9 percent vs. 27.7 percent), reduce hours of work

(22.8 vs. 15 percent), and take time off without pay (24.8 percent vs. 14.1 percent) (Stone, Cafferata, & Sangl, 1987). Among single adult caregivers of elderly parents in England, 37 percent of the women and 5.5 percent of the men of working age were unemployed. Of those retired, none of the men and 50 percent of the women had given up work before retirement age (Wright, 1983). This difference is strikingly illustrated in a series of caregivers' stories collected by Jane Norris (1988). The nine daughters said they were glad that they could quit work, could work part-time, or were not employed at the time the caregiving was required. In contrast, the one male who was the primary caregiver for his elderly mother earned a BA, MA, and PhD, served on a national task force for the handicapped, and was employed in a counseling job during the time he was caring for his mother. When he was out of town his married sister cared for his mother (pp. 173-178). Only relatively privileged women without children to support have the choice of reducing or leaving paid employment. Many women, including younger women with a disabled spouse, and other women whose income is necessary for their family's survival, have a triple role of parent, earner, and caregiver (Chu, 1992). Furthermore, for many of the women who can and do choose to reduce employment in order to become a caregiver, the cost is economic dependency and poverty in old age (Graham, 1983; Medjuck, O'Brien, & Tozer, 1992).

In old age, caregiving is not so exclusively a woman's concern. Faced with a disabled spouse or partner, men are as likely as women to become the primary caregiver. Women are still the majority of elderly caregivers because they tend to live longer and to marry older men. Women comprise about two-thirds of elderly caregivers compared to more than three-quarters of middle-aged caregivers (Miller, 1990; Miller & Cafasso, 1992). However, given the lesser employment commitments of older people, the strong preference to be cared for by a partner, and the strength of the emotional bond and social expectations, both women and men are equally likely to engage in caregiving.

In a number of studies, the reported experiences of elderly, primarily white male and female caregivers have been similar. Men were no more likely than women to institutionalize a disabled spouse (Pruchno, Michaels, & Potashnik, 1990), or to have supplemental caregivers (Miller, 1990). Women and men spent an equal number of hours per week in caregiving (Enright, 1991), were equally likely to quit work or change working hours (Stone, Cafferata, & Sangl, 1987), reported a similar range of skills and coping behaviors (Barusch & Spaid, 1989), and described the effects on their marriages in similar ways (Wright, 1991). On the other hand, women have consistently reported feeling more caregiving burden (Miller & Cafasso, 1992; Barusch & Spaid) and caring for more severely impaired spouses (Miller). Furthermore, in qualitative studies differences have emerged. Women have reported more problems with anger, coping with arguments, and feeling frail (Barusch & Spaid), with assuming authority over a spouse with dementia (Miller), and with sexual demands from husbands with dementia (Wright).

Even though men and women are equally likely to care for a disabled partner in old age, two factors may make this more difficult for women. First, women come to caregiving in old age after a lifetime of caring, whereas for many men this may be their first experience with direct, hands-on caregiving. In one study, 25 percent of the men, but none of the women spontaneously mentioned that they were glad to have the chance to reciprocate the care their partner had given them in the past (Fitting et al., 1986). Second, women are more likely to face a future of poverty after the caregiving is over. Thus worry about the future, especially a worry about the loss of income, was reported more frequently by women who cared for partners (Barusch & Spaid, 1989).

Women and men give care in very specific social contexts. Because most of the research has focused on white, middle-class, heterosexual caregivers of elderly relatives with dementia-related disabilities, we know little about how care given in families is shaped differently by race, class, or sexual orientation. In working-class families the need for care is likely to occur earlier, and caregivers have fewer resources and more rigid work schedules. Given that in the U.S. 66 percent of the elderly pay part of the costs of formal services and half pay the entire cost, working-class people caring for the elderly have much more restricted access to formal services (Abel, 1990).

In some situations, family care in some racial and ethnic communities may serve to resist racism and affirm the strength of the family (Graham, 1993). However, the ideology of strong extended families in minority communities can also be used to justify fewer formal services, with the result that disabled people remain in the community with higher levels of impairment than is true in the dominant white community (Abel, 1990). In one study of black and white caregiving daughters, Ada Mui (1992) found that role strain among the black daughters was related to role overload, their own poor health, and the unavailability of respite services. All of these reflect a lack of medical and support services. In contrast, among the white caregiving daughters role strain reflected interpersonal factors such as conflict about paid work and quality of the relationship with their mothers.

In gay and lesbian communities, issues of care have focused on the AIDS crisis and on the creation of alternative families and patterns of childrearing. The gay male community, especially in urban North American centers, has created significant political and support networks around caring for those with AIDS. An important part of this work is the organization of volunteer buddies who often are primary caregivers for gay men with AIDS (McGarrahan, 1994, pp. 24-25). These community-based programs broaden models of informal caregiving which in most other situations is provided by family members and friends. Heterosexist culture defines gays and lesbians as outside of family. Partly in response to this exclusion, many gays and lesbians have become parents and established families both to emphasize their similarities with and differences from dominant heterosexual culture (Lewin, 1993; Weston, 1991).

Issues of race and class figure prominently in the work of care that women do for pay. Women comprise 98.4 percent of nursery school and kindergarten teachers, 97.4 percent of child care providers, and 96.5 percent of registered nurses. Some of these women, especially professional teachers, nurses, and social workers, are middle class, usually white, and are paid reasonable wages for their work. Among the least well-paid care workers, minority women, many of whom are immigrants, predominate. In a study of New York City home care workers, 99 percent were female, 98 percent were members of racial minorities, and 50 percent were immigrants. They were paid so little that 80 percent could not afford housing and 35 percent could not buy enough food. A high proportion were single mothers (Abel & Nelson, 1990). Timothy Diamond (1992) found that nursing assistants in Chicago nursing homes were almost exclusively women of color, including many immigrants. Given a pay schedule that was at or just above minimum wage, most worked two shifts in different nursing homes in order to support themselves and their families (pp. 35-52).

These nursing assistants were caring for a group of mostly white, elderly women, many of whom were experiencing poverty for the first time in their lives (Diamond, 1992, pp. 53-74). Most receivers of care are disabled women of all ages who are marginalized by their need for care. They have also been neglected by feminist theorists and researchers who focus almost exclusively on the costs to women of caregiving (Graham, 1993; Morris, 1991/92). It is primarily disabled women who have pointed out that women have important concerns as care-receivers. For women with disabilities care policies are important because at their worst they increase oppression and at their best they foster self-esteem and independence (Graham).

Reciprocity is a particularly important concern raised by disabled women. Threats to reciprocity heighten inequality and increase the risks of physical and emotional abuse suffered by care-receivers (Morris, 1991/92). Able-bodied adults who care for a physically or mentally disabled parent or spouse commonly speak of their situation as role reversal in which they become the parent caring for an elderly person who has become childlike. This perception is a threat to reciprocity. If people are perceived as childlike, they can easily be treated as children, undermining respect for them and for the lives they have lived as adults. Perhaps even children should not be treated as childlike; however, for people who are not children the lack of reciprocity is heightened. More appropriate than a vision of role reversal is the goal of maintaining as much of an adult-to-adult relationship as possible with the able-bodied adult viewing herself or himself as someone the care-receiver can rely on to a greater or lesser degree (Hillyer, 1993, pp. 178-179; Silverstone, 1988). An excellent vision of reciprocity in caregiving and care-receiving is the book, *Cancer in Two Voices*, by Sandra Butler and Barbara Rosenblum (1991). The voices of the two women are interwoven as they tell of Barbara's fight with breast cancer and Sandra's support of her. As lovers, one of whom is the caregiver and one the care-receiver, they give care to and receive care from each other and from a wider community.

In conclusion, most paid and unpaid care of children, the disabled, and the frail elderly is done by women. Men can and do give care when the necessity arises, usually in a situation where a female caregiver is not present. Among people paid to give care, the vast majority are women including many minority women who work for poverty-inducing wages. Most care-receivers are also women, and disabled women have drawn attention to the issue of reciprocity as central to caring.

CARE AND THE POLITICS OF RESISTANCE

Caring work for women has often reinforced their social subordination and economic poverty. Motivated by a sense of connectedness, actual care is often given in isolation (Graham, 1983). Although care has often been associated with subordination and isolation for women, women also have organized and resisted dominant institutions using care as a reason to demand rights. At different historical moments and in different cultures, women have organized around traditional roles of care, especially the mother-child bond, and moved together into the public sphere to demand the rights that their family obligations require. In doing so, they have challenged dominant institutions, including the military, as potential and actual destroyers of individual and community life. Feminist theorists of care have argued that care should be taken out of the private sphere and unhooked from gender (Tronto, 1993, pp. 125-155). Paradoxically, some women have provided some of the most useful political visions of resistance based on care by embracing traditional roles and ideologies (Kaplan, 1982).

In order to examine women's use of care for political resistance, I will look in some detail at three examples: (1) the motherist movements in Latin America, (2) political organizations of urban poor in Mexico, and (3) the Women Strike for Peace movement in the United States. I have chosen these three examples because they all emphasize gender difference, particularly women's mothering, as a basis for political resistance. My first example comes from the motherist movements in Latin America. The Mothers of Plaza de Mayo (Madres) in Argentina, the Mutual Support Group (GAM) in Guatemala, and the Group of the Relatives of the Disappeared (Agrupacion) in Chile are groups of women who have organized to protest the capture, torture, and death of their family members at the hands of repressive military regimes.

The Mothers of Plaza de Mayo was formed in response to the forced disappearances which began in Argentina in March 1976. It is estimated that 30,000 people disappeared into 340 secret concentration camps between 1976 and 1983. Thirty percent of the disappeared were women, of whom 3 percent were pregnant at the time of their kidnapping (Fisher, 1993, p. 105; Schirmer, 1993).

At first, mothers of the victims went individually to hospitals, police stations, army posts, and morgues looking for their own children. In this process they met other women and realized that they shared both a desperation and lack of access to normal political channels of protest. As a result they organized and took their protest into the streets. On April 13, 1977, 14 mothers gathered in the Plaza de Mayo. One week later the group had grown to 20 members, and by December 1977, 300 mothers, grandmothers, sisters, and daughters had joined the original women. To the present, the women have continually demanded the return of their relatives and, because so many were killed, that the torturers be brought to justice (Fisher, 1993, pp. 103-124; Schirmer, 1993).

In December 1977, the Argentinean military moved against the Madres and within a few days between 12 and 16 members were taken captive, including the leader of the Madres. None of these women was ever heard from again (Fisher, 1993, pp. 109-110; Schirmer, 1993, p. 36). Unwilling, even in the face of this repression, to give up their fight, the Madres began in 1978 to organize more formally and to seek overseas support for their cause. The election in 1983 of Raul Alfonsin and the return of civilian government created painful disagreements within the group over whether discovering the fate of individuals weakened the collective demand for punishment. In 1986, ten of the original 20 founding members left the Madres to form the Linea Fundador (Founding Line) which has pressured the government to provide information about the desaparecidos (disappeared) and to change the laws concerning benefits for the relatives of the disappeared. The Madres have remained firm in their refusal to cooperate with the government which has granted amnesty to most of the military who engaged in the capture, torture, and murder of their relatives (Fisher, pp. 118-133).

An estimated 400 children were kidnapped or born in captivity in Argentina between 1976 and 1983. Many of these children's parents were killed and the babies who survived were often given to military families as war booty. A group of 12 women formed the Grandmothers of Plaza de Mayo in 1977 with the aim of recovering the children who might still be alive and returning them to their families of origin. They have worked with the Madres and the Linea Fundadora. In 1981 they began to travel abroad in search of a blood test that would allow genetic identification using grandparents and more distant relatives. In 1987 the National Bank of Genetic Data was founded and, by law, must remain in operation until 2050. The Grandmothers have argued that justice requires that these children know the truth about their pasts and be allowed to establish contact with their birth parents' families. So far, 50 children have been found. Of these, 25 have been returned to their original families, 12 remain with their adoptive families by mutual agreement, six were murdered, and seven cases remain in the courts (Arditti & Lykes, 1992; Fisher, 1993, pp. 124-133).

In Guatemala an estimated 38,000 people have disappeared in the past two decades. In response to this violence, three women formed The Mutual Support Group for the Reappearance of our Sons, Fathers, Husbands, and Brothers (GAM) in June 1984. By August 1984 there were 130 members and within a year of the formation of GAM there were 1,000 members, including a small minority of men, one of whom was kidnapped, tortured, and killed. The group has pressed the government for information about the disappeared through the courts as well as through weekly protests at the Public Ministry (Schirmer, 1993).

In 1973 a military coup overthrew the Allende government in Chile. Between 1973 and 1977 an estimated 2,000 people disappeared. As in Argentina, women responded quickly to these disappearances. Meeting each other outside prisons, hospitals, and government offices as they searched for loved ones, they formed the Group of the Relatives of the Detained-Disappeared (Agrupacion) in 1974. The group grew from the 20 original founders to 75 members by March 1975. By the end of 1975 Agrupacion had a membership of 323 women. They engaged in active political protest with demonstrations, hunger strikes, and visits to the United Nations (Chuchryk, 1993; Schirmer, 1993).

These three groups have much in common. They are groups of all women, or in the case of GAM, a large majority of women. The women share a lack of previous political experience, and see themselves as responding collectively to their individual losses. The fathers are absent at the mothers' request because they would be the first victims and because their role as breadwinners would be threatened. These women are desperate as only mothers can be at the loss of their children, and use an ideology of self-sacrifice to explain the risks they are taking. In public demonstrations they carry photos of their children, symbols of a mother's responsibility transformed from private mementos to political tools. All three groups resist ties to political parties, but the women are aware that what they do is essentially political. Many have been transformed by their experiences working in these groups. They do not challenge traditional gender roles and do not consider themselves feminists. However, they have challenged the division of public political roles from private ones. As their concern moved from a focus on their own children to a concern for all children, their work took on a critical political dimension. One member of the Madres remembered as important the day they decided that each woman should not carry the photo of her own child or relative, but rather pick up any photo and carry it in the demonstration (Fisher, 1993, p. 136). These women have remained faithful to traditional symbolism of women as mothers, and, at the same time, have politicized these symbols for use against repressive military states. Exploiting their own marginalization, they were able to express political dissent in situations where it was too dangerous for traditional radical groups to do so (Chuchryk, 1993; Schirmer, 1993). Hebe Pastor de Bonafini, a leader of Las Madres de Plaza de Mayo speaks for many of these women when she says:

> It is as if lions grew inside of me, and I am not afraid. I am determined to carry out this confrontation, and if my life serves that purpose, then so much the better. It means that I

was chosen by God. I am doing all this work to recover all our children. I do not know if I can still recover mine, but I know that there are many others who expect a lot from us. (Chelala, 1993, p. 69)

For my second example, I turn to organizations of urban poor in Mexico. Although these organizations have involved both men and women, authority is claimed differently. Women have claimed their political authority from their roles as mothers. Men, on the other hand, have organized around economic and political concerns that are ". . . not linked to or rooted in their roles as fathers" (Logan, 1990, p. 152). In a culture where women are transformed by the birth of their first child into a person capable of self-sacrifice, and where poor women often have extensive social networks, it is possible for women to politicize their networks rapidly in response to a condition that threatens their right to feed and protect their families and communities (Logan, 1990; Martin, 1990). Joann Martin (1990) lived and studied in the community of Buena Vista in Morelos Mexico in the 1980s. She found that women formed their own ongoing political group in an atmosphere of widespread mistrust of male politicians by both men and women. The women reinterpreted central cultural images, particularly that of the mother-child bond, to reconceptualize politics. Women emphasized the importance of the community over the state, and particularly, over the self-interest of male politicians. Male politicians were corrupt because they lacked connections to the domestic sphere. The mother-child bond was held as providing the paradigm for honest politics. Women presented their special capacity to suffer for their families and community as giving them a deeper understanding of national and international problems.

My third example of women's self-conscious use of care as a basis of political resistance is from a Eurocentric culture. On November 1, 1961, in 68 different cities in the United States, an estimated 50,000 women staged a one-day peace strike to protest the dangers of atmospheric nuclear testing. The idea for the strike came from a small meeting in Washington, DC in late September. Using Christmas card lists, phone books, Parent Teacher Associations (PTA), churches, temples, women's clubs, and peace groups, thousands of women were mobilized in five weeks for the November 1 strike (Swerdlow, 1993, pp. 15-26). Out of this action Women Strike for Peace (WSP) was formed.

The women of WSP were similar and different from the women in the Latin American Motherist movements. The major similarity was that they spoke as housewives and mothers moving out of their homes because of a concern for their own and other women's children. They acted because they cared. Like the Latin American Women's groups, they were outraged at society's betrayal of them as mothers. Yet they also differed in several ways from the Latin American women's groups. One important difference was that most of the founders and major actors in WSP came from highly political backgrounds. These women had been active in leftist and Communist groups in the 1930s and early 1940s. After WW II most of these women, like most people in leftist movements, withdrew from active politics because of the highly reactionary political climate in the United States. Another important difference was that most WSPers, unlike their Latin American counterparts, had been highly educated and had given up potential careers when they returned to the home to raise children. The women of WSP also were more exclusively middle class than many of the Latin American groups have been (Fisher, 1993, p. 107; Swerdlow, 1993, pp. 49-69).

Even in the highly reactionary 1950s atmosphere of red baiting in the U.S., many WSP founders had remained members of peace groups but had become critical of the typical top-down hierarchies of these groups. As a result, the organization of WSP was consciously nonhierarchical. There was no official WSP policy. Each local took whatever action it saw fit without consulting with or reporting to the national office in Washington, DC. No dues were collected, no official votes taken, and no membership lists kept. WSP members paid all their own phone bills, travel expenses, and other expenses associated with WSP activity. As a result, the most active members were those with the discretionary time and money to invest. Disputes arose, but did not gain the visibility they might have in a more formal structure. Because votes were not taken as a part of policy, no one ever lost a vote. Women left WSP in protest over various policies, but as there was no membership list from which one's name was removed, this too remained invisible (Swerdlow, 1993, pp. 70-80).

Whatever the advantages and disadvantages of this structureless format, WSP became a highly visible peace group gaining extensive media coverage.

By 1962, WSP had gained enough public exposure to attract the attention of the most repressive political force in U.S. society at that time, the House Un-American Activities Committee (HUAC). In November, HUAC subpoenaed 14 women from the New York WSP to appear at hearings scheduled for December 11-13. The tactics adopted by WSP were very different from any other group which had appeared before the dreaded committee. WSP's use of traditional domestic culture in confronting the committee was so successful that the hearings were the beginning of the end of HUAC (Swerdlow, 1993, pp. 97-98). Rejecting the strategies of other liberal and radical groups which had appeared before HUAC, WSP was determined that no woman, no matter what her political past, would be isolated or abandoned. In a carefully planned strategy, over 100 women from all over the country wrote to the committee volunteering to testify. All were refused. The confrontation was planned as a contest that pitted the masculine patriotism of HUAC against the feminine patriotism of WSP that focused on the survival of the planet and its children. At the actual hearings, WSP women occupied all of the 500 seats in the visitors' gallery. Some brought their children. During the hearings they stood as a group when the first witness was called, applauded comments of the committee that they liked, gave flowers to witnesses, and hugged them after they left the stand. Each woman was encouraged to say whatever she felt was right and was backed by the group in her testimony. Dagmar Wilson, who was called to the stand as founder and leader of WSP, declared not only that was she not a leader, but also that she did not know what went on in any local WSP chapter, because each local was autonomous and free to engage in any action it saw fit. The women, cleverly and intelligently, challenged HUAC on grounds of their own choosing, refusing to engage in the anti-American rhetoric of the committee. And they won (Swerdlow, 1993, pp. 97-124). After the WSP hearings, fear of the committee receded and in subsequent hearings the balance of power between the political groups and HUAC changed. A HUAC hearing became the opportunity for gaining support for political causes rather than a political liability (Swerdlow, 1993, pp. 97-124).

Through the 1960s and 1970s WSP remained an active political force pushing for nuclear disarmament and working against the Vietnam War. Although critical of male militarists, they remained committed to the political possibilities of using a motherist rhetoric and did not challenge gender roles. However, as individuals they did experience gender conflict. Husbands shared with their wives a radical politics. Conflicts, when they came, were not over politics, but over housework and child care that did not get done or fell to the men when their wives were busy with peace (Swerdlow, 1993, pp. 185-186). For most of the WSP women, these remained individual problems, not political issues.

In the late 1960s and early 1970s, it became less possible for WSP to remain unaware of gender politics. Working with Voice of Women in Canada to bring Vietnamese women to North America, some of the older women in WSP came into contact with radical younger women involved in Women's Liberation who presented a critical analysis of gender roles. This confrontation changed at least some of the WSP women who became sympathetic to feminism (Swerdlow, 1993, pp. 227-230). In turn, many of the tactics and some of the rhetoric of WSP have been adopted by consciously feminist peace activists. Critical of traditional gender roles, these feminists have purposely used stereotypic activities in an attempt to transform them in search of a language and imagery that is not patriarchal but is subversive (Harris, 1989).

A few examples of feminist peace actions include Greenham Common (Kirk, 1989a, 1989b), the Seneca Peace Camp (Linton, 1989), and the Women's Pentagon Action (King, 1989). These actions vary in time. Greenham Common involved a number of years, Seneca a summer, and the Women's Pentagon Action was two demonstrations. The feminist women involved in these and other actions have not used a specifically motherist rhetoric and are uncomfortable with the essentialist aspects of traditional motherist arguments (Harris, 1989; Forcey, 1994). However, consistent with motherist aims, they consciously use feminine symbols in a language of resistance. Humorous use of household articles for resistance is emphasized. At Greenham Common one woman put a potato in an exhaust pipe of a support vehicle, which caused it to break down. Another time the women locked the main gates of the base together with a Kryptonite bike lock. The army's biggest, strongest cutting tools could not dent the lock and eventually they resorted to driving a truck into the main gates, knocking them down in order to restore access to and from the base (Kirk, 1989a). Such activities do not bring the military to a halt. But they do symbolize the weakness of the military and the strength of the everyday individual for resistance.

The use of song, theater, magic, and incantations are common (Harris, 1989; Kirk, 1989a). In November 1980, during the Women's Pentagon Action, women surrounded the pentagon, weaving a ribbon as they went, with photos, poems, pieces of nature, and the names of women attached to the ribbon (King, 1989). On December 12, 1982, when 30,000 women surrounded the base at Greenham Common, each woman brought something that represented life to attach to and transform the fence surrounding the base (Kirk, 1989b). In addition to the attempt to use personal items to symbolize a resistance based on care and concern, many of the feminist peace groups have continued the practice of WSP of struggling with non-hierarchical decision making. The goal is to value each woman's uniqueness and allow many different individual expressions of resistance, making group decisions by consensus (King, 1989; Kirk, 1989b; Linton, 1989). In practice this often has proved difficult or impossible, but nonetheless it remains a goal that defines feminist peace practice (Kirk, 1989b; Linton, 1989).

All of these groups and actions open up possibilities for broadening and transforming both traditional and feminist politics. They show that effective political action can begin with the care women have for their families and community, and move beyond care for particular individuals in their immediate sphere to a care for a broader range of others. All of these groups use gender as a part of their analysis, but this is done in different and complex ways. The women of WSP never did argue that women were more nurturant than men, only that male militarists had run amok (Swerdlow, 1993, p. 235). Some of these women identify as feminist, some reject the label. Some are consciously and directly political, others would see themselves as political only in the broadest, moral sense.

Three qualities these groups do have in common make them important models for possible feminist political visions. First, they challenge the division between public and private. They use a rhetoric of care, based on their experience in the home, to move outside the home and make public demands. Importantly, they are women who have metaphorically and literally left home (Kirk, 1989a). They have learned complicated legal and scientific knowledge necessary for their struggles (Arditti & Lykes, 1992; Swerdlow, 1993, pp. 80-86, 165-171). Having discovered their competence in the public sphere, many WSP women never did return home because they no longer perceived home as the center of their responsibilities (Swerdlow, pp. 125-127, 239). Second, these women moved from acting as individuals to acting as part of a collective. In some cases they began with a concern for their own children and family members. In all cases they moved their care outward from their own homes to embrace a wider community, sometimes including women from other cultures (pp. 187-232).

Third, these women are all involved in confrontation, often of the military establishment or dictatorship. They are not nice. They are not passive. Many take tremendous risks to act on what they believe. Members of the Madres de Plaza de Mayo have been harassed, tortured, and killed (Chelala, 1993; Chuchryk, 1993; Schirmer, 1993). Women have faced the disapproval of their own community for their actions (Linton, 1989). A number have chosen civil disobedience and been arrested. In the Women's Pentagon Action, 120 women were arrested for weaving the entrance to the Pentagon shut with yarn (King, 1989). What some may see as ineffective feminine symbols are often taken seriously by the police and military who move quickly and forcefully to stop them.

IN CONCLUSION: CARE, SUBORDINATION, AND DOMINANCE

Care is an important but difficult issue for feminists. The problem of disconnecting care from gender and moving care outside the private realm is complex. Both caregiving and care-receiving interact with dominance and submission. Although children, the disabled, and the elderly often have a lower status and are marginalized as care-receivers, it is important not to overlook the care that dominant people also receive. What is different is not their lesser need for care so much as their privilege that allows the care they receive to be perceived as supporting and reinforcing their independence rather than their dependence. For example, elderly people who receive Meals on Wheels are dependent because they require this service. In contrast, middle-class men, whose wives cook meals for them because they are busy with more important things, gain dominance and independence. White middle-class heterosexual men regularly receive emotional and instrumental care from their wives at home and from female support staff at work. This care is made invisible by the male's privilege which constructs his activities as individualistic pursuits. Fay Wright (1983) found that frail elderly mothers living with single sons were far more domestically active than similar mothers living with single daughters. Thus, the men who were primary caregivers were receiving more care from their elderly mothers than were women caregivers. Furthermore, mothers of the sons expressed concern that they were not taking care of their sons well enough, a concern that was not expressed by mothers of daughters.

Some privileged women also receive care in ways that reinforce their independence rather than their dependence. In many cultures, privileged women hire less-privileged women as domestic workers. These relationships are always defined by class and often by race as well. The privileged women are middle or upper class, and in racially divided societies, of the dominant race. The domestic workers who care for their employer's house and children live in poverty and are often minority or immigrant women. This caregiving, care-receiving relationship of economic inequality allows privileged women to pursue individualistic career goals by freeing them from many of their direct hands-on caregiving tasks. At the same time the caregiving energies and skills of the minority women are diverted from their own families to the families of privileged women (Cock, 1993, p. 51; Fisher, 1993, p. 187; Graham, 1993; Rothman, 1994; Wong, 1994).

Giving care also reinforces submission or dominance and does so differently depending on gender and other forms of privilege. Much of the care women give defines them as dependent and submissive

(Graham, 1983). Some forms of care by some people, however, reinforce dominance. One example is giving money. Men care for their families by earning money that is necessary for the family to survive. And privileged people, men and women, give money to social causes that provide care for the less fortunate. But money does not directly meet human needs. It must be transformed by human labor into food, clothing, medicine, or other direct forms of care. In this sense providing money for care is taking responsibility for care, but not direct hands-on caregiving (Tronto, 1993, p. 107). Sometimes women's expression of care is emotional and men's instrumental, a distinction that reinforces women's submission (Cancian, 1986). Even within the realm of instrumental caregiving, however, the kind of the care given differentially reinforces dominance and submission. The more instrumental caregiving depends for its success on the subjective response of the care-receiver, the more it reinforces the submission of the caregiver. Thus cooking a meal is defined as successful caregiving if the meal is pleasing to the person who eats it. That it is pleasing depends both on the skill of the cook and the subjective preferences of the eater. In contrast, instrumental caregiving that depends less on the subjective preferences of the care-receiver preserves the dominance of the caregiver. Thus fixing a car for someone is defined as successful caregiving if the car runs (Friedman, 1993, pp. 179-180). Certainly both activities are defined by the dependence of the care-receiver and the skills of the caregiver. However, they differ in that cooking, more than car repair, also requires deferring to the preferences of the care-receiver.

A particularly problematic form of care is protection. To be able to protect someone is to be in a position of dominance over him or her (Friedman, 1993, pp. 181-182). In the public sphere one of the main institutions that relies on a rhetoric of protection is the military. The main image of military care is of men who engage in combat at the front to protect women and children in the rear (Cock, 1993, p. 90; Elshtain, 1987, pp. 205-210; Enloe, 1983, pp. 211-212). Unrealistic as this image is, it is powerful enough that a great deal of military rhetoric and policy is directed at preventing women from engaging in direct combat. Although women do join militaries, they are conscripted in only three of the 75 countries that have a compulsory draft, and nowhere are they used routinely in combat (Cock, pp. 192-193). Protection is problematic enough that Joan Tronto excludes it from the category of care. Although it has some aspects of care, protection is very low on reciprocity. Instead of taking the other person's needs as a starting point, protection assumes that the one protecting knows what the other needs (1993, pp. 104-105). It can easily become self-serving. Thus, the military argues that more weapons are needed in order to preserve a position of power necessary to protect the nation's women and children. Women too, can and do protect, and their power to protect also reinforces their dominance, particularly with children. Mothers use the need to protect their children to justify violence against others (Davion, 1990). From a position of dominance, the vulnerability of another person can incite care or attack (Cohn, 1993), a relationship that victims of abuse understand all too well. Untying care from gender requires that we untie it not only from submission, but also from dominance.

Paradoxically, some of the most successful intrusions of care into the public world have been made by women consciously using female imagery and traditional symbolism to challenge militaristic states. These movements have served to empower individual women, to challenge repressive states, and to open possibilities for a politics of care. Like any political strategy used by oppressed people, they also have important limitations. Many of the motherist movements in Latin America have been more successful challenging dictatorships than elected governments (Fisher, 1993, pp. 206-207). Although these groups can spring into action very quickly, they often focus on a single issue and do not form continuous organizations (Logan, 1990). Either consciously or unconsciously, they do not challenge gender roles and they do not identify as feminists (Kaplan, 1982; Logan, 1990; Martin, 1990; Swerdlow, 1993, pp. 53-54, 185-186). Many have not made connections among women of different backgrounds. The Madres in Argentina have perhaps been most successful in including women of varying social class backgrounds (Fisher, p. 107). The WSP was middle class, white, and heterosexual (Swerdlow, pp. 1-4, 65-69, 76). The feminist peace groups have included lesbian women (Kirk, 1989b; Linton, 1989), but have remained largely white and middle class, failing to integrate the importance of the holocausts committed against people of color into their agenda for world peace (Omolade, 1989).

The paradox of care serves to remind feminists that oppression is complex and that change will not come via any single strategy. Care is connected in Eurocentric culture to relationships of power, including but not limited to gender. It is important both to untie these relationships, and to learn from women who bring care into the public world as women. Neither strategy alone will serve to create a more caring world. Both deserve respect, attention, and honest criticism. The successes and limitations of both strategies suggest a need for a diversity of feminisms which reflects the diversity of women and women's strategies to make the world a more caring place.

NOTE

1. I wish to thank Michelle Buck for the suggestion of a symphony as a metaphor for imagining gender similarities and differences in a conversation at Faye Crosby's Nag's Heart, Martha's Vineyard, May 26, 1994.

Chapter 8

Conclusions: Choices in Contexts

I think the most important thing to do is to expose the exploitation common to all women and to find the struggles that are
appropriate for each woman, right where she is, depending
upon her nationality, her job, her social class, her sexual experience, that is, upon the form of oppression that is for her the
most immediately unbearable.

Luce Irigaray
This Sex Which Is Not One, 1978/1985, pp. 166-167

Feminist theorists search for explanations of gender and
women's experiences, reasons to and methods of struggle
against domination, ways to understand our own complicity in
them and evidence that struggle against domination by ourselves and others is worthwhile.

Jane Flax
Beyond Equality and Difference, 1992, p. 199

I have argued throughout this book for practicing feminist double
visions which include the usefulness of theories of gender differences and gender similarities in creating critiques of existing cultures and visions of new ones. The dilemma of similarities and
differences cannot usefully be resolved or easily transcended. More
is gained by treating it as an ideological dilemma that helps elabo-
rate controversies rather than demand resolutions (Davis, 1992).
However, this does not mean that choices should never be made.
Individual feminists, because of their backgrounds and particular

experiences may well have an affinity for one of the two sides of this divide (Snitow, 1990). Furthermore, even though there is no final resolution, material and ideological constraints often provide good reasons in specific contexts for choosing sides (Davis, 1992). In taking political action in a specific context, with a particular group of people, toward a chosen goal, it may be wise to use a strategy that emphasizes either similarities or differences. In this concluding chapter I will first examine the political dilemma of marginal peoples attempting to gain access to power. Then I will explore three issues that are important for feminist politics that arise out of practicing feminist double visions: (1) the deconstruction of the equality/difference dichotomy; (2) the inclusion of differences among women; and (3) the consideration of the consequences of all political actions.

Marginal peoples who want to be admitted to the centers of power can claim rights either because they are the same as the people already in the center, or because they are different and have something valuable to contribute (Tronto, 1993, p. 15). Both of these strategies have not been designed by marginal people. They are the strategies that are required by those in power. Both leave dominant men at the center of power as the standard (Rhode, 1990). Thus, only limited choices about political strategy are available to marginal people, some political questions cannot be asked using the available political strategies, and the results of any action are deter- mined only partly by the strategy chosen (Tronto, 1991). External factors including the nature of the opposition, prevailing ideologies, economic factors, and political structures will also influence the results of any particular action. In order to be heard, marginal people must use the language of power. And learning this language limits what can be said, often making important concerns unspeak- able (Cohn, 1987, 1993; Forcey, 1994).

Strategies based on differences and similarities are both useful and limited. Historically, both maternal and equal-rights feminisms created as well as closed off opportunities for women (Allen, 1991; Cott, 1987). Any feminist strategy can both undermine the status quo and be subverted by reactionary political movements to support it. What is common to the intent of feminist work is discomfort with and resistance to dominant political ideologies (Allen, p. 241). The expression of resistance can, does, and should happen in many discourses with differing underlying assumptions. Women's lives are multidimensional and although in specific contexts a decision to advocate a particular feminism may be useful and appropriate, there is no single feminism that will serve across a range of women's experiences.

The dichotomy that sets equality in opposition to difference underlies the political thinking of our culture and is problematic for feminist political actions. This is a false but extremely persistent dichotomy and is reflected in both radical and conservative political thinking. The opposition of equality and difference implies the following analogy: Equality is to sameness as difference is to domination. This implies that in order to have equality people must be the same and that if they are different then unequal treatment is justified. Given this underlying assumption, differences strategies can reinforce domination and equality strategies can require the suppression of valuable characteristics.

Feminists and other social critics who desire equality and do not want to forgo difference must confront and deconstruct the difference/equality dichotomy. Often feminists are faced with a forced choice between equality and difference that is neither personally nor politically comfortable. Indeed, many feminists in the past and in the present have used multiple strategies to bring about needed social change (Offen, 1992; Snitow, 1990). An additional problem with setting up an opposition among different feminist strategies is the polarization of feminisms into better and worse (de Laurentis, 1990), repeating the problem of the equality/difference dichotomy at a political and theoretical level. If theories or political stances are different, then they must be hierarchically arranged rather than differently useful.

Feminists have consciously worked to break down the equality/ difference dichotomy. Jane Flax (1992) substitutes justice for equality seeing in justice a more ready inclusion of difference, potentially without domination. Deborah Rhode (1992) replaces difference with disadvantage in order to encourage different questions and more contextual analyses. She argues that by focusing on disadvantage rather than difference we are more likely to address the consequences of a specific action in a particular context. Feminisms cannot be reduced either to equality or to difference. This is neither a satisfactory nor a realistic choice. The essential focus of feminisms is on the commitment to eliminate domination and privilege, subordination and oppression. Although equality can in some of its meanings incorporate difference, it is fundamentally incompatible with subordination in a democratic citizenship (Pateman, 1992). And not all differences involve domination. What is dangerous is not difference or sameness per se but the potential and actual use of either to reinforce anyone's subordination or privilege. Jane Flax says this well: ". . . feminists should seek to end domination–not gender, not differences, and certainly not the feminine" (1992, p. 194). The systems of privilege are so complex, so entrenched, so hard to change that it is important not to eliminate any tool that is useful in some situations in fighting domination. And it is important not to reduce unnecessarily our visions of possible and desirable futures. The goal is a world where all women and men can be both equal and different, a world free of privilege and hierarchy.

Male domination is not the only form of domination. Other forms of domination including but not limited to ethnicity, race, age, sexual orientation, and physical and mental ability are a basis of difference and domination among women. With very few exceptions, the similarities and differences traditions in feminism have involved white, middle-class educated women. Both traditions have been most successful, especially in Europe and North America, when they have been the basis of action by privileged women who share the most with the men in power. German maternal feminists were primarily middle and upper class Jewish or Protestant women (Allen, 1991). Although the North American suffrage movement included working-class women organizing in socialist movements, post-suffrage feminism in the 1920s focused on gender as the only important locus of difference with the result that equal-rights feminisms appealed to a very narrow group of women (Cott, 1987). Modern equal-rights and cultural feminisms have also attracted mostly white middle-class women. Some, like the feminist peace movements, have addressed issues of sexual difference because significant numbers of lesbians have participated (Kirk, 1989b; Linton, 1989).

Where working-class and poor women have organized in mother-ist and specifically women's groups, they have consistently resisted the label of feminism, seeing it as middle class, individualist, and interested in destroying the family (Fisher, 1993, pp. 177-200; Kaplan, 1982; Logan, 1990; Martin, 1990). The motherist organizations in Latin America have involved women from a range of backgrounds. These women who have come together in a common cause to seek justice for the disappeared have rejected affiliation with political parties and feminisms (Chelala, 1993; Chuchryk, 1993; Fisher, 1993, pp. 103-138; Schirmer, 1993).

What divides women from women are not the political strategies of different feminisms, but the economic and social differences that are associated with racial and other forms of domination that operate across gender lines. The issue of domestic workers is illustrative of these differences. When some women can afford to hire other women, who are always of a different class and often of a different race and nationality as well, to care for their children and do some of their domestic labor, solidarity as women or as mothers will be difficult if not impossible (Cock, 1993, p. 51; Fisher, 1993, p. 187; Graham, 1993; Rothman, 1994).

To define some feminisms as better or more correct than others promotes the exclusion of many women from feminism. Although encouraging diversity in political strategies is not sufficient for the inclusion of diverse women in feminisms, it is necessary and important. The real economic and social differences that exist among women need to be addressed directly by feminists. However, recognizing that women will need to organize from their own situation, use a rhetoric that fits their view of the power relations they want to change, and take action that they judge to be effective is an important contribution to honoring differences among women. Poor Mexican women claim political power based on their capacity to suffer for their families, paradoxically using an image of victimization as one of power and pride (Martin, 1990). Lesbian mothers in North America adopt a strategy that includes resistance and accommodation, subversion and compliance in dealing with a dominant culture that defines them as deviant (Lewin, 1994). In the extreme poverty of the Alto do Cruzeiro in Brazil, people cannot strategize in the sense of a consciously organized action based on a clear vision, with knowledge of the opponent and some optimism about success. Instead they organize their lives around tactics of survival that are defined by an absence of power, and defensive rather than aggressive or collective resistance (Scheper-Hughes, 1992, pp. 471-472). Survivors of the extreme oppression of the Holocaust tell stories that reflect not only their perceptions that luck was critical in determining who survived, but also that they actively struggled not to die (Linden, 1993, pp. 95-102). Respecting diversity among women includes respecting the strategies and tactics that they are limited to and that they choose given the contexts of their lives. An important question about any political strategy is ". . . politically strategic *for whom?*" (Fuss, 1989, p. 107). By respect I do not mean an unquestioning acceptance. Rather, I would argue that it is important for feminists to engage in a dialogue in which each is called on to be a listener as well as a careful critic (Allen, 1991, p. 5).

Political action often requires that feminists attend to gender oppression and ethnic or racial oppression at the same time. This integration of political aims is never an easy one and often involves activism within one's ethnic community about gender oppression as well as within one's feminist community about ethnic or racial oppression. As an illustration of the complexity of political action, I return to Bertha Pappenheim who, as I mentioned in Chapter 3, was active in feminist and Jewish politics in Germany from the turn of the century to the time of her death in 1936. She founded the German Jewish Women's Movement (JFB, Judischer Frauenbund) in 1904, a group which remained active in the German feminist movement until 1933 and the Jewish community until 1938. Her most passionate political cause was working against the prostitution of young Jewish women from Eastern Europe and the Middle East. She challenged Orthodox rabbis who were unwilling to speak against these practices for fear of encouraging anti-Semitism. Because she understood their fears, she also sought feminist allies outside the Jewish community in an attempt to diffuse the potential of her work to fuel anti-Semitism. She was clear that it was difficult to avoid negative political consequences of her work. In 1927 she wrote: "If we admit the existence of this traffic, our enemies decry us; if we deny it, they say we are trying to conceal it" (N. Shepherd, 1993, p. 238). An expert lace maker, she used the metaphor of lace for her life: "... our lives should also be made out of fine flawless material and be interwoven in a way which is sometimes simple and sometimes complex, sometimes aesthetic and sometimes ethical, but this is the only longing I have: to live such a life. I hate the clumsy fingers which disturb my beautiful planning and tear my threads or destroy them" (p. 237). She was only too aware of how delicate and fragile her political work was, how subject to perversion by anti-Semitic oppression. In a final and terrible irony the Nazis made the Jewish role in prostitution traffic central to their anti-Semitic propaganda (Kaplan, 1984; N. Shepherd, pp. 208-242).

Just as all knowledge is partial, so all actions are partial. The success of any political action depends only partly on the strategy chosen. It is also determined by a number of factors beyond the control of the political actors, especially if these actors occupy marginal positions in society. Also, what seems a success in the present, may, from a later view seem more ambivalent. Given the power of dominant discourses to appropriate radical ideas to reactionary purposes, it is important to analyze not only the intent and purpose of ideas and actions but also potential and actual consequences. Intent alone does not determine consequences. An important part of doing feminist theoretical work and action is to seek out possible consequences, especially unintended consequences and address them. One way to do this is to pay serious attention to who supports and who criticizes feminist work, both inside the feminist community and in the wider society. Another is to address in any feminist discourse possible reactionary misuses of the work. Of course merely warning about potential misuses does not mean they will not happen. Feminists, like other radical social critics, do not have the power to stop all misuses of attempts to resist. Nonetheless it is an important ethical concern and will promote more self-conscious and effective social protests.

For women and other marginal groups these unintended consequences are often negative. An action for change is either used against women or the change is limited to a few privileged women. I have discussed many examples of such unintended negative consequences in earlier chapters. When Leta Stetter Hollingworth and other equal-rights feminists fought for women's right to combine motherhood with economic independence (1916c, 1927), they did not mean for this to be limited to a very few privileged women, yet this was a consequence of their focus on equal opportunity (Cott, 1987, pp. 191-204). Karen Horney entered into her debate with Sigmund Freud with the intent of replacing his misogynist biological ideas with a theory that would define two different biologies, equal in value and different in form and content (1926/1967). What she did not intend, but what did happen, was that this biological difference was used to devalue women (Westkott, 1986, pp. 53-65). Modern feminist psychologists have used empirical data to prove gender similarities in mathematics achievement (Hyde, Fennema, & Lamon, 1990; Kimball, 1989). However, because of the cultural symbolization of mathematics as masculine, their argument has in many cases not changed people's thinking (Damarin, 1990, 1993; Walkerdine, 1989). Feminist critics of science intend to change science so that women and other minorities feel more welcome in science and science itself contributes to liberation rather than oppression. An unintended consequence of their actions includes the perception that women would not want to enter science and, if they did, would not do science as well as men. Feminist scientists who seek to end discrimination and directly encourage women to enter science as it is structured and symbolized, are puzzled by young women's and minorities' continuing choices to avoid science (Harding, 1991, pp. 51-76; Longino & Hammonds, 1990). Including care with justice in defining moralities is designed to revalue what women and minorities do, not reinforce oppression and promote traditional roles. Yet these latter have been unintended consequences that are difficult to avoid (Friedman, 1993, pp. 145-155; Tronto, 1993, pp. 77-91, 116-117).

These examples are discouraging in illustrating negative unintended consequences of political action. Given the power of dominant discourses and groups, this is to be expected. However, unintended consequences are not always negative. Many of the women in Women Strike for Peace who intended to leave their homes to engage in political action only temporarily, found that they enjoyed the public sphere and continued to be active politically in WSP and other organizations. Furthermore, as a result of their contact with the women's movement, some grew critical of the gender roles they had extolled a few years before (Swerdlow, 1993, pp. 233-243). Many of the Mothers and Grandmothers of Plaza de Mayo who began their action from an apolitical stance, came to see their work as political in a broad sense and many of their lives changed as a result of their actions (Arditti & Lykes, 1992; Fisher, 1993, pp. 103-138; Schirmer, 1993).

The choice of strategy and action is a difficult process. No action can guarantee the intended–and only the intended–outcomes. In evaluating any political action it is important to understand the context in which it arose, listen to the women and men who initiated the action, and analyze possible unintended as well as intended consequences. If we do this with an awareness of the political and theoretical motivations for making this particular choice at this moment in time, in this context we can avoid essentializing claims of truth. And we will remain open to recognizing the limits of our choices, the strength of what we have not chosen, and the dialectics among the contradictory worlds we live in.

References

Abel, E. K. (1990). Family care of the frail elderly. In E. K. Abel & M. K. Nelson (Eds.), *Circles of Care: Work and Identity in Women's Lives* (pp. 65-91). Albany, NY: State University of New York Press.

Abel, E. K., & Nelson, M. K. (1990). Circles of care: An introductory essay. In E. K. Abel & M. K. Nelson (Eds.), *Circles of Care: Work and Identity in Women's Lives* (pp. 4-34). Albany, NY: State University of New York Press.

Abraham, K. (1922). Manifestations of the female castration complex. *International Journal of Psychoanalysis, 3,* 1-29.

Agosin, M. (1992). *Circles of Madness: Mothers of the Plaza de Mayo.* Fredonia, NY: White Pine.

Allen, A. T. (1991). *Feminism and Motherhood in Germany, 1800-1914.* New Brunswick, NJ: Rutgers University Press.

Allen, C. N. (1927). Studies in sex differences. *Psychological Bulletin, 24,* 294-304.

Antler, J. (1980). "After college, what?": New graduates and the family claim. *American Quarterly, 32,* 409-434.

Appignanesi, L., and Forrester, J. (1992). *Freud's Women.* New York: Basic Books.

Arditti, R., & Lykes, M. B. (1992). "Recovering identity": The work of the grandmothers of Plaza de Mayo. *Women's Studies International Forum, 15,* 461-471.

Atwood, M. (1976). *Selected Poems.* Toronto: Oxford University Press.

Atwood, M. (1986). *Selected Poems II: Poems Selected and New 1976-1986.* Toronto: Oxford University Press.

Baier, A. C. (1987). The need for more than justice. In M. Hanen & K. Nielsen (Eds.), Science, morality, and feminist theory. *Canadian Journal of Philosophy, 13,* suppl., 41-56.

Barnes, M. (1994). Investigating change: A gender-inclusive course in calculus. *Zentrallblatt für Didaktik der Mathematik. (International Reviews in Mathematics Education), 26*(2), 49-56.

Barnes, M., & Copeland, M. (1990). Humanizing calculus: A case study in curriculum development. In L. Burton (Ed.), *Gender and Mathematics: An International Perspective* (pp. 72-80). New York: Cassell.

Barusch, A. S., & Spaid, W. M. (1989). Gender differences in caregiving: Why do wives report greater burden? *The Gerontologist, 29*, 667-676.

Baumrind, D. (1986). Sex differences in moral reasoning: Response to Walker's (1984) conclusion that there are none. *Child Development, 57*, 511-521.

Becker, B. J. (1990). Item characteristics and gender differences on the SAT-M for mathematically able youths. *American Educational Research Journal, 27*, 65-87.

Becker, J. R. (1990). Graduate education in the mathematical sciences: Factors influencing women and men. In L. Burton (Ed.), *Gender and Mathematics: An International Perspective* (pp. 119-130). New York: Cassell.

Benbow, C. P. (1992). Academic achievement in mathematics and science of students between ages 13 and 23: Are there differences among students in the top one percent of mathematical ability? *Journal of Educational Psychology, 84*, 51-61.

Benbow, C. P., & Arjmand, O. (1990). Predictors of high academic achievement in mathematics and science by mathematically talented students: A longitudinal study. *Journal of Educational Psychology, 82*, 430-441.

Benbow, C. P., & Lubinski, D. (1993). Consequences of gender differences in mathematical reasoning ability and some biological linkages. In M. Haug (Ed.), *The Development Of Sex Differences and Similarities in Behavior: Proceedings of the NATO Advanced Research Workshop, Chateau de Bonas, Gers, France, July 14-18, 1992* (pp. 87-109). The Netherlands: Kluwer Academic Publishers.

Benbow, C. P., & Stanley, J. C. (1980). Sex differences in mathematical ability: Fact or artifact? *Science, 210*, 1262-1264.

Benhabib, S. (1987). The generalized and the concrete other: The Kohlberg-Gilligan controversy and moral theory. In E. F. Kittay & D. T. Meyers (Eds.), *Women and Moral Theory* (pp. 154-177). Totowa, NJ: Roman and Littlefield.

Benston, M. (1992). Women's voices/men's voices: Technology as language. In G. Kirkup & L. S. Keller (Eds.), *Inventing Women: Science, Technology and Gender* (pp. 33-41). Cambridge, UK: Polity Press.

BenTsvi-Mayer, S., Hertz-Lazarowitz, R., & Safir, M. P. (1989). Teachers' selections of boys and girls as prominent pupils. *Sex Roles, 21,* 231-246.

Bielby, W. T. (1991). Sex differences in careers: Is science a special case? In H. Zuckerman, J. R. Cole, & J. T. Bruer (Eds.), *The Outer Circle: Women in the Scientific Community* (pp. 171-187). New Haven, CT: Yale University Press.

Blum-Anderson, J. (1992). Increasing enrollment in higher-level mathematics classes through the affective domain. *School Science and Mathematics, 92,* 433-436.

Bohan, J. S. (1993). Regarding gender: Essentialism, constructionism, and feminist psychology. *Psychology of Women Quarterly, 17,* 5-21.

Bordo, S. (1990). Feminism, postmodernism, and gender-scepticism. In L. J. Nicholson (Ed.), *Feminism/Postmodernism* (pp. 133-156). New York: Routledge.

Bridenthal, R., & Koonz, C. (1984). Beyond Kinder, Kuche, Kirche: Weimar women in politics and work. In R. Bridenthal, A. Grossmann, & M. Kaplan (Eds.), *When Biology Became Destiny: Women in Weimar and Nazi Germany* (pp. 33-65). New York: Monthly Review Press.

Bridgeman, B., & Wendler, C. (1991). Gender differences in predictors of college mathematics course grades. *Journal of Educational Psychology, 83,* 275-284.

Broad, W., & Wade, N. (1982). *Betrayers of the Truth.* New York: Simon and Schuster.

Brush, S. G. (1991). Women in science and engineering. *American Scientist, 79,* 404-419.

Burton, L. (1994). Differential performance in assessment in mathematics at the end of compulsory schooling: A European comparison. In L. Burton (Ed.), *Who Counts? Mathematics Achievement in Europe* (pp. 1-21). Stoke-on-Trent, Staffordshire: Trentham Books.

Butler, S., & Rosenblum, B. (1991). *Cancer in Two Voices.* San Francisco, CA: Spinsters Book Company.

Cancian, F. M. (1986). The feminization of love. *Signs, 11,* 692-709.

Card, C. (1990). Caring and evil. *Hypatia, 5* (1), 101-108.

Carpenter, J. P., Fennema, E., Peterson, P. L., Chiang, C., & Loef, M. (1989). Using knowledge of children's mathematics thinking in classroom teaching: An experimental study. *American Educational Research Journal, 26,* 499-531.

Carson, C. C., Huelskamp, R. M., & Woodall, T. D. (1993). Standardized tests. *Journal of Educational Research, 86,* 267-272.

Chelala, C. A. (1993). Women of valor: An interview with Mothers of Plaza de Mayo. In M. Agosin (Ed.), *Surviving Beyond Fear: Women, Children & Human Rights in Latin America* (pp. 58-70). Fredonia, NY: White Pine.

Cherry, R., & Cherry, L. (1973, August 26). The Horney heresy. *New York Times Magazine,* pp. 12, 75-80.

Chipman, S. F. (1988, April). *Word Problems: Where Sex Bias Creeps In.* Paper presented at the meeting of the American Educational Research Association, New Orleans, LA. (ERIC Document Reproduction Service No. TM 012 411).

Chipman, S. F., Marshall, S. P. & Scott, P. A. (1991). Content effects on work problem performance: A possible source of test bias? *American Education Research Journal, 28,* 897-915.

Chodorow, N. J. (1978). *The Reproduction Of Mothering: Psychoanalysis and the Sociology of Gender.* Berkeley, CA: University of California Press.

Chodorow, N. J. (1986). Varieties of leadership among early women psychoanalysts. In L. Dickstein & C. C. Nadelson (Eds.), *Women Physicians in Leadership Roles* (pp. 47-54). Washington, DC: American Psychiatric Press.

Chodorow, N. J. (1989). *Feminism and Psychoanalytic Theory.* New Haven, CT: Yale University Press.

Chu, M. (1992, October). *The Triple Role of Women with Disabled Spouses.* Paper presented at the conference on Women's Health Across the Life Span: Research Issues, Centre for Research in

Women's Studies and Gender Relations, University of British Columbia, Vancouver, Canada.

Chuchryk, P. M. (1993). Subversive mothers: The opposition to the military regime in Chile. In M. Agosin (Ed.), *Surviving Beyond Fear: Women Children & Human Rights in Latin America* (pp. 86-98). Fredonia, NY: White Pine.

Clemmens, E. R. (1986). Karen Horney, MD: An early leader. In L. Dickstein & C. C. Nadelson (Eds.), *Women Physicians in Leadership Roles* (pp. 67-70). Washington, DC: American Psychiatric Press.

Cock, J. (1993). *Women and War in South Africa.* Cleveland, OH: The Pilgrim Press.

Code, L., Ford, M., Martindale, K., Sherwin, S., & Shogun, D. (1991). *Is Feminist Ethics Possible?* CRIAW Papers No. 27. Ottawa, Ontario: Canadian Research Institute for the Advancement of Women.

Cohn, C. (1987). Sex and death in the rational world of defense intellectuals. *Signs, 12,* 687-718.

Cohn, C. (1989). Emasculating America's linguistic deterrent. In A. Harris & Y. King (Eds.), *Rocking the Ship of State: Toward a Feminist Peace Politics* (pp. 154-170). Boulder, CO: Westview.

Cohn, C. (1993). Wars, wimps, and women: Talking gender and thinking war. In M. Cooke & A. Woollacott (Eds.), *Gendering War Talk* (pp. 227-246). Princeton, NJ: Princeton University Press.

Cole, J. R., & Zuckerman, H. (1991). Marriage, motherhood, and research performance in science. In H. Zuckerman, J. R. Cole, & J. T. Bruer, (Eds.), *The Outer Circle: Women in the Scientific Community* (pp. 157-170). New Haven, CT: Yale University Press.

Collins, P. H. (1990). *Black Feminist Thought: Knowledge, Consciousness, and the Politics of Empowerment.* London: HarperCollins Academic.

Collins, P. H. (1994). Shifting the center: Race, class, and feminist theorizing about motherhood. In E. N. Glenn, G. Chang, & L. R. Forcey (Eds.), *Mothering: Ideology, Experience, and Agency* (pp. 45-65). New York: Routledge.

Cott, N. (1987). *The Grounding of Modern Feminism*. New Haven, CT: Yale University Press.

Dagg, A. I., & Beauchamp, R. S. (1991). Is there a feminist science? Perceived impact of gender on research by women scientists. *Atlantis, 16* (2), 77-84.

Damarin, S. K. (1990). Teaching mathematics: A feminist perspective. In T. J. Cooney & C. R. Hirsch (Eds.), *Teaching and Learning Mathematics in the 1990s: 1990 Yearbook* (pp. 144-151). Reston, VA: National Council of Teachers of Mathematics.

Damarin, S. K. (1993, October). *Gender and Mathematics from a Feminist Standpoint*. Paper presented at ICMI Study 93, Gender and Mathematics Education, Höör, Sweden.

Danziger, K. (1990). *Constructing the Subject: Historical Origins of Psychological Research*. Cambridge: Cambridge University Press.

Dash, J. (1991). *The Triumph of Discovery: Women Scientists Who Won the Nobel Prize*. Englewood Cliffs, NJ: Julian Messner.

Davion, V. (1990). Pacifism and care. *Hypatia, 5* (1), 90-100.

Davis, K. (1992). Toward a feminist rhetoric: The Gilligan debate revisited. *Women's Studies International Forum, 15*, 219-231.

Deaux, K. (1993). Commentary: Sorry, wrong number–A reply to Gentile's call. *Psychological Science, 4*, 125-126.

de Laurentis, T. (1990). Upping the anti (sic) in feminist theory. In M. Hirsch and E. F. Keller (Eds.), *Conflicts in Feminism* (pp. 255-270). New York: Routledge.

Dench, S. (1990). *Factors Affecting Engineering Students: Similarities and Differences for Females and Males in the SFU Program*. Unpublished master's thesis, Simon Fraser University, Burnaby, British Columbia, Canada.

Di Pietro, J. A. (1981). Rough and tumble play: A function of gender. *Developmental Psychology, 17*, 50-58.

Diamond, T. (1992). *Making Gray Gold: Narratives of Nursing Home Care*. Chicago, IL: University of Chicago Press.

Dick, T. P., & Rallis, S. F. (1991). Factors and influences on high school students' career choices. *Journal for Research in Mathematics Education, 22*, 281-292.

Dorr, R. C. (1915, September 19). Is woman biologically barred from success? *New York Times Magazine*, pp. 15-16.

Eagly, A. H. (1987). *Sex Differences in Social Behavior: A Social-role Interpretation.* Hillsdale, NJ: Lawrence Erlbaum.

Eagly, A. H. (1995). The science and politics of comparing women and men. *American Psychologist, 50,* 145-158.

Eccles, J. S. (1989). Bringing young women to math and science. In M. Crawford & M. Gentry (Eds.), *Gender and Thought, Psychological Perspectives* (pp. 36-58). New York: Springer-Verlag.

Eccles, J. S., & Blumenfeld, P. (1985). Classroom experiences and student gender: Are there differences and do they matter? In L. C. Wilkinson & C. B. Marrett (Eds.), *Gender Influences in the Classroom* (pp. 79-114). Orlando, FL: Academic Press.

Eccles-Parsons, J. E., Kaczala, C. M., & Meece, J. L. (1982). Socialization of achievement attitudes and beliefs: Classroom influences. *Child Development, 53,* 322-339.

Elshtain, J. B. (1987). *Women and War.* New York: Basic Books.

Enloe, C. (1983). *Does Khaki Become You? The Militarisation of Women's Lives.* Boston, MA: South End Press.

Enright, R. B. (1991). Time spent in caregiving and help received by spouses and adult children of brain-impaired adults. *The Gerontologist, 31,* 375-383.

Epstein, C. F. (1988). *Deceptive Distinctions: Sex, Gender, and the Social Order.* New Haven, CT: Yale University Press.

Ethington, C. A. (1990). Gender differences in mathematics: An international perspective. *Journal for Research in Mathematics Education, 21,* 74-81.

Favreau, O. E. (1993). Do the ns justify the means? Null hypothesis testing applied to sex and other differences. *Canadian Psychology, 34,* 64-78.

Feingold, A. (1992). Sex differences in variability in intellectual abilities: A new look at an old controversy. *Review of Educational Research, 62,* 61-84.

Felson, R. B., & Trudeau, L. (1991). Gender differences in mathematics performance. *Social Psychology Quarterly, 54,* 113-126.

Fenaroli, G., Furinghetti, F., Garibaldi, A., & Somaglia, A. (1990). Women and mathematical research in Italy during the period 1887-1946. In L. Burton (Ed.), *Gender and Mathematics: An International Perspective* (pp. 143-155). New York: Cassell.

Fennema, E. (1990). Justice, equity and mathematics education. In E.

Fennema & G. C. Leder (Eds.), *Mathematics and Gender* (pp. 1-9). New York: Teachers College Press.

Fennema, E. (1993, October). *Mathematics, Gender, and Research.* Paper presented at ICMI Study 93, Gender and Mathematics Education, Höör, Sweden.

Fennema, E., & Peterson, P. (1985). Autonomous learning behavior: A possible explanation of gender-related differences in mathematics. In L. C. Wilkinson & C. B. Marrett (Eds.), *Gender Influences in Classroom Interaction* (pp. 17-35). Orlando, FL: Academic Press.

Fennema, E., Peterson, P. L., Carpenter, T. P., & Lubinski, C. A. (1990). Teachers' attitudes and beliefs about girls, boys, and mathematics. *Educational Studies in Mathematics, 21,* 55-69.

Fennema, E., & Sherman, J. A. (1976). Fennema-Sherman Mathematics Attitudes Scales: Instruments designed to measure attitudes toward the learning of mathematics by females and males. *JSAS Catalog of Selected Documents in Psychology, 6,* 31. (Ms. No. 1225).

Fine, M., & Gordon, S. M. (1991). Effacing the center and the margins: Life at the intersection of psychology and feminism. *Feminism and Psychology, 1,* 19-27.

Finley, N. J. (1989). Theories of family labor as applied to gender differences in caregiving for elderly parents. *Journal of Marriage and the Family, 51,* 79-86.

Fisher, J. (1993). *Out of the Shadows: Women, Resistance and Politics in South America.* London, UK: Latin America Bureau.

Fiss, O. M. (1991). An uncertain inheritance. In H. Zuckerman, J. R. Cole, & J. T. Bruer, (Eds.), *The Outer Circle: Women in the Scientific Community* (pp. 259-273). New Haven, CT: Yale University Press.

Fitting, M., Rabins, P., Lucas, M. J., & Eastham, J. (1986). Caregivers for dementia patients: A comparison of husbands and wives. *The Gerontologist, 26,* 248-252.

Flax, J. (1992). Beyond equality: Gender, justice, and difference. In G. Bock & S. James (Eds.), *Beyond Equality and Difference: Citizenship, Feminist Politics, and Female Subjectivity* (pp. 193-210). New York: Routledge.

Flax, J. (1993). *Disputed Subjects: Essays on Psychoanalysis, Politics and Philosophy.* New York: Routledge.

Fliegel, Z. O. (1973). Feminine psychosexual development in Freudian theory: A historical reconstruction. *Psychoanalytic Quarterly, 42,* 385-408.

Forcey, L. R. (1994). Feminist perspectives on mothering and peace. In E. N. Glenn, G. Chang, & L. R. Forcey (Eds.), *Mothering: Ideology, Experience, and Agency* (pp. 355-375). New York: Routledge.

Ford, M. R., & Lowery, C. R. (1986). Gender differences in moral reasoning: A comparison of the use of justice and care orientations. *Journal of Personality and Social Psychology, 50,* 777-783.

Frankenstein, M. (1990). Incorporating race, gender, and class issues into a critical mathematical literacy curriculum. *Journal of Negro Education, 59,* 336-347.

Freedman, E. B. (1990). Theoretical perspectives on sexual difference: An overview. In D. L. Rhode (Ed.), *Theoretical Perspectives on Sexual Difference* (pp. 257-261). New Haven, CT: Yale University Press.

Freud, S. (1961). Some psychical consequences of the anatomical distinction between the sexes. In J. Strachey (Ed. and Trans.), *The Standard Edition of the Complete Psychological Works of Sigmund Freud* (Vol. 19, pp. 248-258). London: Hogarth Press. (Original work published 1925).

Freud, S. (1961). Female sexuality. In J. Strachey (Ed. and Trans.), *The Standard Edition of the Complete Psychological Works of Sigmund Freud* (Vol. 21, pp. 225-243). London: Hogarth Press. (Original work published 1931).

Freud, S. (1964). Femininity. In J. Strachey (Ed. and Trans.), *The Standard Edition of the Complete Psychological Works of Sigmund Freud* (Vol. 22, pp. 112-135). London: Hogarth Press. (Original work published 1933).

Friedman, L. (1989). Mathematics and the gender gap: A meta-analysis of recent studies on sex differences in mathematical tasks. *Review of Educational Research, 59,* 185-213.

Friedman, M. (1987). Beyond caring: The de-moralization of gender. In M. Hanen & K. Nielsen (Eds.), Science, morality and feminist theory. *Canadian Journal of Philosophy*, *13* suppl., 87-110.

Friedman, M. (1993). *What Are Friends For? Feminist Perspectives on Personal Relationships and Moral Theory*. Ithaca, NY: Cornell University Press.

Fry, C. J. (1990, April). *Learning Style Factors and Mathematics Performance: Sex-Related Differences*. Paper presented at the meeting of the American Educational Research Association, Boston, MA.

Fuss, D. (1989). *Essentially Speaking: Feminism, Nature, and Difference*. New York: Routledge.

Garcia, J., Harrison, N. R., & Torres, J. L. (1990). The portrayal of females and minorities in selected elementary mathematics series. *School Science and Mathematics*, *90*, 2-12.

Garrison, D. (1981). Karen Horney and feminism. *Signs*, *6*, 672-691.

Gilligan, C. (1982). *In a Different Voice*. Cambridge MA: Harvard University Press.

Gilligan, C. (1986). Reply. *Signs*, *11*, 324-333.

Gilligan, C. (1987a). Moral orientation and moral development. In E. F. Kittay & D. T. Meyers (Eds.), *Women and Moral Theory* (pp. 19-33). Totowa, NJ: Roman and Littlefield.

Gilligan, C. (1987b). Remapping development: The power of divergent data. In C. Farnham (Ed.), *The Impact of Feminist Research in the Academy* (pp. 77-94). Bloomington, IN: University of Indiana Press.

Gilligan, C. (1988). Exit-voice dilemmas in adolescent development. In C. Gilligan, J. V. Ward, & J. M. Taylor (Eds.), *Mapping the Domain* (pp. 141-158). Cambridge, MA: Harvard University Press.

Gilligan, C., & Attanucci, J. (1988). Two moral orientations. In C. Gilligan, J. V. Ward, & J. M. Taylor (Eds.), *Mapping the Moral Domain* (pp. 73-86). Cambridge, MA: Harvard University Press.

Gilligan, C., & Wiggins, G. (1988). The origins of morality in early childhood relationships. In C. Gilligan, J. V. Ward, & J. M. Taylor (Eds.), *Mapping the Moral Domain* (pp. 111-137). Cambridge, MA: Harvard University Press.

Goldberg, S. (1990). Numbers don't lie: Men do better than women. *Alumnus: City College of New York, 85* (1), 16-17.

Goodfield, J. (1981). *An Imagined World: A Story of Scientific Discovery.* New York : Harper & Row.

Gornick, V. (1983). *Women in Science: Portraits from a World in Transition.* New York : Simon and Schuster.

Gottheil, E. (1987). *Psychoanalysis, Female Ability and Mathematics.* Unpublished manuscript, Stanford University Medical Center, Stanford, CA.

Grady, K. E. (1981). Sex bias in research design. *Psychology of Women Quarterly, 5,* 628-636.

Graham, H. (1983). Caring: A labour of love. In J. Finch & D. Groves (Eds.), *A Labour of Love: Women, Work, and Caring* (pp. 13-30). London, UK: Routledge & Kegan Paul.

Graham, H. (1993). Social divisions in caring. *Women's Studies International Forum, 16,* 461-470.

Greeno, C. G., & Maccoby, E. E. (1986). How different is the "different voice"? *Signs, 11,* 310-316.

Grevholm, B., & Nilsson, M. (1993). *Gender Differences in Mathematics in Swedish Schools.* Unpublished manuscript, Teacher Training College, Malmo, Sweden.

Griscom, J. L. (1992). Women and power: Definition, dualism, and difference. *Psychology of Women Quarterly, 16,* 389-414.

Grossmann, A. (1993). German women doctors from Berlin to New York: Maternity and modernity in Weimar and in exile. *Feminist Studies, 19,* 65-88.

Hacker, S. L. (1983). Mathematization of engineering: Limits on women and the field. In J. Rothschild (Ed.), *Machina ex Dea: Feminist Perspectives on Technology* (pp. 38-58). New York: Pergamon Press.

Hackett, A. (1984). Helene Stocker: Left wing intellectual and sex reformer. In R. Bridenthal, A. Grossmann, & M. Kaplan (Eds.), *When Biology Became Destiny: Women in Weimar and Nazi Germany* (pp. 109-129). New York: Monthly Review Press.

Hall, G. S. (1920). The fall of Atlantis. In *Recreations of a Psychologist* (pp. 1-127). New York: Appleton.

Hanna, G., Kundiger, E., & Larouche, C. (1990). Mathematical achievement of grade 12 girls in fifteen countries. In L. Burton

(Ed.), *Gender and Mathematics: An International Perspective* (pp. 87-98). New York: Cassell.

Haraway, D. J. (1991). *Simians, Cyborgs, and Women: The Reinvention of Nature.* New York: Routledge.

Harding, S. (1986). *The Science Question in Feminism.* Ithaca, NY: Cornell University Press.

Harding, S. (1991). *Whose Science? Whose Knowledge? Thinking From Women's Lives.* Ithaca, NY: Cornell University Press.

Hare-Mustin, R. T., & Marecek, J. (1990). *Making a Difference: Psychology and the Construction of Gender.* New Haven, CT: Yale University Press.

Harris, A. (1989). Bringing Artemis to life: A plea for militance and aggression in feminist peace politics. In A. Harris & Y. King (Eds.), *Rocking the Ship of State: Toward a Feminist Peace Politics* (pp. 93-113). Boulder, CO: Westview.

Hawkesworth, M. E. (1989). Knowers, knowing, known: Feminist theory and claims of truth. *Signs, 14,* 533-557.

Hedges, L. V., & Becker, B. J. (1986). Statistical methods in the meta-analysis of research on gender differences. In J. S. Hyde & M. C. Linn (Eds.), *The Psychology of Gender: Advances Through Meta-Analysis* (pp. 14-50). Baltimore, MD: Johns Hopkins University Press.

Heidbreder, E. (1933). *Seven Psychologies.* Englewood Cliffs, NJ: Prentice-Hall.

Held, Virginia (1993). *Feminist Morality: Transforming Culture, Society, and Politics.* Chicago, IL: University of Chicago Press.

Hillyer, B. (1993). *Feminism and Disability.* Norman, OK: University of Oklahoma Press.

Hinkle, B. M. (1920). On the arbitrary use of the terms "masculine" and "feminine." *Psychoanalytic Review, 7,* 15-30.

Hoagland, S. L. (1990). Some concerns about Nel Nodding's *Caring. Hypatia, 5* (1), 109-114.

Hollingworth, H. L. (1990). *Leta Stetter Hollingworth: A Biography.* Bolton, MA: Anker. (Original work published 1943).

Hollingworth, L. S. (1913). The frequency of amentia as related to sex. *Medical Record, 84,* 753-756.

Hollingworth, L. S. (1914a). *Functional Periodicity: An Experimental Study of the Mental and Motor Abilities of Women Dur-*

ing Menstruation. New York: Teachers College, Columbia University.

Hollingworth, L. S. (1914b). Variability as related to sex differences in achievement: A critique. *American Journal of Sociology, 19*, 510-530.

Hollingworth, L. S. (1916a). Phi beta kappa and women students. *School and Society, 4*, 932-933.

Hollingworth, L. S. (1916b). Sex differences in mental traits. *Psychological Bulletin, 13*, 377-384.

Hollingworth, L. S. (1916c). Social devices for impelling women to bear and rear children. *American Journal of Sociology, 22*, 19-29.

Hollingworth, L. S. (1918). Comparison of the sexes in mental traits. *Psychological Bulletin, 15*, 427-432.

Hollingworth. L. S. (1919). Comparison of the sexes in mental traits. *Psychological Bulletin, 16*, 371-373.

Hollingworth, L. S. (1926). *Gifted Children: Their Nature and Nurture*. New York: The Macmillan Company.

Hollingworth, L. S. (1927, October). The new woman in the making. *Current History, 27*, 15-20.

Hollingworth, L. S. (1929). The vocational aptitudes of women. In H. L. Hollingworth, *Vocational Psychology and Character Analysis* (pp. 329-350). New York: D. Appleton & Company.

Hollingworth, L. S. (1940). *Public Addresses*. Lancaster, PA: Science Press.

Holloway, M. (1993). A lab of her own. *Scientific American, 269* (5), 94-103.

Honey, M. (Ed.). (1992). *Breaking the Ties that Bind: Popular Stories of the New Woman, 1915-1930*. Norman, OK: Oklahoma University Press.

hooks, b. (1990). Feminism: A transformational politic. In D. L. Rhode (Ed.), *Theoretical Perspectives on Sexual Difference* (pp. 185-193). New Haven, CT: Yale University Press.

Horney, K. (1939a). Can you take a stand? *Journal of Adult Education, 11*, 129-132.

Horney, K. (1939b). *New Ways in Psychoanalysis*. New York: Norton.

Horney, K. (1967). On the genesis of the castration complex in women. In H. Kelman (Ed.), *Feminine Psychology* (pp. 37-53). New York: Norton. (Original work published 1923).

Horney, K. (1967). The flight from womanhood: The masculinity-complex in women as viewed by men and by women. In H. Kelman (Ed.), *Feminine Psychology* (pp. 54-70). New York: Norton. (Original work published 1926).

Horney, K. (1967). Inhibited femininity: Psychoanalytical contribution to the problem of frigidity. In H. Kelman (Ed.), *Feminine Psychology* (pp. 71-83). New York: Norton. (Original work published 1926-27).

Horney, K. (1967). The problem of the monogamous ideal. In H. Kelman (Ed.), *Feminine Psychology* (pp. 84-98). New York: Norton. (Original work published 1928).

Horney, K. (1967). Premenstrual tension. In H. Kelman (Ed.), *Feminine Psychology* (pp. 99-106). New York: Norton. (Original work published 1931a).

Horney, K. (1967). The distrust between the sexes. In H. Kelman (Ed.), *Feminine Psychology* (pp. 107-118). New York: Norton. (Original work published 1931b).

Horney, K. (1967). Problems of marriage. In H. Kelman (Ed.), *Feminine Psychology* (pp. 119-132). New York: Norton. (Original work published 1932a).

Horney, K. (1967). The dread of woman: Observations on a specific difference in the dread felt by men and by women respectively for the opposite sex. In H. Kelman (Ed.), *Feminine Psychology* (pp. 133-146). New York: Norton. (Original work published 1932b).

Horney, K. (1967). Maternal conflicts. In H. Kelman (Ed.), *Feminine Psychology* (pp. 175-181). New York: Norton. (Original work published 1933a).

Horney, K. (1967). Psychogenic factors in functional female disorders. In H. Kelman (Ed.), *Feminine Psychology* (pp. 162-174). New York: Norton. (Original work published 1933b).

Horney, K. (1967). The denial of the vagina: A contribution to the problem of the genital anxieties specific to women. In H. Kelman (Ed.), *Feminine Psychology* (147-161). New York: Norton. (Original work published 1933c).

Horney, K. (1967). The overvaluation of love: A study of a common present-day feminine type. In H. Kelman (Ed.), *Feminine*

Psychology (pp. 182-213). New York: Norton. (Original work published 1934).

Horney, K. (1967). The problem of feminine masochism. In H. Kelman (Ed.), *Feminine Psychology* (pp. 214-233). New York: Norton. (Original work published 1935).

Horney, K. (1967). The neurotic need for love. In H. Kelman (Ed.), *Feminine Psychology* (pp. 245-258). New York: Norton. (Original work published 1937).

Horney, K. (1968). The technique of psychoanalytic therapy. *American Journal of Psychoanalysis, 28,* 3-12. (Translated by D. R. Clemmens and reprinted from *Zeitschrift fur Sexualwissenschaft,* 1917, *4,* Fasc. 6, 7, & 8).

Horney, K. (1980). *The Adolescent Diaries of Karen Horney.* New York: Basic Books.

Horney, K. (1994). Women's fear of action. In B. J. Paris, *Karen Horney: A Psychoanalyst's Search for Self-Understanding* (pp. 232-238). New Haven, CT: Yale University Press.

Horowitz, A. (1985). Sons and daughters as caregivers to older parents: Differences in role performance and consequences. *The Gerontologist, 25,* 612-617.

Houston, B. (1987). Rescuing womanly virtues: Some dangers of moral reclamation. In M. Hanen & K. Nielsen (Eds.), Science, morality and feminist theory. *Canadian Journal of Philosophy, 13* suppl., 237-262.

Houston, B. (1990). Caring and exploitation. *Hypatia, 5* (1), 115-119.

Hull, H. R. (1917). The long handicap. *Psychoanalytic Review, 4,* 434-442.

Hyde, J. S. (1986). Introduction: Meta-analysis and the psychology of gender. In J. S. Hyde & M. C. Linn (Eds.), *The Psychology of Gender: Advances Through Meta-Analysis* (pp. 1-13). Baltimore, MD: Johns Hopkins University Press.

Hyde, J. S., Fennema, E., & Lamon, S. J. (1990). Gender differences in mathematics performance: A meta-analysis. *Psychological Bulletin, 107,* 139-155.

Hyde, J. S., Fennema, E., Ryan, M., Frost, L. A., & Hopp, C. (1990). Gender comparisons of mathematics attitudes and affect. *Psychology of Women Quarterly, 14,* 299-324.

Irigaray, L. (1985). *This Sex Which Is Not One* (C. Porter, Trans.). Ithaca, NY: Cornell University Press. (Original work published 1978).

Isaacson, Z. (1990). 'They look at you in absolute horror': Women writing and talking about mathematics. In L. Burton (Ed.), *Gender and Mathematics: An International Perspective* (pp. 20-28). New York: Cassell.

Jacklin, C. N. (1981). Methodological issues in the study of sex-related differences. *Developmental Review, 1*, 266-273.

Jackson, M. (1990). SATs ratify white male privilege. *Alumnus: City College of New York, 85* (1), 17-18.

Jagacinski, C. M. (1987). Engineering careers: Women in a male-dominated field. *Psychology of Women Quarterly, 11*, 97-110.

Jaggar, A. M. (1990). Sexual difference and sexual equality. In D. L. Rhode (Ed.), *Theoretical Perspectives on Sexual Difference* (pp. 239-254). New Haven, CT: Yale University Press.

Jayaratne, T. E., & Stewart, A. J. (1991). Quantitative and qualitative methods in the social sciences: Current feminist issues and practical strategies. In M. Fonow & J. A. Cook (Eds.), *Beyond Methodology: Feminist Scholarship as Lived Research* (pp. 85-106). Bloomington, IN: Indiana University Press.

Jungwirth, H. (1993). Reflections on the foundations of research on women and mathematics. In S. Restivo, J. P. Van Bendegem, & R. Fisher (Eds.), *Math Worlds: Philosophical and Social Studies of Mathematics and Mathematics Education* (pp. 134-149). Albany, NY: State University of New York Press.

Kahn, A. S., & Yoder, J. D. (1989). The psychology of women and conservatism: Rediscovering social change. *Psychology of Women Quarterly, 13*, 417-432.

Kaplan, M. (1984). Sisterhood under siege: Feminism and anti-Semitism in Germany, 1904-1938. In R. Bridenthal, A. Grossmann, & M. Kaplan (Eds.), *When Biology Became Destiny: Women in Weimar and Nazi Germany* (pp. 174-196). New York: Monthly Review Press.

Kaplan, T. (1982). Female consciousness and collective action: The case of Barcelona, 1910-1918. *Signs, 7*, 545-566.

Karp, K. S. (1991). Elementary school teachers' attitudes toward mathematics: The impact on students' autonomous learning skills. *School Science and Mathematics, 91*, 265-270.

Kaur, B. (1990). Girls and mathematics in Singapore: The case of GCE 'O' level mathematics. In L. Burton (Ed.), *Gender and Mathematics: An International Perspective* (pp. 98-112). New York: Cassell.

Keller, E. F. (1977). The anomaly of a woman in physics. In S. Ruddick & P. Daniels (Eds.), *Working It Out* (pp. 77-91). New York: Pantheon Books.

Keller, E. F. (1983). *A Feeling for the Organism: The Life and Work of Barbara McClintock*. New York: W. H. Freeman and Company.

Keller, E. F. (1985). *Reflections on Gender and Science*. New Haven, CT: Yale University Press.

Keller, E. F. (1987). Women scientists and feminist critics of science. *Daedalus, 116* (4), 77-91.

Keller, E. F. (1991). The wo/man scientist: Issues of sex and gender in the pursuit of science. In H. Zuckerman, J. R. Cole, & J. T. Bruer (Eds.), *The Outer Circle: Women in the Scientific Community* (pp. 227-236). New Haven, CT: Yale University Press.

Keller, E. F. (1992a). How gender matters, or why it's so hard for us to count past two. In G. Kirkup & L. S. Keller (Eds.), *Inventing Women: Science, Technology and Gender* (pp. 42-56). Cambridge, UK: Polity Press.

Keller, E. F. (1992b). *Secrets of Life Secrets of Death: Essays on Language, Gender, and Science*. New York: Routledge.

Key, E. (1911). *Love and Marriage* (A. G. Chater, Trans.). New York: G. P. Putnam's Sons. (Original work published 1903).

Kimball, M. M. (1989). A new perspective on women's math achievement. *Psychological Bulletin, 105*, 198-214.

Kimball, M. M. (1994). The worlds we live in: Gender similarities and differences. *Canadian Psychology, 35*, 388-404.

King, Y. (1989). If I can't dance in your revolution, I'm not coming. In A. Harris & Y. King (Eds.), *Rocking the Ship of State: Toward a Feminist Peace Politics* (pp. 281-298). Boulder, CO: Westview.

Kirk, G. (1989a). Our Greenham Common: Feminism and nonviolence. In A. Harris & Y. King (Eds.), *Rocking the Ship of State:*

Toward a Feminist Peace Politics (pp. 115-130). Boulder, CO: Westview.

Kirk, G. (1989b). Our Greenham Common: Not just a place but a movement. In A. Harris & Y. King (Eds.), *Rocking the Ship of State: Toward a Feminist Peace Politics* (pp. 263-280). Boulder, CO: Westview.

Kissane, B. V. (1986). Selection of mathematically talented students. *Educational Studies in Mathematics, 17,* 221-241.

Kistiakowsky, V. (1980). Women in physics: unnecessary, injurious and out of place? *Physics Today, 33* (2), 32-40.

Kittay, E. F. (1984). Womb envy: An explanatory concept. In J. Trebilcot (Ed.), *Mothering: Essays in Feminist Theory* (pp. 94-128). Totowa, NJ: Rowman & Allenheld.

Koehler, M. S. (1990). Classrooms, teachers, and gender differences in mathematics. In E. Fennema & G. C. Leder (Eds.), *Mathematics and Gender* (pp. 128-148). New York: Teachers College Press.

Kohlberg, L. (1981). *The Philosophy of Moral Development: Moral Stages and the Idea of Justice: Essays on Moral Development, I.* San Francisco, CA: Harper & Row.

Kohlberg, L., Levine, C., & Hewer, A. (1984). The current formulation of the theory. In L. Kohlberg, *Essays on Moral Development: The Psychology of Moral Development* (Vol. II) (pp. 212-319). San Francisco, CA: Harper & Row.

Koonz, C. (1987). *Mothers in the Fatherland: Women, the Family, and Nazi Politics.* New York: St. Martins Press.

Koven, S., and Michel, S. (1993). Introduction: "Mother worlds." In S. Koven & S. Michel (Eds.), *Mothers of a New World: Maternalist Politics and the Origins of Welfare States* (pp. 1-41). New York: Routledge.

Kramer, P. E., & Lehman, S. (1990). Mismeasuring women: A critique of research on computer ability and avoidance. *Signs, 16,* 158-172.

Leavitt, J. W., & Gordon, L. (1988). A decade of feminist critiques in the natural sciences: An address by Ruth Bleier. *Signs, 14,* 182-195.

Leder, G. C. (1990). Teacher/student interactions in the mathematics classroom: A different perspective. In E. Fennema & G. C.

Leder (Eds.), *Mathematics and Gender* (pp. 149-168). New York: Teachers College Press.

Lewin, E. (1993). *Lesbian Mothers: Accounts of Gender in American Culture*. Ithaca, NY: Cornell University Press.

Lewin, E. (1994). Negotiating lesbian motherhood: The dialectics of resistance and accommodation. In E. N. Glenn, G. Chang, & L. R. Forcey (Eds.), *Mothering: Ideology, Experience, and Agency* (pp. 333-353). New York: Routledge.

Linden, R. R. (1993). *Making Stories, Making Selves: Feminist Reflections on the Holocaust*. Columbus, OH: Ohio University Press.

Linn, M. C. (1986). Meta-analysis of studies of gender differences: Implications and future directions. In J. S. Hyde & M. C. Linn (Eds.), *The Psychology of Gender: Advances Through Meta-Analysis* (pp. 210-231). Baltimore, MD: Johns Hopkins University Press.

Linn, M. C., & Hyde, J. S. (1989). Gender, mathematics, and science. *Educational Researcher, 18* (8), 17-19, 22-27.

Linton, R. (1989). Seneca women's peace camp: Shapes of things to come. In A. Harris & Y. King (Eds.), *Rocking the Ship of State: Toward a Feminist Peace Politics* (pp. 239-261). Boulder, CO: Westview.

Logan, K. (1990). Women's participation in urban protest. In J. Foweraker & A. L. Craig (Eds.), *Popular Movements and Political Change in Mexico* (pp. 150-159). Boulder, CO: Lynne Rienner Publishers.

Longino, H. E., & Hammonds, E. (1990). Conflicts and tensions in the feminist study of gender and science. In M. Hirsch & E. F. Keller (Eds.), *Conflicts in Feminism* (pp. 164-183). New York: Routledge.

Lott, B. (1990). Dual natures or learned behavior: The challenge to feminist psychology. In R. T. Hare-Mustin & J. Marecek (Eds.), *Making a Difference: Psychology and the Construction of Gender* (pp. 65-101). New Haven, CT: Yale University Press.

Lowie, R. H., & Hollingworth, L. S. (1916). Science and feminism. *The Scientific Monthly, 4*, 277-284.

Luchins, E. H. (1979). Sex differences in mathematics: How *not* to deal with them. *American Mathematical Monthly, 86*, 161-168.

Lyons, N. P. (1983). Two perspectives: On self, relationships, and morality. *Harvard Educational Review, 53*, 125-145.

Maccoby, E. E., & Jacklin, C. N. (1974). *The Psychology of Sex Differences*. Stanford, CA: Stanford University Press.

Malette, L., & Chalouh, M. (Eds.). (1991). *The Montreal Massacre* (M. Wildeman, Trans.). Charlottetown, Prince Edward Island, Canada: gynergy books.

Mandula, B. (1990). Is the SAT unfair to women? *Association for Women in Science Newsletter, 19* (1), 8-16.

Marsh, H. W. (1989). Sex differences in the development of verbal and mathematics constructs: The high school and beyond study. *American Educational Research Journal, 26*, 191-225.

Marshall, S. P. (1984). Sex differences in children's mathematics achievement: Solving computations and story problems. *Journal of Educational Psychology, 76*, 194-204.

Marshall, S. P. & Smith, J. D. (1987). Sex differences in learning mathematics: A longitudinal study with item and error analysis. *Journal of Educational Psychology, 79*, 372-383.

Martin, J. (1990). Motherhood and power: The production of a women's culture of politics in a Mexican community. *American Ethnologist, 17*, 470-490.

Martin, J. R. (1994). Methodological essentialism, false difference, and other dangerous traps. *Signs, 19*, 630-657.

Matthews, W. (1984). Influences on the learning and participation of minorities in mathematics. *Journal for Research in Mathematics Education, 15*, 84-95.

McDougall, W. (1921). The island of Eugenia: The phantasy of a foolish philosopher. In *National Welfare and National Decay* (pp. 1-25). London: Methuen.

McGarrahan, P. (1994). *Transcending AIDS: Nurses and HIV Patients in New York City*. Philadelphia, PA: University of Pennsylvania Press.

McGraw, K. O., & Wong, S. P. (1992). A common language effect size statistic. *Psychological Bulletin, 111*, 361-365.

McIlwee, J. S., & Robinson, J. G. (1992). *Women in Engineering: Gender, Power, and Workplace Culture*. Albany, NY: State University of New York Press.

McLaren, A., & Gaskell, P. J. (1995). Now you see it, now you don't: Gender as an issue in school science. In J. S. Gaskell & J. Willinsky (Eds.), *Gender In/forms Curriculum: From Enrichment to Transformation* (pp. 136-156). New York: Teachers College Press.

Medjuck, S., O'Brien, M., & Tozer, C. (1992). From private responsibility to public policy: Women and the cost of caregiving to elderly kin. *Atlantis, 17* (2), 44-58.

Mednick, M. T. (1989). On the politics of psychological constructs: Stop the bandwagon: I want to get off. *American Psychologist, 44*, 1118-1123.

Meece, J. L., Wigfield, A., & Eccles, J. S. (1990). Predictors of math anxiety and its influence on young adolescents' course enrollment intentions and performance in mathematics. *Journal of Educational Psychology, 82*, 60-70.

Miller, B. (1990). Gender differences in spouse management of the caregiver role. In E. K. Abel & M. K. Nelson (Eds.), *Circles of Care: Work and Identity in Women's Lives* (pp. 92-104). Albany, NY: State University of New York Press.

Miller, B., & Cafasso, L. (1992). Gender differences in caregiving: Fact or artifact? *The Gerontologist, 32*, 498-507.

Mills, C. J., Ablard, K. E., & Stumpf, H. (1993). Gender differences in academically talented young students' mathematical reasoning: Patterns across age and subskills. *Journal of Educational Psychology, 85*, 340-346.

Montague, H., & Hollingworth, L. S. (1914). The comparative variability of the sexes at birth. *American Journal of Sociology, 20*, 335-370.

Morawski, J. G. (1984). Not quite new worlds: Psychologists' conceptions of the ideal family in the twenties. In M. Lewin (Ed.), *In the Shadow of the Past: Psychology Portrays the Sexes* (pp. 97-125). New York: Columbia University Press.

Morawski, J. G. (1985). The measurement of masculinity and femininity: Engendering categorical realities. *Journal of Personality 53*, 196-223.

Morris, J. (1991/92). 'Us' and 'them'? Feminist research, community care and disability. *Critical Social Policy*, No. 33, 22-39.

Moulton, R. (1975). Early papers on women: Horney to Thompson. *The American Journal of Psychoanalysis, 35,* 207-223.

Mui, A. C. (1992). Caregiver strain among black and white daughter caregivers: A role theory perspective. *The Gerontologist, 32,* 203-212.

Noddings, N. (1990a). A response. *Hypatia, 5* (1), 120-126.

Noddings, N. (1990b). Ethics from the standpoint of women. In D. L. Rhode (Ed.), *Theoretical Perspectives on Sexual Difference* (pp. 160-173). New Haven, CT: Yale University Press. [text].

Norris, J. (Ed.). (1988). *Daughters of the Elderly: Building Partnerships in Caregiving.* Bloomington, IN: Indiana University Press.

Oaks, G. (Ed. and Trans.). (1984). *George Simmel: On Women, Sexuality, and Love.* New Haven, CT: Yale University Press.

Offen, K. (1990). Feminism and sexual difference in historical perspective. In D. L. Rhode (Ed.), *Theoretical Perspectives on Sexual Difference* (pp. 13-20). New Haven, CT: Yale University Press.

Offen, K. (1992). Defining feminism: A comparative historical approach. In G. Bock & S. James (Eds.), *Beyond Equality and Difference: Citizenship, Feminist Politics, and Female Subjectivity* (pp. 69-88). New York: Routledge.

Olds, S. (1992). *The Dead and the Living.* New York: Alfred A. Knopf.

Omolade, B. (1989). We speak for the planet. In A. Harris & Y. King (Eds.), *Rocking the Ship of State: Toward a Feminist Peace Politics* (pp. 171-189). Boulder, CO: Westview.

Paris, B. J. (1994). *Karen Horney: A Psychoanalyst's Search for Self-Understanding.* New Haven, CT: Yale University Press.

Pateman, C. (1992). Equality, difference, subordination: The politics of motherhood and women's citizenship. In G. Bock & S. James (Eds.), *Beyond Equality and Difference: Citizenship, Feminist Politics, and Female Subjectivity* (pp. 17-31). New York: Routledge.

Peplau, L. A., & Conrad, E. (1989). Beyond nonsexist research: The perils of feminist methods in psychology. *Psychology of Women Quarterly, 13,* 379-400.

Poffenberger, A. T. (1940). Leta Stetter Hollingworth: 1886-1939. *American Journal of Psychology, 53,* 299-300.

Pratt, M. W., Golding, G., & Hunter, W. J. (1984). Does morality have a gender? Sex, sex role, and moral judgment relationships across the adult lifespan. *Merrill-Palmer Quarterly, 30*, 321-340.

Pruchno, R. A., Michaels, J. E., & Potashnik, S. L. (1990). Predictors of institutionalization among Alzheimer disease victims with caregiving spouses. *Journal of Gerontology: Social Sciences, 45*, S259-266.

Quinn, S. (1987). *A Mind of Her Own: The Life of Karen Horney.* New York: Summit Books.

Raymond, J. G. (1986). *A Passion for Friends: Toward a Philosophy of Female Affection.* Boston, MA: Beacon.

Relke, D. M. A. (1993). Foremothers who cared: Paula Heimann, Margaret Little and the female tradition in psychoanalysis. *Feminism and Psychology, 3*, 89-109.

Reyes, L. H., & Stanic, G. M. (1988). Race, sex, socioeconomic status, and mathematics. *Journal for Research in Mathematics Education, 19*, 26-43.

Rhode, D. (1990). Definitions of difference. In D. L. Rhode (Ed.), *Theoretical Perspectives on Sexual Difference* (pp. 197-212). New Haven, CT: Yale University Press.

Rhode, D. (1992). The politics of paradigms: Gender difference and gender disadvantage. In G. Bock & S. James (Eds.), *Beyond Equality and Difference: Citizenship, Feminist Politics, and Female Subjectivity* (pp. 149-163). New York: Routledge.

Riger, S. (1992). Epistemological debates, feminist voices: Science, social values, and the study of women. *American Psychologist, 47*, 730-740.

Ringelheim, J. (1985). Women and the Holocaust: A reconsideration of research. *Signs, 10*, 741-761.

Roazen, P. (1975). *Freud and His Followers.* New York: Alfred A. Knopf.

Rodgers, M. (1990). Mathematics: Pain or pleasure? In L. Burton (Ed.), *Gender and Mathematics: An International Perspective* (pp. 29-37). New York: Cassell.

Rogers, P. (1990). Thoughts on power and pedagogy. In L. Burton (Ed.), *Gender and Mathematics: An International Perspective* (pp. 38-46). New York: Cassell.

Rosenberg, R. (1982). *Beyond Separate Spheres: Intellectual Roots of Modern Feminism.* New Haven, CT: Yale University Press.

Rossiter, M. W. (1982). *Women Scientists in America: Struggles and Strategies to 1940.* Baltimore, MD: Johns Hopkins University Press.

Rothman, B. K. (1994). Beyond mothers and fathers: Ideology in a patriarchal society. In E. N. Glenn, G. Chang, & L. R. Forcey (Eds.), *Mothering: Ideology, Experience, and Agency* (pp. 139-157). New York: Routledge.

Roweton, W. E. (1990). Leta Stetter Hollingworth: A personal profile of Nebraska's pioneering psychologist. *Roeper Review, 13,* 136-141.

Rubins, J. L. (1978). *Karen Horney: Gentle Rebel of Psychoanalysis.* New York: Dial Press.

Ruddick, S. (1989). *Maternal Thinking: Toward a Politics of Peace.* New York: Ballantine Books.

Russo, N. F. (1983). Psychology's foremothers: Their achievements in context. In A. N. O'Connell & N. F. Russo (Eds.), *Models of Achievement: Reflections of Eminent Women in Psychology* (pp. 9-24). New York: Columbia University Press.

Sadosky, C. (1993, October). The Association of Women in Mathematics. In C. Keitel (Moderator), *The Role of Organizations.* Panel conducted at ICMI Study 93, Gender and Mathematics Education, Höör, Sweden.

Sayre, A. (1975). *Rosalind Franklin and DNA.* New York: Norton.

Scheper-Hughes, N. (1992). *Death Without Weeping: The Violence of Everyday Life in Brazil.* Berkeley, CA: University of California Press.

Schirmer, J. G. (1993). "Those who die for life cannot be called dead": Women and human rights protest in Latin America. In M. Agosin (Ed.), *Surviving Beyond Fear: Women Children & Human Rights in Latin America* (pp. 31-57). Fredonia, NY: White Pine.

Schoenfeld, A. M. (1989). Explorations of students' mathematical beliefs and behavior. *Journal for Research in Mathematics Education, 20,* 338-355.

Schwarz, J. (1986). *Radical Feminists of Heterodoxy: Greenwich Village, 1912-1940.* Norwich, VT: New Victoria.

Secada, W. G. (1989). Educational equity vs. equality of education: An alternative conception. In W. G. Secada (Ed.), *Equity in Education* (pp. 68-88). New York: Falmer Press.

Secada, W. G. (1990). The challenges of a changing world for mathematics education. In T. J. Cooney & C. R. Hirsch (Eds.), *Teaching and Learning Mathematics in the 1990s: 1990 Yearbook* (pp. 135-143). Reston, VA: National Council of Teachers of Mathematics.

Selvin, P. (1992). Profile of a field: Mathematics. *Science, 255,* 1382-1383.

Shepherd, L. J. (1993). *Lifting the Veil: The Feminine Face of Science.* Boston, MA: Shambhala.

Shepherd, N. (1993). *A Price Below Rubies: Jewish Women as Rebels and Radicals.* Cambridge MA: Harvard University Press.

Shields, S. A. (1975). Functionalism, Darwinism, and the psychology of women: A study in social myth. *American Psychologist, 30,* 739-754.

Shields, S. A. (1982). The variability hypothesis: The history of a biological model of sex differences in intelligence. *Signs, 7,* 769-797.

Shields, S. A. (1991). Leta Stetter Hollingworth: "Literature of opinion" and the study of individual differences. In G. A. Kimble, M. Wertheimer, & C. L. White (Eds.), *Portraits of Pioneers in Psychology* (pp. 243-255). Hillsdale, NJ: Lawrence Erlbaum.

Shields, S. A., & Mallory, M. E. (1987). Leta Stetter Hollingworth speaks on "Columbia's legacy." *Psychology of Women Quarterly, 11,* 285-300.

Showalter, E. (Ed.). (1978). *These Modern Women: Autobiographical Essays from the Twenties.* Old Westbury, NY: The Feminist Press.

Silverman, L. K. (1992). Leta Stetter Hollingworth: Champion of the psychology of women and gifted children. *Journal of Educational Psychology, 84,* 20-27.

Silverstone, B. (1988). Feelings. In J. Norris (Ed.), *Daughters of the Elderly: Building Partnerships in Caregiving* (pp. 104-109). Bloomington, IN: Indiana University Press.

Snarey, J. R. (1985). Cross-cultural universality of social-moral development: A critical review of Kohlbergian research. *Psychological Bulletin, 97,* 202-232.

Snitow, A. (1990). A gender diary. In M. Hirsch and E. F. Keller (Eds.), *Conflicts in Feminism* (pp. 9-43). New York: Routledge.

Solar, C. (1995). An inclusive pedagogy in mathematics education. *Educational Studies in Mathematics, 28,* 311-333.

Squire, C. (1989). *Significant Differences: Feminism in Psychology.* New York: Routledge.

Staberg, E. (1994). Gender and science in Swedish compulsory school. *Gender and Education, 6,* 35-45.

Stack, C. B. (1986). The culture of gender: Women and men of color. *Signs, 11,* 321-324.

Stack, C. B. (1990). Different voices, different visions: Gender, culture, and moral reasoning. In F. Ginsberg & A. Lowenhaupt Tsing (Eds.), *Negotiating Gender in American Culture* (pp. 19-27). Boston, MA: Beacon.

Statistics Canada (1993). *Major Fields of Study of Post Secondary Graduates.* 1991 Census of Canada. Catalogue No. 93-329. Ottawa, Ontario: Industry Science and Technology Canada.

Stevenson, H. W., Lee, S., & Stigler, J. W. (1986). Mathematics achievement of Chinese, Japanese, and American children. *Science, 231,* 693-699.

Stipek, D. J., & Gralinski, J. H. (1991). Gender differences in children's achievement-related beliefs and emotional responses to success and failure in mathematics. *Journal of Educational Psychology, 83,* 361-371.

Stockard, J., & Wood, J. W. (1984). The myth of female underachievement: A re-examination of sex differences in academic achievement. *American Educational Research Journal, 21,* 825-838.

Stodolsky, S. S., Salk, S., & Glaessner, B. (1991). Student views about learning math and social studies. *American Educational Research Journal, 28,* 89-116.

Stolte-Heiskanen, V. (Ed.) (1991). *Women in Science: Token Women or Gender Equality?* Oxford: Berg.

Stone, R., Cafferata, G. L., & Sangl, J. (1987). Caregivers of the frail elderly: A national profile. *The Gerontologist, 27,* 616-626.

Storm, C., Storm, T., & Strike-Schurman, J. (1985). Obligations for care: Beliefs in a small Canadian town. *Canadian Journal on Aging, 4*, 75-84.

Striker, L. J., Rock, D. A., & Burton, N. W. (1991). *Sex Differences in SAT Predictions of College Grades* (College Board Report No. 91-2). New York: College Entrance Examination Board. (ETS RR No. 91-38).

Swerdlow, A. (1993). *Women Strike for Peace*. Chicago, IL: University of Chicago Press.

Terman, L. M. (1944). [Leta Stetter Hollingworth: A Biography]. *Journal of Applied Psychology, 28*, 357-358.

Terman, L. M., & Miles, C. C. (1936). *Sex and Personality*. New York: McGraw-Hill.

Thompson, H. (1903). *The Mental Traits of Sex*. Chicago: University of Chicago Press.

Thorndike, E. L. (1914). *Education Psychology Volume III: Mental Work and Fatigue and Individual Differences and Their Causes*. New York: Teachers College, Columbia University.

Thornley, G. (1993, October). *Women's Participation in Mathematics in New Zealand*. Paper presented at ICMI Study 93, Gender and Mathematics Education, Höör, Sweden.

Tong, R. (1993). *Feminine and Feminist Ethics*. Belmont, CA: Wadsworth.

Traweek, S. (1988). *Beamtimes and Lifetimes: The World of High Energy Physicists*. Cambridge, MA: Harvard University Press.

Tronto, J. C. (1987). Beyond gender difference to a theory of care. *Signs, 12*, 644-663.

Tronto, J. C. (1991). Changing goals and changing strategies: Varieties of women's political activities. *Feminist Studies, 17*, 85-104.

Tronto, J. C. (1993). *Moral Boundaries: A Political Argument for an Ethic of Care*. New York: Routledge.

Turkle, S., & Papert, S. (1990). Epistemological pluralism: Styles and voices within the computer culture. *Signs, 16*, 128-157.

Unger, R. K. (Ed.) (1989). *Representations: Social Constructions of Gender*. Amityville, NY: Baywood.

Unger, R. K. (1992). Will the real sex difference please stand up? *Feminism & Psychology, 2*, 231-238.

Unger, R. K. (1993). Alternative conceptions of sex (and sex differences). In M. Haug (Ed.), *The Development of Sex Differences and Similarities in Behavior: Proceedings of the NATO Advanced Research Workshop, Chateau de Bonas, Gers, France, July 14-18, 1992* (pp. 457-476). Netherlands, Kluwer Academic Publishers.

Unger, R. K., & Crawford, M. (1993). Commentary: Sex and gender–The troubled relationship between terms and concepts. *Psychological Science, 4,* 122-124.

Verhage, H. (1990). Curriculum development and gender. In L. Burton (Ed.), *Gender and Mathematics: An International Perspective* (pp. 60-71). New York: Cassell.

Wainer, H., & Steinberg, L. S. (1992). Sex differences in performance on the mathematics section of the Scholastic Aptitude Test: A bidirectional validity test. *Harvard Educational Review, 62,* 323-336.

Walker, L. J. (1984). Sex differences in the development of moral reasoning: A critical review. *Child Development, 55,* 667-691.

Walker, L. J. (1986a). Experiential and cognitive sources of moral development in adulthood. *Human Development, 29,* 113-124.

Walker, L. J. (1986b). Sex differences in the development of moral reasoning: A rejoinder to Baumrind. *Child Development, 57,* 522-526.

Walker, L. J. (1989). A longitudinal study of moral reasoning. *Child Development, 60,* 157-166.

Walkerdine, V., & The Girls and Mathematics Unit (1989). *Counting Girls Out.* London: Virago Press.

Wark, G. R. (1992). *The Effects of Sex, Sex-Role, and Type of Moral Dilemma on Moral Maturity and Moral Orientation.* Unpublished master's thesis, Simon Fraser University, Burnaby, B. C. Canada.

Watson, J. (1968). *The Double Helix.* New York: Atheneum.

Watson, J. B. (1929). Should a child have more than one mother? *Liberty Magazine,* 31-35.

Webber, V. (1987/88, Summer). Maths as a subversive activity. *Education Links,* No. 32, 6-9.

Weisstein, N. (1977). "How can a little girl like you teach a great big class of men?" the chairman said, and other adventures of a woman in science. In S. Ruddick & P. Daniels (Eds.), *Working It Out* (pp. 241-250). New York: Pantheon Books.

Westkott, M. (1986). *The Feminist Legacy of Karen Horney.* New Haven, CT: Yale University Press.

Weston, K. (1991). *Families We Choose: Lesbians, Gays, Kinship.* New York: Columbia University Press.

White, W. L., & Renzulli, J. S. (1987). A forty-year follow-up of students who attended Leta Hollingworth's school for gifted children. *Roeper Review, 10* (2), 89-94.

Willis, S. (1989). *Real Girls Don't Do Maths: Gender and the Construction of Privilege.* Geelong, Victoria: Deakin University Press.

Windall, S. E. (1988). AAAS presidential lecture: Voices from the pipeline. *Science, 241,* 1740-1745.

Wong, S. C. (1994). Diverted mothering: Representations of caregivers of color in the age of "multi-culturalism." In E. N. Glenn, G. Chang, & L.R. Forcey (Eds.), *Mothering: Ideology, Experience, and Agency* (pp. 67-91). New York: Routledge.

Woolley, H. T. (1910). A review of the recent literature on the psychology of sex. *Psychological Bulletin, 7,* 335-342.

Woolley, H. T. (1914). The psychology of sex. *Psychological Bulletin, 11,* 353-379.

Wright, F. (1983). Single carers: Employment, housework, and caring. In J. Finch & D. Groves (Eds.), *A Labour Of Love: Women, Work, and Caring* (pp. 89-105). London, UK: Routledge & Kegan Paul.

Wright, L. K. (1991). The impact of Alzheimer's disease on the marital relationship. *The Gerontologist, 31,* 224-237.

Xu, J., & Farrell, E. (1992). Mathematics performance of Shanghai high school students: A preliminary look at gender differences in another culture. *School Science and Mathematics, 92,* 442-444.

Zuckerman, H. (1991). The careers of men and women scientists; A review of current research. In H. Zuckerman, J. R. Cole, & J. T. Bruer (Eds.), *The Outer Circle: Women in the Scientific Community* (pp. 27-56). New Haven, CT: Yale University Press.

Zuckerman, H., & Cole, J. R. (1991a). [Interview with Andrea Dupree]. In H. Zuckerman, J. R. Cole, & J. T. Bruer (Eds.), *The*

Outer Circle: Women in the Scientific Community (pp. 94-126). New Haven, CT: Yale University Press.

Zuckerman, H., & Cole, J. R. (1991b). [Interview with Salome Waelsch]. In H. Zuckerman, J. R. Cole, & J. T. Bruer (Eds.), *The Outer Circle: Women in the Scientific Community* (pp. 71-93). New Haven, CT: Yale University Press.

Index

SHANAHAN LIBRARY
MARYMOUNT MANHATTAN COLLEGE
221 EAST 71 STREET
NEW YORK, NY 10021

DATE DUE

AUG 0 5 2002			
NOV 1 2 2003			
GAYLORD			PRINTED IN U.S.A.

MARYMOUNT MANHATTAN COLLEGE
THOMAS J. SHANAHAN LIBRARY

3 3203 00071 8073